Readings in the

History of Economic Thought

Paul P. Louis

Associate
Professor of Economics

University of Dayton
Dayton, Ohio 45409

McCutchan Publishing Corporation
2526 Grove Street
Berkeley, California 94704

1699487

CONTENTS

PREFACE

There are many textbooks on the history of economic thought. Then why another? Anyone who has taught this subject knows very well how hard it is to assemble the major teachings of the economic philosophers into a compact and comprehensive whole. This book is intended to present the greatest economists of the world with a short biography, a list of their main teachings, a short analysis of their effectiveness, and a brief discussion of the relevance of the teaching in modern economics. The book also includes selections on the major economic movments from Mercantilism to Socialism.

Textbooks are becoming extremely expensive due to the rise in cost of production and distribution. *Readings in the History of Economic Thought* can satisfy the need of any undergraduate college course. Moreover, many high schools are interested in an inexpensive text that can familiarize their students with the makers of economic science. A paperback publication may well be the answer. Many lay people are apprehensive about economic writings, although they have to make economic decisions almost daily. This book can be an effective way to develop readings in economics.

The author is indebted to Dr. George McKenzie and Professor Frances Tiernan of the University of Dayton, Dr. Cyrin Maus, Dean of St. Leonard College, and Sister M. Alacoque of Miamisburg, Ohio, for reading the manuscript and rendering many constructive suggestions. My typists Mrs. Mary Gillo and Miss Clara Mae Guilfoyle deserve many thanks.

Finally, the author owes a debt of gratitude to Dean William J. Hoben, School of Business, University of Dayton for his continued encouragement from the initiation to the completion of this endeavor.

Respectfully dedicated to my parents

Paulose and Achamma Louis

and my brother

Sextus Louis

THE GREEK ECONOMISTS

It is common knowledge that the Greek culture served as the basis for many fields of study in the Christian civilization. This is true particularly of philosophy, and also of metaphysics and logic and of politics and law. Yet the Greek contribution in the discipline of economics has been overlooked.

The Greek philosophers did not identify economics as a separate discipline: they considered economics to be part of politics and sociology. Nevertheless, ancient Greek philosophers like Socrates, Plato, and Aristotle treated the problems of economics while writing about politics and law. Later, Xenephon, in his discussions on agriculture, ownership of land, sharing of crops, and obligations between landlords and tenants, examined the problem of meeting the man's material needs, which, after all, is what economics is all about.

The Greeks dealt extensively with political and sociological relationships. With high integrity and sophistication, mainstream Greek writings accepted the task of defining production, distribution, and consumption functions. Those Greeks, at least, who enjoyed the life style of the aristocracy, cultivated an atmosphere of leisure. Leisure, as the Greeks viewed it, was not pure inertia or lascivious indulgence but time set apart from physical works. This type of leisure promoted literary and philosophical curiosity, which led to the formation of the world philosophies handed down by Socrates, Plato, and Aristotle.

They did not write complete economic treatises per se; probably they did not conceive of economics as a science independent enough to assume its own origin, growth, and operation. Their economic thoughts stem from, and exist within, their treatises on ethics and government.

These philosophers lived in a world of their own in which their

1

economic needs were met by other classes without any real interaction. They had no reason to build or plough, or even to learn basic
economic realities. In fact, the upper classes do not seem to have
been aware of how their own material needs were being satisfied.

Plato laid down principles of operation for philosopher kings, war-
riors, farmers, and slaves. No one was to interfere in the activities of
the other classes. Despite this stratification of Greek society, the
philosophers delved into many economic concepts that remain the
foundations of this discipline. The ancient Mesopotamian civilization
of the Tigris and Euphrates valleys shows evidence of economic dicta
borrowed from the Greeks. They kept records of business transactions, rural-urban trade relationships, and contractual arrangements
of community efforts in irrigation with estimates of costs and modes
of sharing these costs. Still, no organized form of treating economics
as a science can be found in their archives. This is also true of the
Egyptian civilization along the Nile.

The major post-Hellenic culture—that of Rome—developed trade
relations, a tax system, a monetary system, and a commercial law far
more than the Greeks. Yet Roman writings in economics never go
beyond the production and distribution of agricultural products. The
historian Cato wrote the earliest economics book. His composition,
Farming, concerned itself with the management of rural estates. The
statesman Cicero makes random reference in his vast writings to
agriculture. He praised the farmer as the backbone of the nation but,
ironically, downgraded the craftsman "who only changes the shape
and form of things produced by the farmer in conjunction with
nature."

Economic considerations were different in Greece, notably in the
city-state of Athens. In the Athenian universities, where students
from all over the known world gathered, the spirit of critical inquiry
flourished. Dialogues on ethics and politics produced a concern with
the practical problems of law and justice. When law and justice become dominant themes, economics recedes and becomes their practical reflection. Justice was a matter of *suum cuique*—to each one his
due. This then became the guideline for distribution and sharing. Is
economics anything different from just distribution?

Thus, despite the sophistication of Greek life, ideals treated in law
and justice did not remain exclusively within the universities. They
filtered down to the common life, into the wheat fields and market
places. They became yardsticks for measuring intrinsic values of commodities that were then applied to barter and trade. Many modern
economists have called the Greek economists "simplistics," possibly

because they overlooked the manifold economic veins involved even in the forms of bartering. To be sure, knowledge of the intricate mechanism of supply and demand, marginal costs, and marginal revenue was gained only in the time of the classical economists. But these pioneers did formulate elementary notions that served as guides for posterity. The Greeks talked about things that befitted their life style. Modern writers coin better terminologies to suit the demands of their times. Yet the Greek economists treated the same things without the professional jargon the modern economists use.

Plato

Plato (427 B.C.-347 B.C.) was one of the greatest political theorists of all time. Two of his major works are the *Laws* and the *Republic*. Plato understood the intricacies involved in the art of lawmaking and enforcement. His work *Republic* treats various aspects of government, but the main theme is the enforcement of law to serve all levels of society.

Greek society evolved from a collection of households to the city-state ("polis"), which is the origin of political economy. Indeed, Plato saw the origin of the state as not only a social phenomenon but also an economic necessity.

A state arises, as I conceive out of the needs of mankind. No one is self sufficing, but all of us have many wants ... Then as we have many wants, and many persons are needed to supply them, one takes a helper for one purpose and another for another; and then these helpers and partners are gathered together in one habitation, the body of the inhabitants termed a state ... And they exchange with one another, and one gives and another receives; under this idea the exchange will be for their good ... The true creator (of the state) is necessity who is the mother of our inventions.[1]

In the city-state, land was held by the aristocracy who divided it into fragments that could be cultivated by single households. The tenants, members of these households, accepted the task of tilling the land for the landlords. The term "economics" is derived from the Greek term for "household." Xenephon wrote an economic treatise called *Oikonomikes*, which means "the management of households." From the tenants a new class of merchants gradually evolved. The landlords made certain savings over their consumption. This saving needed to be brought back into circulation by offering more items for consumption. The merchant class served the function of circulating wealth.

Plato espoused rules for all these classes, and he wrote particularly about the division and specialization of labor. The doctrine of division of labor was befitting to the structure of state management. There were three groups involved in the government: (1) statesmen who ruled the states with their political wisdom; (2) soldiers who defended the state through their military training and physical strength; and (3) artisans who worked in the fields and traded the yields of the fields to meet the material needs of all three classes. The division of labor was intended to bring about the self-sufficiency of each district. If each cell could take care of itself, the entire body would remain healthy. Plato believed that people have innate talents to pursue, and they produce certain types of goods or services. He wrote that

All things are produced more plentifully and easily and of a better quality when one man does one thing which is natural to him and does it at the right time and leaves other things.[2]

If jobs of a different nature were imposed on these people, the total productivity would be depressed. Wisdom, according to Plato, was the ability to pursue the innate talent, which was the end and rule of life carried out by the mind.

In essence the principle is that one man should undertake only one trade. Plato stated this principle as one of the major prerequisites of a well organized community. Innate talents would determine the type of vocation each man should go into. Otherwise a person might waste a lot of natural gifts in pursuing another avocation for which he might not be gifted by nature. Present educational philosophy distinguishes innate talents and acquired talents as two separate areas of human aptitudes. By prolonged education a person can develop many talents, not only in the direction of natural endowment but also in areas where he is less gifted. Sometimes his effort and constancy can equip him with "acquired" talents that are better than his undeveloped natural talents. Plato would see it differently. He measured utility by the lowest wastage, and efficiency depended on the lowest expenditure of energy.

Thus he sees the doctrine of division of labor and specialization as the infallible ways of maximizing the common good. Plato did not permit mobility from one class to another. But the population was small, land was plentiful, and there was freedom to travel. If the social consequences of a caste system dissatisfied any member of the system he could leave for greener pastures elsewhere. Plato did not think that the teachers or philosopher kings in their wisdom would ever exploit the working class. This belief was based on the principle of communal property. In the guardian classes, Plato did not permit private property or ownership by a private family. Since there was no accumulation of private possessions, there was no fear of the exploitation of the weak and the aggrandizement of the privileged classes. The guardian class was totally devoted to the growth of the public welfare, they were supported by public funds, and therefore, the growth of the public funds became their chief concern.

Random thoughts like these are strewn about Plato's writings. For him, slavery was a normal economic factor. In *Laws* he described how slaves were to be treated, so that their lives would also be happy. He recommended division of labor among slaves according to their individual abilities.

Plato could not find anything to respect in craft (manufacturing) or commerce (dealing in goods produced by the farmers). He expected identical wages for men and women and openly condemned excessive profits as mere exploitation of another person's indigence. He argued further that excessive profit-taking was a deliberate abdication of the dictates of the intellect, and since one should have the full enjoyment of his moral, intellectual, and ethical values to attain fullest happiness, an act against the intellect was the worst sin a person could commit. It is clear that Plato's economic science was really only an extension of his philosophical ethics.

Aristotle

Aristotle (384-322 B.C.) was a disciple of Plato, and like Plato, he was the founder of a school and a prolific author. Besides *Politics* and *Nicomachean Ethics*, he wrote on biology, ethics, psychology, metaphysics, and logic. Aristotle observed the world about him and wrote to communicate with the real world. Thus, Aristotle was a realist while Plato remained an idealist.

According to Aristotle, the household is the beginning of economics. He said that the science of household management, *oikonomika*, is the most proper part of the economy. If each household were managed properly the state would be able to maximize happiness. The state should be completely self-sufficient, but Aristotle realized that not all households would be self-sufficient. In that case, the state had the duty to subsidize them so that their standard of living could be brought up to par. Wealth, according to Aristotle, amounts to the necessities of life that are at the command of the household or the state. Man owns and exchanges material goods in pursuit of the "good life," or in Aristotle's words, "the natural act of acquisition which is practiced by households and statesmen arises at first in the natural manner from the circumstances that some have too little and others too much. . . ."[3]

By the good life Aristotle did not mean an abundance of wealth but having enough leisure time to contribute to the fulfillment of duties. He perceived a dual system operating in households, one which was unbecoming for good household management. He called it *chremastistics*—money making. He had no kind words for those who were accumulating money at the expense of others. He thought that the amount of money one could accrue by skill alone was limited; but the amount of money resulting from trade alone was unlimited and to exploit trade to accumulate unlimited gains was wrong. Aristotle insisted that trade was not necessary to maintain the community's self-sufficiency. Today no one would go along with this opinion. Aristotle in some way combined the idea of profit with usury.

The most hated sort, and with the greatest reason, is usury, which makes gain out of money itself, and not from natural object of it. For money was invented to be used in exchange but not to increase the interest. . . . Of all modes of getting wealth, this is most unnatural.[4]

This attitude was not unusual. Until the modern era, most people considered money sterile and unproductive. The entire Judeo-Christian tradition protested severely against usury. In essence, Aristotle thought that an exchange should happen when there was an equality of wants on both sides. A surplus item would be exchanged for some other product which in itself was a surplus for the person who wanted to exchange. When trade happened between the two, both parties possessed equivalent values, or as Aristotle put it, "a sharing of goods through the equivalency of exchange."

He also thought that each commodity had two values. One was its primary value in use, which he called the subjective value; the other was its value in exchange, which he called the secondary or objective value.

Politics and *Ethics* contain the cream of Aristotle's economic thinking. He found three uses of money: (1) medium of exchange; (2) storage of value; (3) measure of value. He supported money because of its intrinsic value, usefulness, and easy applicability to the acquisition of goods. Money might become the medium of mutual contract, but he could not accept a specific value for money. To him money was a commodity that would fluctuate according to the market value of specie contained in the coin.

Plato advocated communal property, but his disciple could not accept this view. Aristotle studied the codes of 150 cities. This study convinced him that the right to private property was essential to advance the common good and wealth of the nation. He argued that common ownership would deprive the individual of his self-esteem and incentive to work, "for that which is common to the greatest number has the least care bestowed upon it."[5] He thought that private ownership engendered a special pride rooted in the "generosity of man" or in what Plato considered the innate talents.

Aristotle could not visualize the problem of scarcity that the world would have to face in centuries to come. He thought the world had ample resources to sustain both animals and people. Economics was the way an orderly distribution of these resources could be implemented so that all animals and people would have their just share. Aristotle did not understand the market mechanism, especially the supply and demand functions. He could not envision the relationship between domestic markets and foreign markets. This may be the reason why he called commercial profits unnatural profits.

Aristotle disapproved of trade and industry. He thought that industry was only changing the form of a product already in existence. Agriculture was the real thing, producing wealth out of nothing. Trade should not be considered a natural act since it involved taking a profit, exploiting the needs of consumers. He agreed with Plato and called trade a "dishonorable" function.

On the other hand Aristotle thought that a true economist must be able to acquire a certain level of wealth, and expected four qualities in this well-to-do economist: "He ought to be able to acquire it, and to guard it, otherwise no advantage in acquiring it; . . . further he ought to be able to order his possessions aright and make a proper use of them; for it is for these reasons we acquire wealth."[6] The "right" order in which a household should operate was exemplified in the way the wealth was exhibited and the members of the household protected against physical and moral dangers.

Aristotle complained about population explosion, and called for legal control over marriage and birth rate. He wanted, first, to limit the inhabitants of the city, and second, to limit the population of the state.

A state then begins to exist, when it has attained a population sufficient for a good life in the political community; it may indeed if it somewhat exceed this number, be a greater state. But, as I was saying, there must be a limit.[7]

The size of the population should never exceed the desirable level in which all people can live in peace and harmony.

Aristotle recognized four types of economies:

(1) Royal economy. This type had to do with the right of preeminence for coinage, exports, imports, and taxes to pay the bills;

(2) Seraphic or Provincial Governor economy. The cities survived only through the flow of goods from the farmland, for the farmer is the backbone of a nation. Based on the fact that city goods were always priced higher than farm goods, the Provincial Governor economy assured the flow of farmgoods to feed the urbanites by balancing the outflow of manufactured goods from the cities and the inflow of agricultural goods from the farmland.

(3) City economy. The concentration of people in the cities necessitated jobs to keep them occupied. The City economy had to do with the government's obligation to supply jobs for urbanites so that they could buy the farmgoods necessary for survival.

(4) Personal economy was the ordering of the individual household.

Summary

Plato's economic theories were those of an idealist while Aristotle was as a realist. Aristotle approached economics with a sociological understanding. Plato viewed economics as an auxiliary of politics. Economics was important only as a contributor to the well-being of the supreme state. Both Plato and Aristotle claimed that production and distribution were ethical only when the products met a "necessary use." Both considered agriculture the prime economic action.

Footnotes

1. Bell, John Fred. *A History of Economic Thought*, New York: Ronald Press, 1967, pp. 17-18.

2. Soule, George. *Ideas of Great Economists*, New York: Viking Press, 1953, p. 6.

3. *Ibid.*, p. 14.

4. Bell, *op. cit.*, pp. 4-5.

5. Spiegel, Henry. *The Development of Economic Thought*, New York: John Wiley & Sons, 1952, p. 7.

6. Monroe, Arthur Eli. *Early Economic Thought*, Cambridge: Cambridge University Press, 1930, p. 1344.

7. Whittaker, Edmund. *A History of Economic Thought*, New York: Longman Green, 1940, p. 322.

MERCANTILISM

Any analysis of the term mercantilism should include the sharp distinction between English mercantilism and the German cameralism (see p. 15). Beyond this important distinction, the student of economics will note three powerful forces at work in the building of mercantilism:

(1) The rise of the national state. As national states took shape, the thinkers who elaborated the economic system in each nation showed deep concern about making their own state both powerful and wealthy.

(2) "The commercial revolution." This "revolution" was characterized by a growth of money and credit economy that filled the coffers of the rich, who in turn distributed their wealth to businessmen in need of capital.

(3) The decrease of the medieval economy. The disappearance of the medieval institutions enriched the state, which then took up commercial pursuits or directly backed trading companies in maritime commerce by offering them charters with monetary subsidies and military protection.

External Policies

England especially was interested in asserting its power over the other states of Europe by entering their markets and wielding financial superiority. The fundamental position of foreign trade—to create a favorable balance of trade over the buyer nations—was explicated by Thomas Mun.

The ordinary means, therefore, to increase our wealth and treasure is by Foreign Trade, wherein we must ever observe this rule to sell more to strangers yearly than we consume of their's in value ... That part of our stock which is not returned to us in wares must necessarily be brought home in treasure.[1]

Almost a century after Thomas Mun wrote this doctrine, Bishop Berkeley was asking in the *Querist* whether that trade should not be accounted most pernicious, wherein the balance is most against us.[2]

Indeed, the doctrine antedates Mun's famous statement by well over a century and Bishop Berkeley's query by more than two. The idea had been supported by a consistent defensive tariff policy. The guilds had demanded the protectionists tariffs and custom laws. All of Europe was rocked by the outflow of gold, silver, and precious stones to Spain and Portugal who were the most aggressive merchants of early modern times. England, baffled by the loss of her intrinsic wealth, enacted laws forbidding the export of gold, silver, wool, and other items of recognized value. While they permitted the shipment abroad of manufactured goods and corn, they imposed import duties on luxury items and textiles. It was not until the latter half of the nineteenth century that these elaborate intricacies of customs and tariffs were abolished.

England, meanwhile, was trying hard to increase its shipping power. Under the Navigation Act the trading companies were permitted to sail their own ships under the English flag. Thus, the navy and the merchant marine became almost identical. The navigation laws were excellent examples of the mercantile policies in vogue at that time.

The old colonial system is another example of the external policies of mercantilism. England as a state was eager to expand its colonies wherever the merchants established markets. The takeover of lands that belonged to others was truly based on the economic gains the English expected to realize from distant countries. The colonies were also to be the source of essential raw materials and of exotic goods like cotton, tobacco, and spices. The home demand could be satisfied by importing raw materials from the colonies where the state had a favorable balance of trade.

Mercantilism also overhauled population policies. In many parts of England there were more people than were needed for the farming of expected arable lands. England wisely transplanted the surplus population to the colonies where they could find respectable jobs. These new employees of the colonies looked after the national interests as a means of safeguarding their own interests in the colonies.

By thus juggling resources and population, monopolizing colonial trade, and assigning new world manufacturers to a subordinate and supplementary place, England established a secure and thriving mercantile empire. To protect it, she entered into trade treaties with the other European countries, fought a war with the Dutch, kept the

Netherlands and France always at bay, and intimidated the lesser
powers from crossing her naval routes.

Internal Policies

In order to strengthen themselves the mercantile nations subjected
their citizens to sometimes voluntary, but most often involuntary
austerities. The appointment of governors within colonial regions and
districts was geared to enforce blind obedience to the decrees and
policies contained in white papers. The state also regulated prices and
qualities of goods. In addition, the government supervised the rate of
productivity, quotas, and even wages; sometimes it also enforced the
"iron law of wages," keeping wages at mere subsistence level. One
should bear in mind that this occurred when the total economy was
improving in England, because of profits from commerce and revenues from the colonies.

The state also meddled with the freedom of the people by urging
them to consume whatever they could afford. At the same time the
mercantilists kept constantly demanding some sort of sumptuary regulations. "If we were not too much affected to pride, monstrous
fashions and riot, above all other nations, one million and a half of
pounds might plentifully supply our wants," lamented Mun. There
were sumptuary laws in the reign of Edward I and during the rule of
Queen Elizabeth. Burleigh revised the fish laws requiring the entire
nation to eat fish on certain days. The tariffs aimed at restraining the
taste for foreign goods, going so far as to stop the importation of
foreign buttons and buttonholes from France, along with French lace
and cambrics. In spite of all this legislation—and perhaps because of
its inconsistency with the government's exhortations to conspicuous
consumption mentioned above—the mercantilists really failed to control the taste of an opulent populace. The government said, "Buy
English," but all the people heard was, "Buy."

The mercantile system was not at all remarkable for its coherence.
No writer insisted simultaneously on the balance of trades, sumptuary laws, or other related rulings. The nationalistic character, however, of the fundamental teachings of mercantilism was visible in all
the writings of the time. The state was expected to legislate for the
growth of its own power and wealth. As Malynes put it, "Nevertheless, (as a commonwealth is nothing else but a great household or
family) it ought to keep a certain equality in the trade or trafficke
between his realm and other countries."[3]

This excerpt shows the typical attitude of the mercantilists. The
interest of the households are subordinate to the dominant interests

of the family, and, as such, unequal treatment seems justifiable. The servants must accept a much more modest living than their masters. The state is the master of all households; consequently for the good of the state, all households must forego some of their preferences and comforts.

Mercantilism can be considered as a planned economy put into action. Even though at the beginning the science of economics did not enjoy a widespread acceptance, there is already evident a measure of ingenuity in ordering things under certain socialistic principles; this seems besides to have succeeded greatly in the twentieth century under Lenin and Stalin. The rich were permitted to spend but only for objects sanctioned by the state. Farmers and merchants were to cooperate with the state to produce an abundance of items that would fill the coffers of the state making it possible to restrict imports to what was strictly necessary to satisfy human wants and would least cause a depletion of the state treasury. While the farmer was expected to supply the raw materials needed for manufacturing, it was incumbent on the laborer to turn out the end products at the least possible cost.

The corn law provided for steady rent to be paid to the landlord. The merchant was permitted to take some profits, but always under the vigilant eyes of the state. All of these developments clearly point up the interdependence of politics and eocnomics. Political proposals were implemented by economic devices and economic questions were answered in the light of political gains. Even though politics seemed to be the sole determining factor with mercantilists, in the practical order economics held sway over politics. The economic activities of the individuals contributed to the stability of the state. Possibly this is the reason the state emphasized the idea of accumulating treasures and of enforcing the favorable balance of trade.

One special thought of the time seems strange. Economists wanted to create the power of a nation by keeping domestic order and building up international anarchy. The nations of Europe like France, Holland, and Spain, were self-contained and self-seeking. Their parochial mentality created an almost constant atmosphere of war and discontentment among them. Britain exploited this murky state of affairs in Europe to procure wealth, treasure, trade, and colonies on other continents.

One last feature of the mercantilists' political philosophy is worth consideration. They designed a structure of the state that they regarded as almost the primary goal of their system. Yet it is quite clear that the state, to which they assigned such a prestigious role, was structured on a foundation that had no connection with the political philosophy of the time. They confined themselves to fashioning an expedient, practical, and working mechanism—a device as unstable as the empires of the Roman era. One can see the display of a national household in the state they created. Its permanence depended on the acuteness of the business rivalries of the economy.

The main tenets of mercantilism were the following:

1. Mercantilists regarded gold and silver as the most desirable form of wealth.

2. Mercantilists promoted nationalism.

3. Mercantilists advocated importing raw materials without duties.

4. Mercantilists believed in dominating and exploiting the colonies.

5. Mercantilists believed in free movement of goods and services within the country.

6. Mercantilists believed in a strong central government.

7. Mercantilists favored accumulation of wealth for the nation but failed to legislate an equitable distribution of wealth for its citizens.

Footnotes

1. Mun, Thomas. *England's Treasure by Forraign Trade*, ed. Sir William Ashley, New York, 1895, pp. 7-8.

2. Berkeley, George. *The Querist*, ed. John Hallander, Baltimore, 1910, question no. 167.

3. Malynes, Gerard de. *A Treatise of the Canker of England's Common Wealth*, London, 1601, pp. 2-3.

CAMERALISM

While mercantilism flourished in England, the same philosophy had its impact on other parts of Europe. The term *cameralism* is applied to the associated political ideas regarding administration, finance, economic policy, and trade, which characterized the absolute monarchy in Germany and Austria during the eighteenth century. The term also has some reference to the political ideas of the same period. Cameralism is the version of mercantilism that existed under the German and Austrian kings. The primary distinguishing feature of cameralism was its emphasis on internal political consolidation to the exclusion of external policies for foreign trade or colonization outside. Under Frederick William I, the process of unification of the political elements started in Prussia. Later Maria Theresa in Austria tried to reform what had been started in Prussia. These reforms had some common denominators: (a) centralization of administration, (b) liberation of industry from guild organization, (c) creation of a uniform municipal law, and (d) formulation of a common mercantilistic philosophy. Austria started with absolute control, which was effected by the centralization of financial legislation that emphasized issuance of tax ordinances, designation of agencies of the central government for the collection of taxes, and reorganization of the Royal Exchequer as a national treasury. One can see two distinct phases in cameralism. For the first phase under Leopold I, it is easy to identify the great political economists of the time, namely Becher, Schroeder, and Hornick.

Becher concentrated on internal policies to coordinate all economic agents in pursuit of uniform goals. Schroeder advocated absolutism under a monarchical state. Hornick wrote about the unification of all Austrian states under the king. One can see in his writings a shadow of the "Federated States of Austria" as created in the new

15

continent. In cameralism there is a shadow of the "business science" that has become very prominent in the twentieth century. In fact, the university of Austria established a chair for administrative science under cameralism. The rising power of states demanded the principles of delegation, division of labor and specialization. In order to extend effectively the central power to all parts of the state, it was necessary to establish bureaus in the name of the state with equal executive power. The only obstacle to this pervading power of the state was the existence of powerful guilds that arose during the medieval period. The state abolished these guilds and paved the way for free trade within the state with mobility of labor and capital. The expansion of the states into every facet of individual life became a source of vast discontent among the people. In order to pacify them the state fabricated ingenious heresies like the "Natural Right of Kings" and the "Divine Right of Kings."

What characterized the natural rights of kings was the concept of "union of wills" not individual freedom. The state existed because of the joining together of the individual wills in a social contract—the "will of the state." The doctrine of natural rights as developed by Pufendorf formed the theoretical basis for enlightened absolutism. It interpreted the extent of state power to provide legal sanction for state intervention in private life.

. . . Cameralism (was) a series of proposals devised first, to help the quasi absolutist states recover from the ravages of endless wars; second, to bring about a self-sufficiency that would be beneficial both to the people and the state. The civic and economic problems were to be treated as one, and both were bound up in the mystical unity of the prince with the people . . .[1]

The most distinguished representatives of later cameralism are J. H. B. von Justi and Joseph von Sonnenfels. Their doctrines are founded on the natural rights theories of the state. For them the general happiness of the subjects is the object of the state. Unlike the mercantilists of England, the cameralists advocated increasing the population. The food supply and the population are in direct relation to each other. National wealth increases by increasing the population; the more people there are to work, the greater will be the increase in national wealth. The cameralists encouraged aliens to immigrate with promises of tax exemption and subsidies. The cameralists did not envision commercial expansion and manufacturing centers. Balance of trade was considered only as the relationship of available employment and available number of workers; freedom of trade meant only the abolition of price control by the state. On the practical side, cameralism was effective for over two centuries. The rulers regulated labor, industry, trade, and commerce. They encouraged skilled craftsmen to immigrate to Germany and also regulated money and credit.

The importance of knowledge of Kameralism to an understanding of German economics remains to be observed. Without its peculiar background of *Kameralwissenschaft*, German theory would probably have been other than it is. One of the most obvious effects appears in the division into general and special economics and finance, and in the emphasis on the technical and financial aspects. Again the early prevalence of the distinction between public and private interests, and the general recognition of the importance of legal advantages, special privileges, business arrangements and credit, may be traced to Kameralism.[2]

Cameralism existed as an economic idea in Germany until the close of the nineteenth·century. Adam Smith's doctrines were spread in Germany through the writings of Jacob, Sodan, and Hufeland and Kant exploded the natural right doctrine held for ages without challenge. But the philosophy was slow to die. Even Rau, who followed Adam Smith, could not force himself out from the cameralistic ideas he incorporated. Lorenz and Stein also show the same taint of cameralism in their writings. Cameralism as a science helped to develop the science of state administration, and with that came the disciplines of statistics, foreign trade, and public finance.

Footnotes

1. Sommer, Louise. "Cameralism," in *Encyclopedia of Social Sciences*, vol. 3, New York: Macmillan Co., 1951, pp. 158-60. And see Bell, John Fred. *A History of Economic Thought*, New York: Ronald Press Co., 1953.

2. Haney, Lewis H. *History of Economic Thought*, Chicago: University Press, 1909.

SIR WILLIAM PETTY

Sir William Petty, British economist, statistician, and mathematician was born on May 26, 1623, in Ramsey, England. At the age of 15 he joined the Hampshire merchant marine but was later abandoned on the French coast by his shipmates for reasons unknown. There he was educated by the Jesuits in their college. After a few years he returned to England and enlisted with the Royal Navy, but soon returned to civilian life to continue his education in medicine. In 1646 he received his diploma from the medical school at Leiden and was appointed a professor of anatomy at Oxford. There he collaborated with John Wilkins in the formation of the Royal Society, which was an informal scientific club.

In 1652, Petty was appointed Physician General of the Royal Army in Ireland. At that time, England was making a land survey of Ireland. The Irish charged that the survey was being done in a prejudiced manner by the English committee. Petty asked for and got the directorship of that survey and completed it to the satisfaction of the Irish people.

Petty was serving in Ireland when Charles I became king of England. Charles knighted him in 1662 for the many works he had done for the government and for being the charter member of the Royal Society. His reputation was further enhanced by the publication of his first work in political economy, *A Treatise of Taxes and Contributions*.

Petty belonged to the school of the Physiocrats; he accepted land as the major wealth of any nation. Taxes accrued from the productivity of the land were the major form of revenue for a nation. He did not accept that gold, silver, and precious stones were the basis of the wealth of nations as the mercantilists later contended. Petty reasoned further that the land received its productivity through the labor in-

19

vested in it. Hence the source of value was really the labor spent on the land, which alone is capable of reproduction. Later, Adam Smith and David Ricardo accepted the same thinking and perfected it to suit their schools of thought. In the same year 1662, Petty wrote *Natural and Political Observations made upon the Bill of Morality*, a study of population in London. Statistically oriented, this study analyzed the problem of the mass exodus to cities of the farming population and the subsequent problems of housing, schooling, health, and even morality. Statistics was a game for Petty; he called it, "political arithmetic." Petty used his statistical knowledge in studying agriculture, population, industry, commerce, and labor. These studies were published under various titles: *Political Anatomy of Ireland* (1672); *Observations upon the Cities of London and Rome* (1683-89); and *Political Arithmetic* (1687). Charles H. Hall published Petty's writings on economics and political science in 1894. The University of Cambridge published another volume of Petty's works in 1899. The Down Survey is still kept in the archives of Ireland and it was published in book form by the Archeological Society of Ireland in 1851.

Petty's writings evolved into the discussion of land, wages, tenants, manorism, and share cropping. They were directed more toward cameralism than mercantilism. He did not think too much about foreign trade, though he leaned toward a free trade system and could not find anything unreasonable in the exportation of coins and bullion. Petty did not grasp fully the meaning or operation of the foreign trade, so his utterances are never based on a definite logic. But when treating taxes and revenue, he speaks like an expert because he had the occasion of learning about them at first-hand. The Down Survey helped him to understand the need for taxes, and at the same time it revealed the shortcomings of the uniform tax on land. His work, *Verbum Sapienti* shows both the reason and the cause for discontentment among taxpayers: "Unequal taxation is the true and proper grievance of taxes." The land differed according to its topography, and since productivity depended on the quality of the land, Petty proposed taxing according to quality rather than quantity. He also realized the importance of revenue to meet the commitments of the exchequer. A nation's strength was, and is, its ability to meet its obligations of defending itself and also of supplying the various public services of education, health, transportation, and the like. Petty planned a tax system that would help the government meet its needs without burdening the farmers excessively. He recommended a thorough survey of land as the basis for establishing the size and plan for foreign trade. He demanded the study of land and its produce. Until this was done, he said, "trade will be too conjectural a work for any man to employ his thoughts about." His work, *Treatise of Taxes*, deals with the distribution of taxation, which is a key to the national wealth.

Petty used the tools of political arithmetic in describing the national wealth. He considered the population as wealth. Therefore, scarcity of people was the cause of poverty and vice versa. In an agricultural society every man able and willing to work added to the total productivity of the group. As Petty stated it, "hands are the fathers and land is the mother" of wealth. He built up a formula between hand and land, so that the right combination could maximize productivity, and he accepted money as the common denominator. It is not easy to arrive at the money value of people, who are in fact, not bought or sold. Petty's formula of the monetary value of hand is only conjectural, yet it shows that he had a good understanding of capitalization.

In 1664, Petty did a study of the trade rivals of England, France and Holland. He wrote a booklet, *A collection of Frugalities of Holland* and he asked the British Commonwealth to establish in England some of the austere practices of Holland. In the *Treatise of Taxes*, the Dutch system was held up as a model for England to emulate. In the *Political Arithmetic and Five Essays*, Petty praised the Netherlands as a model but gave first place to France as a power to be feared by the superior life style in England.

The major issues of Petty's work were taxes and revenues, i.e., the amount shared with the farmer by the state. Petty could not explain the reason for other types of income such as rent and interest. He brought out the question: "Why does the right to receive a definite annual payment throughout an infinite succession of years, command in the market only a finite sum?" He never took the time to answer this question in any of his works. He did recognize that the value of the fee depended on the rent that the land would yield. The capital value of the land then was based on the rent, which in turn was based on the productivity. His political arithmetic, therefore, could assign an exact value in money for land, calculated from the rent.

A Treatise of Taxes and Contributions was written when England was going through a series of sudden transitions. The prohibitionists opposed the exportation of gold from England. They believed that gold and precious metals should be the real wealth of a nation and should never be parted with at any cost. The bullionists claimed that gold and precious metals were mere commodities and should be sold at a profit like any other merchandise. Petty believed that the precious metals were the basic wealth of a nation. Yet, he asserted that labor and land took precedence over gold and precious metals. Thus his oft repeated dictum, "land the mother and hand the father" of wealth!

Petty approved the "free port system" like the ones that existed in the Netherlands, which levied taxes on all articles of consumption. He had several reasons for supporting a free port tax system: (1) It decreased smuggling since trade was open for all without any hindrance; (2) by taxing imported consumer goods, the quantity imported would decrease due to the rise in prices; and (3) raw materials could be imported without excise tax at the seaboard. He encouraged more exports and fewer imports so that the nation might enjoy a continuous favorable balance of trade.

Since labor was one of the chief ingredients of wealth, Petty exhorted the total utilization of all available labor. Unemployed people should be directed to public works on roads, making rivers navigable, planting trees, building bridges, mining, and, when possible, manufacturing. He preferred a large population and endorsed the mercantilists' idea of full employment. He advocated a poll tax with the statement: "It seems to be spur unto all men, to set their children to some profitable employment on their very first capacity, out of proceeds thereof, to pay each child his own poll tax money."[1] He thought rent was surplus from land; yet he failed to distinguish the difference between 'return to capital' and 'return to land.'

The corn rent system was predicated on "the excess of the produce over the expense of the cultivation." Petty must have borrowed from Hobbes the labor theory of value. Petty found that a permanent tax on land forced the farmer to pay tax even though the year's crop might have failed. The Down Survey exempted a farmer from paying taxes in the years the expenses of production were greater than the income received from the farm. Petty thought that with a proper method of cultivation any land could be made productive. Clearly, no farmer would waste his land's productivity to avoid paying taxes, and the farmer would also be interested in the surplus value, that is, revenue over capital expenses.

Petty's taxes were not rigid or inflexible demands. "The amount of rent per acre is determined by the density of the population dependent for food upon the land and varies inversely as the said density." This kind of legislation encouraged parents to have larger families, since each of the farmer's children increased the density of population on the land, and decreased the rent he was bound to pay. Technical fertility was not the only measure of establishing a tax structure. Later, Ricardo perfected Petty's formula of rent.

Interest is another economic factor Petty examined. He set out a twofold basis for interest: (1) compensation for risk, and (2) payment for the inconveniences of the lender. When a person lent money for a definite period of time, he was postponing the use of that money for that determined period of time. Having given up the use of the money, the lender might, in the meantime, meet with many unforeseen emergencies requiring the use of the money. Petty felt that this type of personal hardship must be remunerated.

The amount of interest depended on the amount of land the money could buy and also the return on the investment in land. He believed the interest should never exceed five percent. There should be some benefit to the borrower when he used the borrowed money in productive pursuits. If the revenue from land was big, the farmers would borrow money at a higher interest rate and vice versa. In the twentieth century, John Meynard Keynes coined the technical term, "marginal efficiency of capital," which is the expected rate of return on investment. Petty was expressing the same thing in the construct of his age. Exchange was considered as "local usury" meaning, apparently, a compensation for the cost of moving money. Moving money underwent risk, but this risk was eliminated by exchange. Hence one had to pay for that service. Petty did not condemn interest and exchange as usury; he condoned them as the just payments for services rendered.

The idea of wages also had a place in Petty's discussions. In treating rent, the idea of income was introduced. This income was the difference between the expenditures and the total revenue. Size of the income would depend on the smallest cost and highest revenue. A capricious producer would employ workers and give them the minimum to keep the cost down; the wider the chasm between cost and revenue, the richer the land owner would be. But Petty was against underpaying the workers. He thought that profit was not the entire prerogative of the landowner; It had to be shared by employer and employee. This sharing could be done by increasing the wage rate. Similarly, when the expenditures and revenues were almost the same, or the difference was minimal, wages would have to be lowered to make room for a legitimate profit for the employer.

Petty built his concept of rent from the same source, namely, the difference between expenditures and total revenue. The same area became the determinant factor for establishing wage rate. The rent was an additional cost to the employer. If the profit margin decreased because of less revenue, there were two possible alternatives: (1) depress the wage level, or (2) depress the taxes. Petty said, "When the wages of husbandsmen rise, rent of land must consequently fall." This might have been a good thing, if governments had been able to carry on their duties when the wages of husbandsmen rose and the rent fell. The amount of services a government can extend depends on the size of its revenues. By limiting taxes, the lawmakers limit what the government can do for its citizens. This is where Petty's theory of taxation becomes ineffective.

Footnotes

1. *Dictionary of National Biography.* Oxford University Press, London, vol. 15, p. 25.

RICHARD CANTILLON

Richard Cantillon (1685-1734) is considered by some to be the greatest economist before Adam Smith. Cantillon was born in Ireland in 1685. There is much confusion about his identity, stemming from the fact that there seem to have been two Cantillons. Young Richard, the economist, lived with his uncle, the Chevalier Richard Cantillon who was a banker and a man of political importance. Richard Cantillon, the economist, was murdered in London in 1734 by his former cook, who resorted to fire to destroy his former master. Many of Cantillon's economic writings perished in that fire.

Cantillon seemed to have engaged chiefly in banking; he was also involved in an import-export trade in wine, silk, and metals. He started his banking career with his uncle in Paris, but in 1720 he left the French capital for an extensive European tour. Meanwhile he amassed great wealth, succeeding in his many and varied careers, and eventually returning to France to write his views on economics. His fortune at the time of his death was extensive, varied, and dispersed; it included houses and holdings in a number of countries and places.[1]

Cantillon's works remained unnoticed for over 50 years after his death. In 1881, Stanley Jevons edited the unorganized manuscripts and published them in book form. For the first time, the world understood Cantillon's genius. It was he who coined the word, "entrepreneur"—one who purchases goods at a certain price to sell them again at an uncertain price, because he cannot foresee the extent of the demand.[2]

Cantillon's most outstanding work is the *Essai sur la Nature du Commerce en General*.

The *Essai* is divided into three parts. The first develops a general introduction to political economy. It deals with a definition of wealth and then discusses the association of people in societies, in

25

villages, towns, cities and capital cities, the wages of labor, the theory of value, the dependence of all classes upon landed properties, the multiplication of population and the use of gold and silver.[3] The second part discusses barter, prices, circulation of money, and interest; also it contains a treatise on currency. Foreign commerce, foreign exchange, banking, and refinements of credits comprise the third part.

The influence of *Essai* on the development of economic thought is immeasurable. James Stuart, Adam Smith, David Ricardo, and a host of economic writers of the eighteenth century were familiar with Cantillon's writings. They used his definitions, interpretations, and channels of thought in their own writings, without giving due reference to their source of discussion.[4]

The *Essai* deals with the reactions of the contemporary writers in economics, to the world in which they live. Cantillon's views on population fall into five categories:

(1) The mechanism by which members are adjusted in time and space;

(2) The demand for labor and population;

(3) Foreign trade, population capacity, and population growth;

(4) The genesis of living standard; and

(5) The distribution of population in geographic areas.

Cantillon described the relationship of total population to the available labor force. He thought that the migration of people was a natural effect of labor surplus and that people should be free to move wherever they liked. Excess population, he presumed, was eliminated by nature itself through increased infant mortality and occasional adult mortality resulting from pestilence and other contageous diseases. He was of the opinion that nature had a built-in stabilizing mechanism. If man did not tamper with nature, the population would remain adequate at all times. Great famine and poverty, he asserted, were nature's way of controlling population.

Cantillon based his population theory on the cost-of-production theory of value. He said that labor, whose supply depended on the number of people in a certain community, was the main cost of production. He thought that the demand for labor depended on the consumption pattern of the rich. Should these spend their money on the building and furnishings of the cities, the workers could not apply themselves to the production of food; only if the rich subsidized them could the workers produce agricultural products. Affluence, he thought, would accompany this production, whereas famine threatened should the money go for "guns instead of butter," to borrow a current phrase. He considered an economy "closed" that functioned independently of the economies of foreign markets. Conversely, he saw in an "open" economy a constant flow of goods and services. Each good was a "labor imbedded" object, so by trade a nation exchanged labor for labor. Cantillon concluded, "By these induction and examples, I think, we can understand that the price or the intrinsic value of a thing is the measure of the quantity of land and labour which enter into its production, regard being had to the goodness or productiveness of the land and the quality of the labour."[5]

Cantillon saw that money and market mechanisms were the immediate factors that established price and value. He used the notions of supply and demand to arrive at the market price of an item. There is a difference between current price and intrinsic price. The inherent value of the commodity is the intrinsic price, while what is offered in the market is the current price. Even though Petty, North, and Locke mentioned the distinction between current and inherent price, it was Cantillon who perfected this very essential economic idea. The place where the commodity originates and the time when the same commodity is offered for sale, have serious effects on the determination of its price. Cantillon did not comprehend the possibilities of monopoly or oligopoly forces entering the determination of price. He presumed pure competition as the norm of market system.

Cantillon also treated the relationship of money to the quantity of money available to the economy. He agreed with Petty that the intrinsic value of money depended on its cost of production. Cantillon thought that more money makes "land and labor dearer." He analysed the velocity of money and who knows whether Keynes borrowed the term from Cantillon and perfected the idea? Cantillon held that an increase of velocity of money did the same job as the increase of quantity of real money. He went further as to say that timing, manner, and bulk of money supply would have an autonomous effect on price and demand in the market. In his words, "the great difficulty of this question . . . consists in knowing in what way and in what proportion the increase of money raises the prices." Microeconomists find three ways of price discrimination in the present day practice, which come close to Cantillon's theories of location, time, and money velocity.

Cantillon thought that exportation of manufactured goods led to the financial growth of a nation; under the exportation system foreign buyers supported the workers of the exporting state. He did not favor the mutual exchange of surpluses between trading countries, but expected payment to be made with the gold and silver of the importing country. He considered bilateral trade a mere exchange of labor for labor. An arrangement of this sort, he felt, prevented a nation from acquiring sufficient wealth to improve the standard of living of its people.

Cantillon also described the change in prices due to the dynamics of the living standard. As a result of rising prices, he thought that the real income of the proprietors declined. Moreover, he felt that increases in the quantity of hard money in circulation tended to increase the objective and the subjective standard of living. "I conclude," he said, "that an increase of money circulating in a state always causes there an increase of consumption and a higher standard of expenses."[6] He further stated that things did not always sell at their intrinsic value, but according to their abundance or scarcity. Further, he argued that it was impossible to accommodate supply to demand.

Cantillon discussed the economic aspects of country and city life. The prices and cost of living were and are higher in the city than in the country. He attributed this to the fact that, "balance of payment is almost always due from the country localities to the cities and the capital of the country; and that the commodities with which this balance is practically discharged, include the cost and risk of conveyance."[7] Cantillon applied the same theory of the flow of processed goods from cities to the country districts, in exchange for the products from the latter. The same principles apply to the cause of foreign trade. "Any state which sells manufactured goods to neighboring states in such quantity as to draw a balance of specie toward itself, will eventually raise its own scale of prices."[8]

Cantillon wrote about the art of banking when the banking system was rather primitive. Although he himself amassed millions of pounds during a short week on the exchange market, he did not have any kind words for the speculators of the time. The Law's paper currency, he felt, made an abnormal impact on the quantity of money in circulation.

An abundance of fictitious and imaginary money causes the same disadvantages as an augmentation of the real money in circulation. By raising the price of land and labour, or by making works or manufacture more expensive at the risk of subsequent loss. By this occult abundance vanishes at the first shock to credit and predicts disorder.[9]

Cantillon did not stress that increment in income always resulted in a higher standard of living and consequently in higher prices. He implied that the increase in a nation's income tends to condone greater imports from the outside. The only way to solve this dilemma, he wrote, was to produce more to satisfy domestic needs. Production required an ample supply of trained workers as well as a ready supply of raw materials. It was impossible to realize these stipulations in a short period of time and, as a consequence, imports were needed. Increased imports would, however, wipe out the higher supply of money and the higher standard of living, experienced by the importing country. It is evident to the student of economics that trade does not always remain unilateral. The higher standard of living of the exporting country would generate a commensurate flow of imports to stabilize the economies of both countries involved.

Cantillon was the first writer to describe the self-adjusting mechanism of demand, supply, prices, costs and other vital economic functions. In addition he thought that the legislative power of a nation should not tamper with the natural function of the economic system. Adam Smith, David Ricardo, Thomas Malthus, and James Mill quoted extensively from the writings of Cantillon. His ideas touch every aspect of economics. Even great French schools of economics hailed Cantillon as the father of economics. Cantillon must be considered as one of the foremost authorities on economic thought, for on his ideas rest much of modern economic theory.

Footnotes

1. Cantillon, Richard. *Essai sur la Nature du Commerce en General*, (Trans. Henry Higgs) New York: A. M. Kelley, 1964, p. 365.
2. Spiegel, Henry. *The Development of Economic Thought*, New York: John Wiley & Sons, 1952, p. 67.
3. Cantillon, op. cit., p. 106.
4. Jevons, Stanley. *Principles of Economics: a Fragment of the Treatise on the Industrial Mechanism of Society*, New York: A. M. Kelley, 1964, p. 52.
5. Spiegel, op. cit., p. 49.
6. Higgs, George H. *The Physiocrats*, New York: Macmillan, 1897, p. 58.
7. Jevons, op. cit., p. 205.
8. Spiegel, op. cit., p. 52.
9. Ibid., p. 56.

DAVID HUME

There is very little written about the early life of David Hume. His autobiography, *My Own Life*, is simple and concise. Hume was the second son of the Home family of Ninewells, an estate near Berwick, Scotland. David disliked the name Home and later changed to Hume. David lost his father when he was very young and his care was left to his mother, "a woman of singular merit."

Hume's description of his education is also meagre: "I passed through the ordinary course of education with success." One of his letters tells of the type of education he had: "as our college education in Scotland, extending little further than the language, ends commonly when we are about fourteen or fifteen years of age. After that, I was left to my own choice in my reading."

Hume was "seized with passion for literature" that continued throughout his life. According to primogenital rights of succession, John Home, David's elder brother succeeded to the Ninewell's estate after the death of their father. Since the family was, in Hume's words, "not rich," his patrimony was "very slender." His studious disposition, sobriety, and industry prompted him to pursue law education, but he soon gave that up to study philosophy and literature. He avoided physical activities and spent his time delving into Voet, Vinnius, Cicero, and Virgil.

Hume wrote only seven essays in economics, yet these seven essays received great acceptance among economists. Some writers place Hume among the classical economists like Adam Smith, but others think that he was more a mercantilist. Usually a writer bequeathes to the world the richness of his intellectual prowess, and the followers of the writer finally analyze and criticise his writings and enshrine him in various niches according to their whims. So Hume is a great philosopher to some; to others, one of the stalwarts of the education-

31

al philosophy; and to still others, one of the proponents of mercantilism.

Hume's essays contain not only themes of proposals, but also criticisms of the existing systems. His economic thoughts are inseparable from his political ideas. He believed the politics of a free society was the assurance of the economic growth of its members, and the economic system he proposed was founded on liberty.

Civil Liberty, the first essay, characterizes some great advances in the realm of human civilization. Hume found that a peaceful and constitutional government opens the way for the progress of all sciences, which in a true sense measures the civilization of that time. He thought of peaceful coexistence as the best outward sign of human maturity and of war as the overt expression of the primitive hostility of man. He wanted a peaceful society in which "a number of neighboring and independent states, connected together by commerce and policy" work together for mutual progress. The next essay he published, *Of Balance of Power*, is a continuation of the thoughts on peaceful coexistence. He proposed a free trade system in which all states involved would refrain from deterring the free flow of goods and services.

Of Commerce, the third essay, demonstrates the importance of freedom in trade and commerce. Rulers must consult the people they rule, before they proceed to legislate for all. Individual interests of the rulers can hamper the common good of the people. Therefore, free trade is a sign of the rulers' willingness to permit their citizens to pursue the advantages of division of labor and specialization. Hume believed that this freedom must benefit the state. Everything in the world is purchased by labor and our passions are the only causes of labor. The more labor, therefore, that is employed, the more necessities there are, and the more powerful is a state.[1]

Of Money

This essay is a study of price and value. "It seems," said Hume, "the prices of everything depend on the proportion between commodities and money, and that any considerable alteration on either has the same effect either of heightening or lowering the price."[2] This natural relationship depends on a good government which permits freedom of enterprise. When this freedom is restricted in any form, the whole society becomes crooked and confused. The result of such a development is the creation of monopolies, cartels, and other unethical means of maximizing and exploiting profits. Hume believed the functions of the merchants were very important for the economic growth of a state. "Merchants beget industry, serving as canals to convey it through every corner of the state."[3] In his time, there were writers, such as the great physiocrats, Quesnay, Turgot, and Petty, who depressed the positions of the merchants and considered them to be parasites. Hume, however, thought that the profit motive was a natural instinct of all enterprises, and he defended the merchants' right to take risks to earn a profit legitimately.

Of The Balance of Trade

In his previous essay, Hume mentioned that overproduction in one state can create imbalance between the neighboring states. He developed the theme in this essay. Production is for consumption. Overproduction by a state would force that state to impose its surplus on other states and thus accumulate wealth for itself. This spirit of accumulation of wealth by a state, destroys the original understanding and cooperation between the community of states. It is only natural that the more powerful a state, the more it would look down on other states like an overlord and later demand unquestioned conformity to its demands. Intervention in other states is the embryo of imperialism. Hence Hume's dictum: "What happens in small portions must take place in greater."

Hume also discussed the policy of monetary devaluation, depreciation, and revaluation. He recommended the issuance of paper money as a way of lowering the value of money. The revaluation of national currency imposes hardships on other countries in buying goods and services of the revaluated nation. Similarly, devaluation has the effect of increasing the exports of the devaluated country. Internally this makes no difference to the actual wealth of any particular individual. Still, monetary changes have a general result of giving further "encouragement to industry." Hume did not want any state to amass wealth. He warned that states possessing hoards of wealth were likely to use such wealth," in dangerous and ill-concerted projects." The degeneration of the overly wealthy would engender the loss of a sense of civilization and "thereby probably destroy with it what is much more valuable, the industry, morals and numbers of its people."

Hume wrote that it is not the accumulation of wealth that is important for any nation; it is the free circulation of goods and services, which implies a sharing of the bounties of nature by as many people as possible. This, in a true sense, is the wealth of a nation. What a lofty idea for a man of the eighteenth century! And what an astute observation. The present generation is surrounded by object lessons in reverse. Accumulation of wealth by one nation, one class, one race, has indeed created conflict and undermined our sense of civilization.

A credit system is considered a way of overcoming economic fluctuations for an individual or society at large. "Merchants," Hume writes, "acquire a great facility in supporting each others credit, which is a considerable security against bankruptcies." However, credit also has some evil effects on society. It can be an inducement to overspend, and merchants can exploit the extravagance of the thoughtless consumers. Hume says, "Merchants adopt many contrivances, which serve no other purposes but to check industry and rob ourselves. . . ." The same theme of thinking led Hume to write *Of the Jealousy of Trade*. Hume could see the English tradesmen exploiting everyone with their unfair competitive practices. He was so utterly disgusted with the way business practices were deteriorating that he said publicly, "not only as a man, but as a British subject, I pray for the flourishing commerce of Germany, Spain, Italy and even France." When a British subject prays for the economic prosperity of "even" France, the situation is serious indeed.

Of Taxes

The essential thoughts of Hume's economics can be found in all his essays. In *Of Taxes* he addressed the problem of national debt. "Posterity will pay off the encumbrances contracted by their ancestors," he wrote. He condemned national leaders who borrow on the hope of never paying back in their lifetime and wage war against other countries with borrowed wealth. Hume was a strong opponent of war, because "modern war is attended with every distructive circumstance; loss of men, increase of taxes, decay of commerce, dissipation of money and devastation by sea and land"[4] Many of these destructive circumstances are caused by the deficit spending attendant on any war through the selling of negotiable war bonds.

In the domestic economy of a nation, the practice of deficit financing has many disadvantages:

1. The rural population migrates to the cities.

2. Public securities drive out private financing.

3. Taxes and interests increase and raise the wage structure disproportionately.

4. The large holdings of the securities will be in the hands of the

rich, who undertake an idle life of wasteful leisure. Hume said, "our funds, give greater encouragement to a useless and inactive life."

5. The greater part of the securities of a nation will fall into the hands of other nations and make the debtor nation "a tributary of other nations" who are creditors.

Hume demands setting upper limits to public debts. Every war creates increasing debts, which normally can never be repaid. The loser has no way of paying back; the winner becomes a total bank-rupt after winning the war. The war can be financed only by borrow-ing, mortgaging, and selling precious materials of wealth at cut-rate prices. In similar circumstances a private individual has no recourse other than bankruptcy. In the same way a national debt will lead the nation to total insolvency.

Hume wanted balance between nations and balance between every form of human activity. Is this not the same idea Keynes talked about in the General Equilibrium Theory? Hume did not use the semantics of Keynes, but the fundamental idea was displayed in the statement of 'balance' and 'limitation' in his discussion. Hume's bal-ance embodied every form of interaction of man, like balance in opinion, balance between interests and rent, balance of wages and prices, and balance of commerce. The major function of the govern-ment is to establish this type of balance where all parties have the resources and freedom to excel. He envisioned the world community as one entity and wanted harmony between the members based on a balance of power between them.

Footnotes

1. Hendel, Charles. *David Hume's Political Essays,* New York: The Liberal Arts Press, Inc., 1953, pp. 325-26.

2. Green, T. H. and Grose, T.H., eds., *Essays, Moral, Political and Literary,* London: Longman, Green & Co., 1898, pp. 316-19.

3. Ibid., pp. 331-34.

4. Green and Gross, op. cit., p. 362.

References

Greig, J.Y.T. *The Letters of David Hume,* London: Bouverie Press House, 1932.

Laing, B.M. *David Hume,* London, Clarendon Press, 1932.

Mossner, Earnest Campbell. *The Life of David Hume,* Austin: University of Texas Press, 1954.

Oser, Jacob. *The Evolution of Economic Thought,* New York: Harcourt Brace and World, Inc., 1970.

FRANCOIS QUESNAY

Quesnay was born at Mere, France, the son of a prominent lawyer. Francois lost his father when he was quite young, but his father had provided for the education of his children. Quesnay was a genius from the very beginning and earned a license to practice medicine at the age of 16. He continued his medical education in Paris and became a master surgeon at the age of 24. He earned his doctor's degree in. medicine in 1744. By 1749, he had become the physician of Madame de Pompadour and Louis XV. Joseph Schumpeter wrote about him, "as being thoroughly upright and honest."[1]

Eighteenth century economics saw a new system of thought develop in the works of Francois Quesnay. Like William Petty, who started as a physician and then became an economist, Quesnay by dint of circumstances made himself into an economist. Quesnay is the father of politico-economic individualism. He wrote a book for the use of his royal patients called *Tableau Economique* in 1758, which was immediately followed by his second publication, *Maximes Generales*. Some of his articles like "Fermiers" and "Grains" appeared in the Encyclopedia in 1756. In 1888, Onkenon edited his articles into one and published them simultaneously in Frankfurt and Paris under the title *Oeuvres économiques et politiques*. Mirabeau and Turgot were primarily responsible for advocating and extending Quesnay's economic doctrines, and although his theories spread slowly, Quesnay lived to see them in the ascendancy in Europe.

Quesnay is identified with the physiocrats. He held that the right to property is a part of human freedom. He borrowed some of his ideas from the English writers Shaftesbury, Locke, and Cumberland. Some say, "as Locke was the father of political individualism, Quesnay was the father of economic individualism."[2]

Physiocrats emphasized the individual right and believed that the individual knew best what is good for him. The principle of self-interest was the core of their economic philsophy. The politics of France was totally against individualism. Hence the physiocrats took it on themselves to achieve changes in politics and society.

Quesnay's *Tableau* was the first attempt to change the notion of political supremacy and introduce *ordre naturel*. He identified three classes: (1) the productive class or cultivators; (2) the proprietors or landowners, who were considered semiproductive; and (3) the non-productive or, as Quesnay put it, *la classe sterile,* including merchants and professional people. Quesnay organized various professions and occupations according to their importance and this is how his work got the name *Tableau.* Quesnay's ordering of occupations was totally in line with his preferences and prejudices and thus cannot be reckoned as foolproof. He expected his table to be a compass measuring and directing priorities in the political policies.

Like Aristotle, Quesnay regarded agriculture as the prime occupation, and he thought that the land and cattle are the primitive wealth of all great states. He was the author of the dictum, "The wealth of the agriculturalists beget the agricultural wealth." In his essay "Fermiers" he wrote about the problems of farmers. He pointed out two alternative choices at the command of the farmers: to use horse or oxen to plough the field. It was obvious, he said, that the horse-ploughed field had a better yield than oxen-ploughed fields. He pointed out the national loss caused by the inability of many farmers to use horses to plough their fields. He found three main reasons for the rural poverty:

1. Immigration of peasant children to the cities (once in the city, children do not support their parents);

2. The arbitrary taxation which causes agricultural investments to be insecure; and

3. The restriction on corn trade.

Quesnay advocated the abolition of an arbitrary tax on agriculture. He said, "The true national economic policy was to turn to the productive power of the soil of France, and buy luxuries from abroad . . . exactly the reverse of what was being attended."[3]

Quesnay and the physiocrats introduced the idea of *produit net*, which means the surplus that is received from the cooperation of land and labor. Into the distribution of this *produit net*, come the landowner, tenant, and workers who contributed to the "staff making" or surplus of the bounty of nature.

Quesnay did not recommend any better wages for the workers. Physiocrats as a whole advocated a subsistence wage. Quesnay's value theory also depended on the *produit net*. Value and price were intimately affixed to cost. The same goes for taxation; all who shared *produit net* should pay tax. Since land is the only source of value, the burden of taxation rested on the productivity of the land. The land tax became the single direct tax. Quesnay also proposed indirect taxes, not on the landowner, tenant, or worker, but on the business man who imported and exported and did various functions for a profit. There was clear distinction between the land-profit, or *produit net* and the profit derived from commerce. The land produces from nothing but commerce produces profit from things already existing in one form or another. Hence, the reason for the indirect tax on merchants.

Quesnay stood for *laissez faire, laissez passer, le monde va lui-même* (let do and let be, the world goes of itself), a principle that emanates from the self-interest doctrine. He wanted freedom of occupation, freedom of consumption, and freedom of movement from place to place. The center of all these freedoms was the freedom of private property.

In America, Benjamin Franklin became a disciple of Quesnay; in France, Turgot accepted Quesnay as his teacher; and in England, many writers in economics and politics accepted Quesnay's views. Some writers, however, were displeased with Quesnay's writings and refuted his major theories. In Italy, Galiani opposed Quesnay's claim of natural order; Condillac opposed Quesnay's assertion that manufacturing and commerce are sterile; and the clergy considered him as a rebel, since Quesnay could not accept the clergy as a productive class nor the existence of a primary spiritual or mental, rather than corporal, productive activity.

Physiocrats under Quesnay made some real contribution to the time and were indirectly responsible for the beginning and growth of mercantilism. Some of the benefits accruing from the physiocrats can be summarized as follows:

1. They put economics on a scientific basis by applying scientific methods and by separating it from sociology and politics.

2. Their emphasis on the surplus of agriculture or *produit net* led the way for the surplus value theory.

3. Their analysis of capital or factors of production led to the notion of rent, interest, wage, and profit.

4. They developed the theory of taxation.

5. Their thought opened the way for individual freedom and the abolition of many social practices, policies, and laws that discriminated against people on the basis of economic disparities.

6. Their insistence that "land is the source of all values" initiated the scrambling for more land and the establishment of many colonies.

The idea of *laissez faire and laissez passer* became the soul of the economic growth of the New World. This freedom theory, is the philosophical justification of the natural right. The United States Constitution is written with the preamble of inalienable human right, which is the outcome of the *ordre naturel*. Spann has described this matter in his forceful and eloquent style:

Since economic laws cannot run counter to the natural laws of the social life, since they likewise are manifestations of the determinisms inherent to the natural laws of the "ordre naturel" action in accordance with the natural law, which prescribes that a man should obey the dictates of self-interest cannot fail to bring about the most natural (and, therefore, the best) development of economic life.[3]

Footnotes

1. Spann, Othmar. *The History of Economics*, New York: Norton, 1930, p. 75.
2. Higgs, Henry. *The Physiocrats*, London: Macmillan, 1897, p. 46.
3. Ibid., p. 29.
4. Spann, op. cit., p. 85.

References

Haney, Lewis H. *History of Economic Thought*, New York, Macmillan Co., 1936.

Schumpeter, Joseph A. *History of Economic Analysis*, New York, Oxford University Press, 1955.

Encyclopedia Britanica, Vol XVII, XVIII and VI, New York, Harcourt, Brace & World, 1966.

ANNE ROBERT JACQUES TURGOT

Turgot was born and educated in Paris. At the early age of 22, he joined the University of Sorbonne as an instructor. After some time, he was elected prior (president) of that celebrated institution. He remained there only three years, relinquishing his presidency in 1761 to assume the civil service job of *intentent* (like city manager) of Limoges. There he got his first chance to apply some of the economic theories he learned in class-rooms and private reading. He published his first writings, *Reflexion sur la formation et la distribution des richesse (The Reflections About the Formation and Distribution of Wealth)*. This timely publication won him profound admiration among the elite. The civil authorities recognized his talents and made him the General Comptroller of France in 1776.

It was customary at the time for city managers to demand free labor from the citizens. Most cities were economically unable to pay for the various services needed for the public welfare, for people were too poor to pay city taxes in money. So free labor contributed to the city worked for the benefit of the city and its citizens. This practice, seemingly beneficial to both parties, caused numerous problems for the public and the city. Sometimes, when the city needed bricklayers, it got carpenters, and similar situations made the practice onerous to everyone involved.

While serving as the city manager of Limoges, Turgot abolished the practice of "contributed service." Turgot introduced money payment for all public works, and to meet the needs, he introduced a new system of taxation. While serving as the General Comptroller, Turgot abolished *octoris*, the tax on foods and drinks brought into the cities. He also abolished the *droit d'auliane*, a residency tax on foreigners which discriminated against people within the same city.

It was not only the abolishing of taxes that made Turgot famous.

41

The new system of taxes he levied on all segments of the society made him known as a great administrator. He found that the old guild system of France had outlived its usefulness. They had already become a barrier to free trade and free enterprise. The guilds or, as they were called, *jurandes* perpetuated monopolies with clan and class biases. Hence, Turgot decreed the liquidation of all guilds in France.

Turgot thought that yield on money as interest is always greater then the yield on land. The money lender would invest his money on land if the rate of return from the land exceeded the existing interest rate. Interest presupposes a certain amount of risk. Hence an attractive interest rate is the only compelling reason to lend money to borrowers.

One should not forget that Turgot was writing at a time when most schools forbade interest on loans as sinful. Turgot defended the interest rate as a legitimate reward for the use of money. He wrote, "Interest is the sum paid for the use of land or any object of commerce, and depends in either case, on the supply and demand."[1]

Turgot condoned only a land tax. He argued that all forms of taxes in the final analysis, rest on the land revenue. This opinion was founded on the rejection of commerce as an unnatural pursuit that did not deserve even the honor of being taxed. However, Turgot did find a few reasons for the existence of commerce:

1. Unequal distribution of land;
2. Diversity of soil and its fitness for production;
3. Multiplicity of human race; and
4. Advantages of division of labor and specialization.

Turgot preferred farmers over other artisans. His argument was, farmers can exist without artisans, but artisans cannot exist without farmers. This is an opinion that can have some meaning in a closed society with no foreign trade. Turgot can be considered as the originator of the "wage-fund" theory, *l'unique fonds des salaries.* Wage-fund theory is now understood as a predetermined amount of money set aside to be distributed as wages and salaries, which never increases or decreases regardless of the change in the labor force. Turgot did not foresee such a definition of wage-fund theory. He defined the term quite simply: "The commodities which he buys are the exact equivalent of the produce which he gives in exchange."

Again he commended the farmer as the only producer of surplus value, since "nature does not higgle with him for subsistence wage." Hence the farmer is that privileged person, *l'une productive,* while the artisans are only salaried people or *l'autre stipendiée.*

Turgot discussed the principle of diminishing returns. He thought that the nature has the habit of resisting the extra pressure put on it. Any productive factor can accept only a limited amount of other factors as complements. Beyond that line or mark, additional factors would be rejected as superfluous, and that would show up as the process of diminishing returns. Hence, the common saying "Too many cooks spoil the broth."

One cannot really separate Quesnay and Turgot. Both are physiocrats and have the same feelings about the economic process. Their value theories are the same, extolling farmers and depressing all other occupations.

Footnotes

1. Higgs, Henry. *The Physiocrats*, New York: Macmillan, 1964, p. 96.

THE INDUSTRIAL REVOLUTION

Whenever there was a sudden transition from hand industry to machine production, historians called this process, industrial revolution. Basically, the industrial revolution was a succession of technological changes that took place in three areas: (1) substitution of machine or technological skill for human skills; (2) replacement of manpower by motive power; and (3) accelerated use of natural resources which from the beginning of time had been ignored as infertile. Europe was already well-advanced before the dawn of the industrial revolution. This cultural heritage was the real reason behind the exploration of the unknown. There is an inherent thirst in every human being to find ways to lessen the hardships involved in fulfilling any task. This quest for new methods of resolving problems opened the way for inventions.

Europe had already established the right of private property and private enterprise, which some consider the bases for freedom. The spirit of inquiry flourished under the benevolent philosophy of *primo capienti* or first finder rights. As the economies expanded, so did the desire for innovation and creativity. If people as a whole set out doing things in a different way, better ways of doing things will follow. Growth provides for creativity and creativity provides for growth. Another reason for the industrial revolution was the high value attributed to the use of natural resources. Natural resources are of no value unless they are found useful. The industrial revolution enhanced the wealth of nations by finding uses for neglected natural resources and thus increasing their monetary value.

Religion also made its contribution to the industrial revolution. Inertia or laziness was counted as the major sin a human could commit. Writers like Thomas Mun denied to the indolent the right of sharing the bounties of nature. This social castigation of laziness was a strong motive to be active and working. Then religion associated work with prayer and made heaven the reward for the work we do on earth. Thus was work ennobled and labor given its dignity by religion.

The technological changes of the industrial revolution included (1) the use of basic materials like coal, ore, and natural gas; (2) the use of energy sources like electricity; (3) the invention of new machines, such as the spinning jenny and the power loom; (4) the development of the factory system, which entailed the division of labor, specialization, and standardization; and (5) the increased application of science to industry. All these innovations prepared the way for present day mass production and use of natural resources.

There were other areas that showed the profound influence of the industrial revolution. For example, it was now possible to experiment with intensive and extensive cultivation of the land, thus allowing a small labor group to supply an entire population with farm products. The economic changes abolished the old feudalism and effected a wider distribution of wealth. Certain political philosophies appeared that resulted in the concentration of wealth and power in the hands of the central governments. Other sweeping changes were reflected in the growth of markets, the formation of cities, and the rise and emancipation of the working class. Along with these changes, men strove for higher skills, better education, and nobler appreciation of the finer things in life.

There were certain basic realities that guaranteed the success of the industrial revolution. These included sufficient capital investment, mobility and adaptability of labor, an active market system, a merchant marine for foreign trade, plentiful natural resources, new inventions and techniques, a monetary system of dependable banking and credit, and, finally, a strong government, faithful to political philosophies honoring private property and free private enterprise. The industrial revolution began in the textile industry. The cotton, jute, and calico shipped to Europe by the East India Company, required immediate spinning and weaving to supply the lucrative markets abroad. The shipbuilding industry expanded with the expansion of foreign trade. Changes happened fast. Thomas Mun once said, "Necessity is the mother of invention." The textile industry is a good instance in point. John Kay as it happened, invented the flying shuttle, a mechanical device that automatically ejected the weaving shuttle to accelerate the making of cloth. Later James Hargreaves developed the spinning jenny, which mechanically produced the action of the hand spinner. In 1769, Richard Arkwright patented the water frame for making ropes, which as the name indicates was driven by water power. Later, Samuel Crompton devised a "mule" which was a cross between the water frame and the spinning jenny. The mule and the water frame produced an abundant supply of ropes and yarn. In an effort to capitalize on this abundance, the Rev. Edmund Carwright succeeded in mechanizing the weaving process by inventing the power loom. The increased use of these raw materials lifted the price of cotton and jute and agriculture experienced a new phase of prosperity. The finished goods were marketed all over the world. Only one problem baffled the cotton growers; hand labor could not separate the seeds from the cotton with satisfactory speed, and as a result the supply of cotton remained very limited. Eli Whitney solved the problem with the invention of the cotton gin. The effect on the Southern cotton growers was instantaneous. They expanded enormously the cultivation of cotton, which in turn was partially responsible for the increase in slave trade.

The textile industry was the first to introduce the factory system. The workers were forced into a confined area where they fell subject to the ruthless discipline of the machine. In an effort to increase productivity, the managers applied the principles of business administration in their dealings with the workers: division of labor, specialization, channels of communication, span of control, vertical and horizontal delegations, line and staff divisions, and many other business techniques were discussed and applied under the factory roof. With the workers gathered together in one group, the way was open for dialogues about their mutual interests. This in turn opened the door for unionization. The power-driven machines produced goods in such abundance that local markets could not consume the entire output. The search for distant markets gave rise to the maritime trade.

The textile industry was not the only industry thriving at this time. There were also rapid advances in mining and metallurgy. By 1700, Abraham Darby and his son had found the way to reduce coal to coke; Henry Cort's invention of "puddling" with a rolling mill had simplified the production of wrought iron; and John Wilkinson had found a way of boring cylinders to precise dimensions in wrought iron. All of these inventions paved the way for the final success of James Watt's steam engine. Matthew Boulton was another person to be remembered since he financed the efforts of Watt. By 1800, there were more than five hundred Watt and Boulton machines on the market. Roads and canals became the arteries for transporting industrial goods for domestic consumption. Steam boats were built to carry the cargo from city to city, and Richard Trevithick invented the high pressure steam engines for river boats. By 1800, workmen had already laid rails in England; within a short time a network of railroads ran in all directions in Europe. In 1807 Robert Fulton's steam boat appeared on the Hudson River. Nevertheless, it took a long time to replace the commercial sailing boats with steam boats.

Not all the changes associated with the industrial revolution were technical ones. They included large scale industrial investments, accelerated population growth, and new ways of saving money for the rich through banking and credit. The need for heavy investment is crucial during the initial stages of development or industrialization. Prerevolutionary economies showed only a limited amount of saving after meeting the current expenses. The need for investment at that time was small. The postrevolutionary economy realized extensive production, which guaranteed greater profits. It is interesting to observe that countries passing through the initial stages of the industrial revolution must strain for large profits at the same time that the bulk of their production is rather meager.

The industrial revolution that occurred successively in separate countries followed much the same pattern. The time element ran from 30 to 60 years. The demand made on natural resources was always heavy; investments finally exceeded any possible profits; as a result, the real income remained static. The latter factor is not surprising since no one has ever devised a way of keeping investments on a par with personal income. No one, in fact, seems able to curb the growth pattern of an industry with reasonable bounds or in harmony with the possibilities of a given geographic area.

There are many reasons for the acceleration of investment. Some derive from sudden favorable discoveries or inventions; others depend on an "engineering invention" that may necessitate heavy investment. In the case of the "chemistry invention," the goal aimed at by investment is the manufactured product. The first of these two inventions is evident in the material development of the industry in the same locality. Since new working populations gather together in towns, huge investment finds its way in housing, road construction, markets, and recreational facilities. The same is true in agricultural developments; irrigation, drainage, storage, fencing, and fertilizers call for sizable capital investments. To stabilize or even to increase the public demand for a product, the industry must expand into markets in proportion to the volume of production it intends to realize.

The industrial revolution is a concrete example of what authors have called "developmental block." This is in reality a "primary growth sector," which in turn serves the users in the "secondary growth sector." Briefly, it represents a minimum momentum of investment.

Many factors acting on present elements influence the course of industrial revolution in a given country. These include the duration of intensive industrialization, the ease with which the peak of stabilization is passed, and the social problems subsequent to growth. Some of these pressures can be eased by an adequate legal system, a flexible social structure, a wealth of natural resources, and successful penetration into foreign trade. In some nations, the misuse of resources, false starts that failed to take into account the market conditions, business fluctuations, human errors, and rapid obsolescence, greatly increased the cost of industrialization. Some countries underwent spontaneous industrial revolution. These countries already accumulated profits or surpluses over consumption and had at their service a certain amount of technology. In France, for example, there occurred a spontaneous buildup of the entire complex of basic industries in metals, textiles, food processing, and chemicals, as well as in methods of transportation. Other nations, on the contrary, had to struggle with their infant economies. They felt incapable of surmounting foreign competition and were burdened by the tariff and custom laws at home.

Errors in forecasting the volume of production can damage any effort to grow. Countries like China and India are seemingly defeated by a population that grows at a faster rate than the process of industrialization. Investment increases in these nations are absorbed by the increase in population; a situation of this kind tends toward the lessening of man-hour equipment. The result is an ever growing rate of unemployment. Adam Smith dealt with this feature in 1776. "Wealth per head, given the soil, climate and the extent of the land, must be regulated, first by skill, dexterity and judgment with which labour is generally applied; and secondly by the proportion between the number of those who are employed in useful labor and that of those who are not so employed." When money is invested to buy a plant and equipment to produce other products, it becomes a capital investment. This kind of capital investment demands many workers. When no money is invested to produce luxury products, the volume of consumption becomes limited and hence the number of workers needed is also limited.

While analyzing the conditions of industrialization in England and Germany, Frederick List pointed out that the United States government gave the necessary protection to business, which was the main reason for the economic growth of the United States. While in France, Saint-Simon asserted that the logical allocation of capital is the basic reason for economic growth. Russia worked out a shifting balance with capital goods and consumer goods to achieve economic growth. It is clear from the foregoing instances that a planned economy can effect a balanced economic growth.

The industrial revolution, among other things, engendered a thirst for knowledge as nations realized that the extent of their know-how would determine their economic growth. Education in science and technology received added emphasis in an industrial society. Germany, for example, opened a large industrial chemical plant as an adjunct to a university. The difference between pure research and applied research seemed to disappear in education. During the second stage of the industrial revolution, science became the key factor for growth. Precision tools opened the way for the computer age. Henry Maudslay's slide-rest, working on all metal lathes, facilitated the accurate cutting of metals. The screw-making machine was one of the byproducts of this invention. At New Haven, Connecticut, Eli Whitney's factory assembled muskets, using a system that foreshadowed the mass production technique that would give industrial preeminence to the United States. The Seimen-Martin process of purifying steel by means of "open hearth," the Thomas Gilchrist method of smelting iron ores with high phosphorous content, and later the Bessemer process, all contributed to the growth and perfection of the steel industry.

One major drawback of these advances in the industrial revolution was the depersonalization of ownership through the creation of corporations. Moreover, mass production methods depersonalized employees and reduced them to numbers and statistics. Markets became a bone of contention among nations and many wars were fought over the issue. All in all, however, the industrial revolution brought new vigor and vitality to economic systems that had stagnated for centuries.

ADAM SMITH

The exact date of Adam Smith's birth is not known, but he was baptized at Kirkcaldy, Scotland, in 1732. At the age of 14 he entered Glasgow University. At that time three professors, Alexander Dunlop, Robert Simon, and Francis Hutcheson, were attracting students to Glasgow from all over Europe. Adam Smith was strongly influenced by all three of them. The most powerful influence was Hutcheson. Smith acquired a great respect for "natural liberty and justice" from the lectures of Hutcheson. After three years in Glasgow, Smith received a fellowship at Baliol College, Oxford.

Baliol, however, did not appeal to Smith because of the intellectual stagnation he met there. The inefficiency of Oxford left Smith on his own resources. Baliol possessed one of the best libraries in England and Smith delved deep into that gold mine of knowledge. Even so, he left Oxford with bitter feelings which were expressed later in his work, *Wealth of Nations.*

Smith wanted to accept a private tutorship for a living but that was hard to come by at that time. Under the sponsorship of Lord Kames, a prominent leader in the Edinburgh Bar Association, Smith was invited to deliver public lectures at Edinburgh. The lectures were primarily on poetry and rhetoric. Later he took up the subject of progress and opulence, which naturally led him to the economic thoughts he later developed. Later he accepted a professorship at Glasgow. That led the way to writing. His first publication, *The Theory of Moral Sentiments*, appeared in 1759 and established a reputation for him as a philosopher. The theme of that writing was, as he said later, "what prompts men to be benevolent as well as self-interested, to be virtuous as well as mundane, to be human as well as humane." Smith rejected the idea put forth by his predecessors, including his professor, Hutcheson, that every man is endowed with an innate moral sentiment. Smith held that identity of sorrow and happiness of others in us is not an innate propensity but something cultivated by self. The book brought him respect and a name, and Charles Townsend offered him the job he really wanted, that of a private tutor. He reminisced later, "the life I led in Glasgow was a pleasurable and dissipated life in comparison of that which I lead here at present. I have begun to write a book in order to pass away the time." The product of this leisurely writing was the immortal *Wealth of Nations*. Later he took a job as Commissioner of Customs just to spend the last part of his life among his own kind. Smith died on July 17, 1790.

Smith shared some of the popular prejudices evident in the writings of the physiocrats. (Physiocrats recognized an inherent natural order that governs all societies. They counted land as the basis of wealth and taxation, and also advocated industry and trade at the start of mercantilism.)

Wealth of Nations has two fundamental principles: (1) Money is just an instrument of trade; and (2) the real source of a nation's wealth is based on its annual labor, and its wealth or well being could only be increased by making its labor more productive.

It is important to look at the type of "Economic Man" that Smith saw as surrounding the economic system. The productive man in Smith's eye was industrious and imaginative. The nonproductive man was not a common element in the British society. He pictured the average man as somewhat discontented with the status quo *and constantly striving to upgrade himself.* Smith opposed too much government control since that would destroy the inherent nature of man to strive to better himself and face greater hardship.[1]

Another characteristic of the average man was a propensity to trade or, as Howard S. Marshall puts it, "truck and barter." The economic man was also a thrifty person who gained wealth by the simple process of postponing consumption or in other words by saving. Smith thought that basic qualities in man differ with different people. Even then by education one can bridge this gap to a greater extent. Still, something like an "invisible hand" called "chance" plays a part in a man's life. The reason why one man is a philosopher and another, a street cleaner is to some part dependent on "chance" in terms of family background and varying opportunities for education.

An Inquiry Into The Nature And Cause Of The Wealth Of Nations is the full title of Smith's book. The book deals with the methods of acquiring wealth as the title states, although Smith climbed many branches to deliver this fundamental message. The mercantilists held that a measure of a nation's wealth was determined by the quantity of gold it possessed. Smith held that the actual wealth of a nation depended on the capacity it has in producing goods and services.

Wealth

In the first chapter of *Wealth of Nations*, Smith defined wealth by the division of labor. The definition consists of three parts: (1) increase in skill, (2) saving of time through specialization, and (3) replacement of hand labor with machinery. The division of labor is limited by the extent and activity of the market. Money becomes a necessary medium of exchange as the market becomes more active. It is the immense increase in the production of goods and services resulting from the division of labor that results in the universal prosperity. Every workman has a great quantity of his own product for sale and can exchange it, through money, for the products and services of other workmen. The amount of production and exchange which takes place in a country accounts for the wealth of that country. "This was similar to the 'natural order' theory of the physiocrats in France which stated that individual action as a social force would promote the general good."[2]

Smith did not accept the arguments of the mercantilists that the eternal supervision of the government is needed to increase the production and trade of a nation. Smith argued that the government should refrain from interfering with the worker, so that he is able to exert his maximum productive capacity freely.

Price

The word value has two different meanings. Usually, it expresses the utility of a particular object and sometimes the power of obtaining other goods by its exchange. The former value is called "value in use" and the latter "value in exchange." The things that have the greatest value in use may have least value in exchange and vice versa. Value in exchange is based on cost, real price, utility, resale value, and so on. The cost is based on the factors of production that make a product's input. The real price is the cost, plus expected profit. The value depends on the willingness of the consumer to pay money in exchange for the product.

There were two basic assumptions in Smith's concept of price mechanism. First, he believed that the consumer was rational and capable of judging his own best interest. Smith's second assumption was that the order of consumer choice is formed by the existence of vigorous competition in the market. Smith assumed a society composed of a vast array of small businessmen, each incapable of controlling the market.[3]

He thought that the owners of productive resources would invest in something that would bring the highest return. The same principle will force another businessman not to enter an industry that has been already taken over by others. When each industry is balanced with sufficient numbers of investors, the total economy will reach a balance, which Smith called the "equilibrium of investments" or "market equilibrium."

Money price of anything is composed of three elements: (1) the wages of labor; (2) the profit on capital; and (3) the rent of land. In the rude society, value was based on the quantity of labor involved. Smith criticized the mercantilists because they demanded government intervention in controlling the wages of labor and denying mobility of labor from place to place. Smith expected equilibrium of wage to achieve prosperity for all or, as he termed it, "universal prosperity." Any government intervention in controlling wages and denying mobility of labor would lead to exploitation of labor and a poor labor class in the nation. When the sellers offered their products below cost to face the competition, the first group to suffer would be the worker who is at the mercy of the employer for his survival. The employer naturally would cut wages to lower the cost. Smith strongly repudiated this iron law of wages or subsistence wage theory of the mercantilists.

Wages, profit, and rent are the three original sources of income. All other incomes ultimately are derived from one or the other of these. To Smith, land was only an instrument enabling man to earn a wage for his labor and make the profits on his capital. The profit of capital is only a different name for wages for "the labor of inspection," now called management, risk taking, or entrepreneurship.

Both mercantilists and Smith recognized the role of population expansion in fostering economic growth.[4] The mercantilists could not see the improvement in the rate of productivity of labor and they supported the idea of more laborers to achieve a higher quantity of products. Smith differed from this view. He expected the productivity of labor to increase through better training, higher education, and use of machines. He contended, as we do today, that production is the result of labor and resources. In this he took basic issue with the mercantilists' doctrine that the nation's wealth is derived from an excess of exports.[5]

Smith accepted the "invisible hand" theory with two assumptions. He thought that there exists a social force that causes individual action, regardless of motive, to promote the general good. Its implication is twofold:

1. The individual worker, through selfish motives, continually strives to find the most advantageous employment, which contributes to the welfare of the total economic system.

2. The rich with their abundant supplies and resources are faced with their own dilemma. Whether rich or poor, the capacity to consume is limited. Even if the rich had insatiable desires and irresistible urges they still could not consume the entire competency of fortune. They have to face the reality and have to share with the poor some fruits of the laborer. Charles Gides and Charles Rist explained this phenomenon by paraphrasing Smith's labor theories. "In seeking a theory to explain the level of wages, Smith came up with several explanations, including subsistence explanation, a wage-fund theory, a productive theory, and the theory that wages were determined by bargaining between combinations of labor and employers."[6]

Smith accepted certain inequalities of wages to be inevitable. These are (1) agreeableness to work; (2) difficulty of learning the trade; (3) regularity of the employment; (4) amount of trust given to the person performing the task; and (5) possibilities of success in the trade.[7] These factors are still guideposts to wage differentials.

Rent

Smith claimed rent to be the reward to the third party of production over land. He gave three separate explanations for the reasons for rent. First, it was the monopoly return paid because land was scarce and owned by a relatively small proportion of the population. Secondly, it was the result of the abundant generosity of nature. Thirdly, rent was paid in different degrees depending on the fertility of the land. He never treated the relationship of rent to the price discrimination.

Book I

Book I deals with the analysis of the effects of economic process and progress on wages, profits, and rents. This analysis provided the pattern for subsequent attempts on these subjects.

Book II

This book is concerned with capital, saving, and investment. Smith classified capital as fixed and circulating. Money was part of the circulating capital of the nation. He brought in the interrelationships of money, credit, and banking and emphasized the importance of saving as the backbone of investment. The banks stand as an intermediary between the savers and investors. Smith discussed productive and unproductive labor, concluding that agriculture is the major productive labor and most others are unproductive, except trade.

Smith also believed in the profit motive as an inducement for production. Private property and laissez-faire ideas went against state control of production and distribution. But to Smith, the individual freedom meant a lot to increased productivity. He said, "No regulation of commerce can increase the quantity of industry in any society, beyond what its capital can maintain." Smith did believe in a legal ceiling on the interest rate rather than complete freedom to extort higher interest rates according to the intensity of the borrower's need.

Book III: Different Progress of Opulence in Different Nations.

This book is composed of speeches given by Smith at Edinburgh and seems like the oldest part of the *Wealth of Nations*. In it Smith discussed alternative approaches to improve the economic conditions of Europe as a whole through agriculture and commerce. He fixed some priorities of investment, namely agriculture taking the precedence over manufacturing and then commerce. To him any other arrangement could only retard development.

Book IV: Systems of Political Economy

This book is devoted to Smith's attack on mercantilism through a review of commercial policies. His main target was the manifold restrictive regulations and monopolistic control the mercantilists held. Smith thought there would be the state of "natural liberty" if these privileges were abrogated. He defended internal free trade and the abolition of apprenticeship laws. He also attacked duties levied through tariffs and customs, which hindered the natural flow of international trade. He thought that England as a state could not capitalize on colonies because of the burden of defense invested with the states. He thought that the chartered companies were exploiting the colonies to their advantage instead of the common good of England. He hoped for an Utopia where, "the colonies and the mother country remain faithful, affectionate and as generous allies."

Book V: The Revenues of the Sovereign or Commonwealth

This book deals with the expenditures of the state and describes how by taxation the state can meet the obligations of public debts. Smith confined the state to three functions: (1) defence; (2) justice and civil government; and (3) erecting and maintaining public institutions and public works. Regarding taxation, he was not very definite; he stated a taxing policy according to ability, more or less the present graduated taxation. Then he changed his mind and wanted to dump the burden of taxation on the rich alone. "It is not very unreasonable that the rich should contribute to the public expense, not only in proportion to their revenue, but in something more than that proportion."

Smith advocated the system of natural liberty. This idea was rather unique at the time when kings, churches, and feudalistic practices looked after classes rather than masses. This trumpet call for universal prosperity was the main reason the *Wealth of Nations* attracted so much attention. He advocated the removal of all systems that upheld preferences and restraints. He demanded that everyone should have the freedom to pursue his own interests in life, as long as he did not violate the laws of justice.

In the last few pages of *Wealth of Nations*, Smith discussed the problems of the American colonies. He thought that the British government's desire to extend taxation all over the empire could never materialize or be practical. He even made a study of the possible amount of tax the British government could levy from the various colonies under it to prove the futility of regimenting tax levies on colonies. But there were many vested interests with more influence than Smith. As a result, some colonies felt compelled to break loose from the thraldom of the empire.

Of these former colonies, the United States, at least, did not accept Smith's work with any enthusiasm. After the Revolution, the United States did not really favor free trade. It settled into a strong policy of protection, influenced by the contemporary statesmen. Even after 1860 when Europe moved toward free trade, the United States did not join that movement, but remained the most protected country in the world.

The Value of Wealth Of Nations

Smith's *Wealth of Nations* was not original thinking. Smith himself acknowledged indebtedness to over one hundred writers. It was not a theoretical model of economics either. He tried hard to accumulate data to substantiate his major proposals. Inexplicably, he left some questions unanswered. He also failed to look at any alternate ways, which could have avoided the practical difficulties in implementing some of his recommendations. He painted a cheerful society and a world at large that spontaneously would drift into place to create the mosaic of "natural liberty" and "universal prosperity."

The particular trend that enriched Britain, after Smith, was largely due to the special characteristics of the world they encountered—the wars in Europe, progress in navigation, and the opening of Asia as a vast market to buy as well as to sell. These factors had no relevance or dependence on Smith's thinking and exhortations. Adam Smith's work had tremendous influence on all countries except the United States. One can see some influence on the change of the United States' commercial policies with other nations. But no one can say that this happened because of *Wealth of Nations*. The current was favorable to these changes as the United States gradually came to be a world power.

In spite of all these criticisms, let no one conclude that Smith's work had no lasting value. His contribution lies imbedded in the manner in which he combined a broad variety of complex problems into a study of "Human Economic Welfare" rather than a random glimpse at economics itself.

Footnotes

1. Marshall, Howard D. *The Great Economists*, New York: Pitman Publishing Co., 1967, p. 29.
2. Whittaker, Edmund. *School and Streams of Economic Thought*, Chicago: Rand McNally and Co., 1960, p. 101.
3. Marshall, op. cit., pp. 42, 44.
4. Clark, J.M. *Adam Smith*, Chicago: Chicago University Press, 1928, p. 82.
5. West, E.G. *Adam Smith*, New York: Arlington House, 1969.
6. Gide, Charles and Rist, Charles. *A History of Economic Doctrines*, New York: Heath Publishing Co., 1949, p. 39.
7. Marshall, op. cit., pp. 52 & 54.

JEAN-BAPTISTE SAY

Say was a product of religious persecution. His parents fled from France at the revocation of the Edict of Nantes. When Napoleon came into power, Say gained some public acceptance, but was considered a liberal philosopher and many of his writings were viewed with suspicion by the orthodox schools. No one really forgets his early childhood experiences. The hardships of his early life caused Say to turn to extreme liberal views, which were adamantly opposed by vested interest groups.

Say's economic theories were based on two simple assumptions:
1. Desire for commodities is infinite.
2. Supply creates its own demand.

There are some desires for goods that cannot be infinite, like the desire for food. The limitations of the stomach make consumption limited. But there are a million other things man can aspire to without any limit, like money, comforts, fame, love, etc.

The goods produced are priced according to the scale of the cost of production. Cost of production for the employer becomes the income of the employees. Hence Say's famous slogan, "Every cost is someone's income." Whether the cost be wages, salaries, rent, or interest, it is income to the persons on the other side of the ledger. Income is purchasing power, and man will accept any form of income to raise his standard of living. In other words, every income is expected to be spent, now or later. With this idea in mind, Say asks, "How can a glut happen in the economy?" Hence supply has to find its own demand.

Say published his famous work, *Traité d'économie politique* (*The Political Economy*) in 1803. In this work is a dialogue worth presenting:

Should a tradesman say, "I do not want other products for my woolens, I want money" he may be told, "You say, you only want money, I say, you want other commodities and not money. For what, in point of fact, do you want money? Is it not for the purchase of raw materials, or stock for your trade, or victuals for your support? Wherefore, it is products that you want, and not money."

From this quote one can see how Say built his theory, "supply creates its own demand" or, as it is called, the "law of market." Today, obviously no economist accepts Say's law, because technology has made possible relatively infinite quantities of production carrying a surplus value that wage earners collectively are unable to consume. Moreover, many producers are not interested in consuming any units produced by themselves or by their competitors. Men producing Salk's vaccine, for example, do not think in terms of consuming the product of their labor.

Say did not negate the possibilities of money being hoarded or given away to totally alien consuming groups. Before the banking system came into existence, quite a bit of income was hidden away for future needs. Say was confident that even the buried treasures would surface when appropriate needs for consumption arose. So every dollar earned would, inevitably, join the circular flow of the economy.

The Treatise on Political Economy was the first economic writing that appeared in Europe with definite compartmentalization of production, distribution, and consumption, which caused many later economists to define economics as a science that deals with production, distribution, and consumption of wealth. Say's writing introduced Adam Smith to the French speaking populace. Say did not follow Adam Smith word by word, but in some ways created his own separate school of thought in economics.

Say considered economics a natural science. Wealth is the creation of nature in all three stages: production, distribution, and consumption. As a natural science, Say believed that economics must not be impeded by government, management, or unions. In fact, the law of market was based on totally free enterprise. Then only supply can create its own demand or market. The French writers had already lost appreciation for the labor theory of value proposed by Ricardo and later augmented by Karl Marx. Galiani and Condillac had already established that value depended on scarcity and utility. Say professed himself to be a follower of Galiani and Condillac. He pointed out that there would be inevitable conflict in the market due to the two different stands the seller and the buyer take in clearing the market. The seller would price his products on the basis of his cost of production, while the buyer would buy the product primarily on the basis of utility. These two value systems create the inability of the market to sell out its entire inventory. Say said that the conflict between the seller and the buyer would cause the inventory to pile up and force both sides to reexamine their positions. Then either the seller would lower his price, or the buyer would see greater utility in the commodities and offer more money for the merchandise, and thus the market law would operate, as certain as physical laws.

Marx and Mill found Say's law a meaningful tool under free and competitive systems. Malthus and Sismondi challenged Say's law from its very inception. In spite of the opposition, Say's law won more followers as time passed. John Maynard Keyne's *General Theory* of 1936 overturned Say's law totally. Present economists view Say's law merely as a once flourishing antique.

JEREMY BENTHAM

Jeremy Bentham was born in England, in a little town called Houndsditch, in 1748. His father was a prosperous lawyer, and he wanted his son to follow in his footsteps. However, he arranged for special education in trade so that Jeremy could succeed as a business man if he chose that as his career.

Jeremy was a brilliant child who could read history at the age of three, write letters to his friends at the age of five, and had a working knowledge of French, German, Latin and Greek before he was 15. People nicknamed him, "Little Philosopher" to the delight of his proud father. Bentham started his formal education at the Westminister School at the age of seven. Young Jeremy was very unhappy at school. He suffered from poor health and did not take any interest in physical education. He studied hard to compensate for bad health by higher accomplishments in academics. Finally Jeremy left the school to study with his father who mapped out a career for him and was able to prepare him to join a college at Oxford.

His father had the first look at every book that came into Jeremy's hands. It cannot have been easy to follow his father's plans. Jeremy did so but his biggest thrill was to go on vacation to his grandmother's place where he could read whatever he wanted, listen to the music of his choice, and engage in social activities without the scrutinizing eyes of a father who was also his tutor.

Jeremy attended the Queen's College at Oxford, where he found certain incursions on students' rights, especially in the practice of forcing every student to sign the notorious "Thirty-nine Articles" of the college. He did not want to be a conformist but to speak out as he saw best. He hated the meaningless tests offered at Queen's and the rituals that surrounded the educational system. Naturally, the administrators of the college tried to squash Bentham's ideas and liberal views. And although Bentham did not approve the compulsory signing of the "Thirty-nine Articles," he signed to satisfy his father's wishes.

Bentham did not have any pleasant memories of Oxford. He wrote "the streets of Oxford were paved with perjury." He became a lawyer and in some ways paid off the love lavished on him by his father. While practicing law in the courts of England, he got his chance to be a reformer. The judicial system was very antiquated, and as a consequence not only inefficiency but also open corruption crept into the system. Bentham vowed to clean up the judiciary system. His success can be measured by the words of John MacCunn: "He (Bentham) has by general admission, done so much to make the law what it is, that it has become impossible without special knowledge to realize what before Bentham it was."[1]

It is not an easy task to reform the law. There are written laws, but they become meaningful only through court decisions. There were so many contradictory court decisions that it was not easy to sift the right ones to give precision and direction to the written laws. It was Bentham's job to discriminate between legal rights and legal fictions and build a new code that would serve justice.

The sad condition of the prisons was another area of his scrutiny. Incarceration itself is the deprivation of the cardinal human rights. If prison life is debased below bestial standards, it becomes worse than death itself. Bentham offered a reform plan in which, although confined, the prisoners could work and play like normal people. He borrowed from his brother Samuel a model house, *Panopticon*, which Samuel had designed as an inspection house for the Russian government. The Panopticon was a circular edifice with cells for prisoners around the circumference. The warden had his office in the center, and from the office windows he could keep a constant watch over the prisoners without being noticed by them. The warden was to be paid a certain amount of money to look after the necessities of the prisoners. Whatever was left after the monthly expenses was supposed to be a remuneration for the warden. Meanwhile the state had to set up a minimum standard of life for the prisoners. In order that the warden might not exploit the prisoners, a tax was imposed on the income of the warden. This plan was offered to King George III who commissioned Bentham to pursue and implement the plan, but later he changed his mind. This infuriated Bentham, and he wrote *History of the War Between Jeremy Bentham and George III*, by one of "The Belligerents." The publication of this book did not do Bentham any good, and it caused some derisive criticism from the press.

England underwent an economic recession during the 1790s. Slums became a common sight. Bentham reintroduced his idea of the Panopticon to house the poor and remove eyesore slums from the big cities. He drafted thousands of pages of a national network of housing programs, which were supposed to be self-sufficient units with the cooperation of government and industry. Each unit had everything to make it self-sufficient, with farms, transportation facilities, hospitals, schools, and recreation facilities. As recently as the 1950s Bentham's Panopticon ideas reappeared in a series of community projects that succeeded in temporarily rebuilding India's teeming villages.[2]

In 1780, Bentham wrote *An Introduction to the Principles of Morals and Legislation*. This was one of the best of his writings and probably the best remembered by people who recognize him as an economist. In this book, Bentham brought out the concept of utilitarianism. Utilitarianism was not mere expediency, but a systematic effort to define human acts and motives in terms of pleasure and pain. Joseph Priestly had already published and publicized the dictum, "the greatest happiness for the greatest number," and Bentham borrowed that theme to build the school of utilitarianism. David Hume and the French writer Helvetius had already defined utility but not to the extent to which Bentham and later his disciple, John Stuart Mill, analyzed it.

Is there a correlation between pain and pleasure? Pain is something that people want less of in their lives and pleasure is something that people want more of. Even though pain is something that all want to avoid, many elect willfully to undergo pain. A farmer may work in the rain without compulsion in order to finish something he started. In order to attain some goals in life, man elects every day to perform arduous feats. The attainment of the goal is the pleasure and the hardship involved, the pain. The undertaking of fearful feats can be a pleasure to some. Working in the mines, or underwater, or even as a test pilot involves pain, but it may bring pleasure to the man who accepts it as his cup of tea. Bentham considered pain as anything to which a man had an aversion.

The greatest happiness to the majoirty of the people has become the basic norm of a democracy. Any system—whether democracy, socialism, or communism—must deliver maximum happiness to the majority of the people, or it will not last. Bentham brought out four general principles for a government to use in assuring the general happiness. The four factors were: subsistence, abundance, equality, and security.

The government should be capable of providing at least a subsistence level of happiness to all. Any government that cannot afford to give the minimum survival rate to its citizens should immediately abdicate. If this is a true assumption, how many political powers should give up their scepters and unload their crowns? Further, Bentham believed that happiness is a state that can be limitless. The purpose of civilization is to raise the people to that realm of abundance where all of their needs and many of their wants would be satisfied. It is the bounden duty of political entities to ensure that the people can freely move into the higher steps of the economic ladders.

Bentham's principle of equality needs more analysis than those of subsistence, abundance, and security. He admitted that men are far from being equals. Each one has his own capacity to produce and enjoy. Even the assimilation of pleasure from the same object is different in different people. The Swiss mathematician Bernoulli proved that the pleasure derived from the use of one dollar by a millionaire is much different from the pleasure enjoyed by a poor man in spending one dollar. Bentham used the term equality only in regard to the application of law. If a criminal willfully kills a storekeeper, he should be liable for his crime. In the same way, if the son of a head of state commits murder willfully, he should be subjected to law and should not be given any preferential treatment.

The utilitarian principles were hopelessly misunderstood by the public. Bentham intended the notions of pleasure and pain to be used in a general sense only. Knowing what was happening to his basic premises, he understood that prompt explanations were necessary to support his thoughts. So he explained again, "The distinction between pleasure and happiness is that happiness is not susceptible to division, but pleasure is. A pleasure is single, happiness is the blended result like wealth."[3] Bentham's further explanation of his ideas only confused the public more. Moreover, many thought that he was playing with words to salvage his theories. Even though people talked against his theories, his fame spread into Europe and America. Many called on him to get advice about many political and economic issues. Misunderstood and ignored in his own country, he was made an honorary citizen of France.

Bentham wanted to revise the English Law and possibly to find a tool to measure pain and pleasure. But his attempts needed the full support of the government; what he got was the cold shoulder. He tried to find a calculus and in fact invented a model that to some extent succeeded in measuring the pain and pleasure of some people.

Since Bentham preferred empirical sciences, he himself abandoned that project.

Jeremy Bentham was more than a century ahead of his time. Since his writings went against the long-standing traditions of his time, he was considered a utopian philosopher. That misunderstanding is still alive in educated circles. Bentham wrote too much for one man, and he did not organize his thinking beyond refutation of his opponents. He never did full justice to one train of thought and often changed his attack in the middle of a discussion without any reason. Hence his writings are flawed by repetitions and disorganized ramblings. He entrusted his manuscripts to the publishers, who were charged with editing his thoughts. Most of the time the publishers did not clearly comprehend Bentham's ideas, and they hurriedly revised the manuscript according to what the ideas meant to them.

Bentham was involved in the formation of the British Royal Society with James Mill, father of John Stuart Mill, and other notables of England. The prestige of this contact with the higher circle and, to some extent, the encouragement of this exclusive club made Bentham forget some of the weaknesses of his writing.

Jeremy Bentham died in 1832, willing his body to medical science so that the world could benefit even from his death. It was a befitting act of a very generous man, dedicated to improving the living conditions of the human race.

Footnotes

1. MacCunn, John. *Six Radical Thinkers*, New York: Russell & Russell, Inc., 1964.
2. Mack, Mary P. *Jeremy Bentham: an Odyssey of Ideas*, New York: Columbia University Press, 1963. And see *International Encyclopedia of the Social Sciences*, David Sills, ed., New York: Macmillan, 1968, vol. 2, p. 55.
3. Mack, op. cit. p. 223.

References

Baumgardt, David. *Bentham and the Ethics of Today*. Princeton, New Jersey: Princeton University Press, 1952.

Dictionary of National Biography. Volume II. Oxford, England: Oxford University Press, 1921.

Keeton, George W. and Schwarzenberger, Georg. *Jeremy Bentham and the Law*. Westport, Connecticut: Greenwood Press, 1970.

Mill, John S. *On Bentham and Coleridge*. New York: Harper and Brothers, 1962.

Sills, David L. Editor. *International Encyclopedia of the Social Sciences*. USA: The Macmillan Company, 1968.

THOMAS ROBERT MALTHUS

Thomas Robert Malthus was born in 1766. His father was a lawyer and a friend of Rousseau and Hume, distinguished philosophers of the time. Malthus was sent to the School of Theology at the University of Cambridge. After his graduation, he was ordained a minister in the Anglican church. It was not uncommon at that time for ministers to accept civil employment, and in 1805 Malthus accepted a professorship in history and political science at East India College. He gained acquaintance with David Ricardo, which led to the founding of the Political Economy Club in 1821 and the Royal Statistical Society in 1834.

Society was boiling with heated arguments for and against the industrial revolution. Adam Smith's *Wealth of Nations* became the bible of the industrial world. Improved methods of production and transportation, new forms of business organization, and many improvements in banking and credit operations, as well as the consequent evils of the factory system were marks of the era. Technological improvements displaced manual laborers; population concentrated in urban areas; intellectual liberalism questioned age-old traditions and beliefs of people; and in some ways these changes destroyed the order and tranquility that had existed before. As can be seen even today, social upheavals such as these reflect on the commodity price structures and result in violent business fluctuations. Say's law of supply finding its own demand did not work in an economy where the machines overproduced, leaving a sizable portion of the labor force unemployed. People feared the possibility of a revolution like the one in France. England, worrying about a class uprising, concentrated on improving the conditions of the working class. Malthus could not stay in his campus office and simply observe the passing stream of events. He entered the social front with his lectures and writings. His first book was entitled, *An Essay on the Principles of Population as it Affects the Future Improvement of Society.*[1]

The Law of Population

Malthus had a debate with his own father about the doctrine of Godwin, a utilitarian who advocated the abolition of private property. Godwin had said that population growth is an unqualified blessing. He based his argument on a notion of sharing happiness; the more there are to share happiness, the better it is. Godwin did not see any problem in feeding a large population. If the land were controlled by society, all the fruits of the land would be available for the entire population. He thought poverty was due to the rich freezing the distribution of goods. In short, Godwin thought that a social utopia can be built with the reorganization of social and political structures.

Malthus refuted Godwin with two principles: (1) that food is necessary for the existence of man; and (2) that passion between the sexes is necessary, and will remain nearly at the present state. The first principle is self-evident, and Malthus argued that Godwin failed to disprove the second. He maintained that the instinct for marriage is permanent, and that the operation of the principles of population would make it impossible to attain the millenium Godwin foresaw.

Malthus argued that the population, unless checked, would tend to double every 25 years, thus growing in a geometric progression—1, 2, 4, 8, etc. Food production, on the other hand, could at best be expected to grow at an arithmetical rate of 1, 2, 3, 4, etc., each 25 years. This difference in the rate of fertility and productivity would end in famine and poverty unless there were some checks on population. Malthus suggested two checks, that of raising the mortality rate, and of reducing the birth rate. He thought that all these checks would lead to "moral restraint, vice and misery." He defined moral restraint as "restraint from marriage which is not followed by irregular gratification." He approved this check but doubted its feasibility. "Vice" included promiscuous intercourse, unnatural acts, and other sex deviations. Of course misery is the total breakdown of the family order.

Although Malthus brought the problem to light, society was not ready to accept his postulates. It was only in the twentieth century that John Maynard Keynes gave widespread acceptability to Malthusian theory. Keynes lamented "the almost total obliteration of Malthus' line of approach and the complete domination of Ricardo's for a period of a hundred years, a disaster to the progress of economics.[2]

There had been forerunners of these population discussions in the writings of Benjamin Franklin and Robert Wallace. Wallace considered population growth a catalyst for the creation of a socialistic society. Benjamin Franklin, like Godwin, rejoiced at the population growth. Wallace's open advocacy of limiting population led William Godwin to refute his ideas in the "Inquirer." Malthus defended Wallace in his *Essay*, which later was contested by the Marquis de Condorcet. Malthus protested "that human institutions appear to be obvious and obtrusive causes of such mischief to mankind, yet, in reality they are light and superficial; they are mere feathers that float on the surface, in comparison with those deeper seated causes of impurity that corrupt the springs and render turbid the whole stream of human life."[3]

Most of Malthus' published works dealt strictly with economic matters: food, prices, corn laws, and rent. He is credited with the formulation of the concept of diminishing returns, although Ricardo's more explicit exposition gained popular acceptance.

Malthus believed that the principles of population constituted a natural law. Its ill effects could be removed by appropriate individual or social action. Otherwise the population would increase beyond subsistence. "The struggle for survival" would lead the world to misery.[4] Malthus demanded the abolition of the "Poor Law," which encouraged the poor to marry even though their income was insufficient to support a family.

Malthus opposed birth control explicitly. As an Anglican Minister he could not in conscience support artificial birth control. He expected individual restraint, social laws that promote late marriages, and a blind obedience to the Sixth Commandment as the cure for population growth.

Malthus refused to identify corn as food and thus he differed from Adam Smith's treatise on the corn laws. Malthus thought that a rise in the price of corn would discourage consumption and lead to letting the land lie fallow.[5] He thought that an abundance in corn production in England would foster foreign trade and would enable the surplus to be sold at more expensive markets. "A free trade in corn secures a steadier as well as cheaper supply of grain."[6]

Malthus could not see the rationale of changing the occupation of people from agriculture to manufacturing. He thought that would change the essential character of the people. He thought that "manufacturing industry conduces to mental activity, to an expansion of comforts, to the growth of the middle classes . . . fluctuation of fashion, which lead to chronic destitution and discontent . . ."[7]

Malthus wrote a second corn law pamphlet where his true sentiments about this matter became more evident. In *Grounds of an Opinion on the Policy of Restricting the Importation of Foreign Corn* he urged a temporary duty on imported corn, "to get rid of that price which belongs to great wealth, combined with a system of restriction."[8] He warns the government not to take advantage of a particular trade. It should concentrate on the public benefit. His book, *The Political Economy,* is not a continuous essay, but a compilation of many essays he wrote at different times. Malthus disagrees with Smith in spite of the fact that Smith wrote *Wealth of Nations.* Malthus considers wealth as man, or more definitely, in relation to man.

Rent

Malthus defined rent as "the excess of the value of the whole produce, above what is necessary to pay the wages of the labor and the profits of the capital employed in cultivation."[9]

Malthus' first reason for rent was the fact that fertile soil yields produce that can more than feed the producer. Therefore production should exceed the cost, the difference between cost and production providing the rent.

In agricultural lands, demand exceeds supply. There can never be overproduction of food materials. Overproduction becomes measurable only because of underconsumption. If the surplus were given out as rent, the needy would consume it and there would not be any overproduction. This transfer of surplus is the second basis of rent.

Malthus' third reason for rent was the scarcity of good land. There was not enough fertile land to supply all the wants of the people. When the land becomes depleted, the willingness to cultivate that land decreases. Malthus in some way treated marginal cost and marginal revenue ideas when he said the inferior land will be left without prouduction when the producer cannot meet the cost of tillage. If the landlord still demands payment of rent, then that rent should be paid only after the due cost of the farmer's labor is taken out. Naturally the farmers will move into more fertile areas and the wealth of the nation as a whole will decrease.

Malthus concludes his chapter on rent in his book, *Principles of Political Economy,* thus: "In every point of view, then, in which the subject can be considered, that the quality of land which, by the law of our being, must terminate in rent, appears to be a boon, most important to the happiness of mankind; and I am persuaded that its value can only be underrated by those who still labor under some mistake, as to its nature and its effect on society. [10]

Meaning of Value

Value is a term defined by many writers in many ways. Value has become something undefinable, because of the subjective and objective measurement of value. In the objective definition, no one can disassociate the subjective estimation, creating age-long conflicts in value. Malthus came to distinguish three types of value: (1) value in use—the intrinsic utility of the object whether it be a free good or economic good; (2) nominal value in exchange—the value of commodities estimated as intrinsic, like that seen in precious metals; and (3) value in exchange—the power to exchange an object or commodity for other products or the purchasing power arising from intrinsic causes. The desire to possess a product in exchange for one in hand results from the mutuality of wants. The offeror and offeree should feel a share in the buyers' surplus or the sellers' surplus, in order to exchange a product. This value may depend on the ease or hardship in supplying a product. Hence, Malthus accepted the principles of supply and demand as the cause of the third type of value. Most products are priced according to the cost of production involved in ordinary wages, profits, and expected rent. The price of raw materials should differ from the price of finished products, because of the extra factors of production invested in the raw materials. In the market places one may see the cost of production controlling a monopolistic price structure. Manufacturing is only changing the shape and quality of the raw materials, altering existing material. Yet the final product wields exclusive right to establish a price of its own.

Law of Markets

Many people remember Malthus under the construct of his population and, possibly, agricultural theories. A student of Malthus can easily see that he addressed himself to most of the facets of the economic society. Thus he also had his own ideas about the market system. The economists of the time accepted the principles of self-adjustment of markets. Smith spoke of the "invisible hand" that determines what to produce, when to produce, and for whom to produce. The principles of market adjustment are graphically illustrated by Samuelson's *For Whom the Bell Tolls*. Jean-Baptiste Say proffered the self-adjusting mechanism of markets. In the writings of John Mill one can see the same idea spelled out differently.

Most classical economists believed in the complete turnover of the business cycles into all four phases. So they (Say, Ricardo, and James and John Mill) regarded recessions and depressions as inevitable concommittents of prosperity or economic progress. Still, in the long run, they could not see any possiblity of over-production or over-accumulation of capital investments. Every commodity produced would find a buyer just because of the inequalities of the market structure. According to them, the goods had to flow from cheaper markets to dearer markets. In other words, water seeks its level, but since it never makes it, we have low tides and high tides, or a system of continuous flow from one sector to another. Prices also tend to level off, but never attain complete equilibrium. This is the fundamental basis for the classical economists' assertion that supply makes its own demand. Even the neoclassicists agree to some extent with the notion of aggregate supply equaling aggregate demand, not always in a single market, but in the international market as a whole. Malthus drives home a different idea when he notes, "If the supply of a given commodity is excessive, the losses incurred in its production will soon diminish its supply; while conversely, if the supply falls short of current demand, the resulting high profits will expand output so that individual demands and supplies tend to be balanced."[11]

From the above, one can see that Malthus did not accept the principles of spontaneous creation of markets for anything and everything produced. He realized that profit-seeking businessmen will leave less profitable pursuits or industries and seek higher-profit-yielding industries to maximize their profits. This market law is visible especially in modern times under monopolistic competition.

Conclusion

Malthus influenced the public policy of his time through the logic of his philosophy and the burning problems he brought to the public's attention. His predictions of population growth on a geometric ratio and the productivity growth on an arithmetic ratio were not substantiated in the years that followed. He could not foresee the tremendous technological advances to come or the diseases and wars that would curtail population growth.

But today Malthusian theory is beginning to make more sense. India and China are groaning under unsupportable population increases. Death rates have slowed by reason of dissemination of education and distribution of sophisticated medicines. Peace has been established every 25 years to let one generation propagate freely. This has resulted in formidable increases in population. On the other hand, the Western world has accepted Malthus' notion of controlling population by planned parenthood, and modern society also follows some of the methods of controlling population which were frowned on by Malthus.

The impact of an individual's work may manifest itself in a variety of ways. It may directly or indirectly influence subsequent works leading into the main stream of thought. It also can be incorporated into policies and legislation of future generations. It may lead into further studies in the same discipline. Malthus succeeded in all these areas.

Reverend Thomas Robert Malthus wrote in a time when society needed changes and new actions. He followed the "dismal science" and proved it true to its name with writings pessimistic from start to finish. Yet in the economic thoughts of Smith, Ricardo, Hume, Rousseau, and Mill an empty niche was left where Malthus fitted in.

Footnotes

1. Malthus, Thomas Robert. *An Essay on the Principle of Population as it Affects the Future of Improvement of Society*, London: 1926.

2. Semmel, Bernard, ed. *Occasional Papers of T. R. Malthus*, New York: Burt Franklin Publishers, 1963. See also, Keynes, J. M., "Robert Malthus: First of the Cambridge Economists," *Essays and Sketches in Biography*, 1951.

3. Himmelfarb, Gertrude, ed. *On Population and Thomas Malthus*, New York: Random House, 1960, pp. 18-19.

4. Flew, Antony. *The Structure of Malthus' Population Theory*, New York: 1963, vol. 1.

5. Semmel, op. cit.

6. Ibid.

7. Ibid.

8. Glass, D. V. *Introduction to Malthus*, London: 1953. See also Bonar, James. *Malthus and His Work*, New York: Kelley, 1924; idem, *First Essay on Population*, 1798, New York: 1965.

9. Levin, S. M. "Malthus and the Idea of Progress," *Journal of the History of Ideas*, vol. 27, no. 1 (1966).

10. Levin, S.M. *Principles of Political Economy*, New York: Kelley, 1964.

11. Bonar, James. *Malthus and his Work*.

DAVID RICARDO

David Ricardo was born in 1772, the third child of Abraham Israel Ricardo, a stockbroker in the Netherlands. Shortly before David was born, Abraham Ricardo immigrated to London and David began his education there. David was far from being an outstanding child except for being an avid reader. When he was twelve, David went to the Netherlands to continue his education. Spending only two years there, he returned to England and joined his father's business. David made up for the wasted years in education by showing excellent abilities and imagination in finance. After marrying Priscilla Ann Wilkinson and changing his religion from Orthodox Judaism to Unitarianism, he started his own brokerage firm. In the stock market he became very successful and amassed immense wealth. At the tender age of 30 he was ready to retire from business and enter the world of literary pursuits.

In 1799 David became an outspoken follower of Adam Smith. He suddenly became interested in the scientific approaches to the problems of finance and banking. In 1797 he met James Mill, the father of John Stuart Mill. The Mills were involved in the dialogues of utilitarian economics under the leadership of Jeremy Bentham. This contact opened the door for Ricardo to be accepted among the circles of economists of the time. It seems that Mill was not fully aware of Ricardo's financial knowledge and urged him to write literary poems!

Ricardo's early venture in writing came in the form of letters to the *Morning Chronicle*, the leading newspaper of the time. These letters were later compiled and reedited in the form of a booklet entitled *The High Price of Bullion: A Proof of the Depreciation of Bank Notes*. Ricardo touched on many economic problems confronting the businessman in everyday life. The gold standard was the accepted mode of issuing paper currency. Meanwhile the commodity value of gold fluctuated violently, throwing into imbalance the real value of the paper currency. Ricardo's experience in the stock market and the pure trade of currency exchange made him authoritative in discussing these problems. The renowned economists of the time were pure academicians and thus unable to address problems of such vitality and magnitude. In 1810 the Committee on Bullion issued a report that coincided with Ricardo's assertions concerning the problems of the inflated English currency. Thus Ricardo influenced the Bullion Report and later defended the report against attacks from all directions. In fact, Ricardo was considered controversial by many, and Parliament refused to repeal the Bank Restriction Act in spite of his vehement support of the Bullion Report.

In 1816, Ricardo proposed a revolutionary "gold bullion standard" in England. Under the standard any holder of English notes was free to exchange the notes into gold bar and vice versa. This free exchange was adopted by the British Parliament in 1819, but it was later abandoned because the economy was inundated with forged currency the forgers hoped to exchange immediately into gold bars. Ricardo wrote a paper supporting the free exchange standard called *Proposals for an Economical and Secure Currency*. Students of history can see how the British Government used the proposals contained in this paper, to balance the currency right after World War I.

One of Ricardo's noteworthy works was *Essay on the Influence of a Low Price of Corn*. This essay was primarily leveled against Malthus who was writing extensively about economic problems at that time. Ricardo introduced a new interpretation of rent different from the idea Malthus and Anderson had expounded. In his essay, Ricardo proffered his major economic thoughts. Accepting them as a base, he then wrote his greatest work, *On the Principles of Political Economy and Taxation*, which was published in 1817. *Principles of Political Economy* explains the value theory held by Ricardo. The exchangeable value of commodities depends on the quantities of labor necessary to produce that item and bring it to the market. One person can add to the commodity any amount of profit, but that does not change the intrinsic value or exchangeable value of that product. Establishing prices purely on the labor involved in production is not always a correct analysis. Dealing with this Hoselitz says:

Ricardo has very generally overlooked the influence of increased prices in diminishing consumption and stimulating industry, so that his conclusions, though true according to his assumptions, do not always harmonize with what really takes place.[1]

Ricardo answered many questions about economic growth or the capital formation, contingent on the productive powers of labor. The production depended on the skill of the laborer, the fertility of the land, and the cooperation of the natural forces. He discussed the quantity of money supply and its impact on wages and prices. Increase in capital would tend to increase wages due to greater demand for labor. Ricardo thought that higher wages necessarily depressed profits. This misconception was the reason for his 'iron law of wage' theory. He stood for slow population growth and ascribed the backwardness of the colonies to the imbalanced and accelerated increase of their population. He found a correlation between the fertility of land and fecundity of humanity. If land produces abundance of harvest, family heads would become more able to support more children. Farmers usually accepted the big family style, because it produced more hands to work in the field.

Ricardo ignored his philosophical, rhetorical, historical and literary tastes in writing this book and stuck to the essential principles of economics alone. He treated in depth the study of value, rent, wages, price, and profit. A reader of the book will notice that Ricardo used the writings and thoughts of contemporary and past economists. Still one can see the forcefulness, clarity and completeness he showed in discussing the cardinal points of economics. This book was not written for the lay person. It was acclaimed as the masterpiece of economic writings and was revised and reissued within a short while.

Ricardo publicly attested that he was a loyal student of Adam Smith. Yet he did not hesitate to express his personality and identity in treating the major principles dealt with by Smith, and he courageously differed with his master on occasion. In Smith one can see a realistic approach to economic issues. Ricardo approached the same problems with premeditated sophistication and abstraction.

In the value theory, Ricardo diverted the attention from the short run to the long run. He supported Say's law that supply created its own demand and that accordingly, there could be no overproduction. Everything produced would be consumed with the force of purchasing power realized as wages and salaries. He said that a temporary undersupply of one commodity might exist which would be offset by a temporary oversupply of other goods for which it could be exchanged. Ricardo, like Smith, discussed the "value in use" and "value in exchange." He saw a deterioration of wage rates due to the subsistence level of income. In his theory of equilibrium, he said that if the exchange rate was greater than the real value, consumers would resist by a slowdown in consumption or a shift to substitute goods. This would result in the piling up of inventories. Ricardo thought this market imbalance was the cause of recessions. The theory of rent held by Ricardo made him break with the physiocrats who believed that rent came from the "bounty of nature." Ricardo found some conflicting interests within the nation because the interests of the landed rent earners did not always coincide with the interests of the landless and the state at large. Ricardo said that the landowner did not produce the rent but only accepted the rent. This is a crucial departure that created radical changes in the creation of socialism and communism. Henry George used this idea to support taxation of landlords, and Karl Marx used the theory as the basis for his surplus value theory. Ricardo held that the value of all products should be determined by the amount of labor involved in producing them. Smith believed that value should be based on the rate of productivity of the labor not just the quantity of labor alone as Ricardo advocated.

Ricardo revised his ideas as time went on. He had accepted unquestionably many of the ideas given by Smith and his predecessors, but as his capacity for critical thinking sharpened with age and experience, he tried to extricate himself from many of the assumptions he had taken for granted. Ricardo's subsistence theory of wages or pure theory of wages is tenable as theory but seldom attainable in real life. Smith discussed the absolute advantage theory as the basis for international trade. Ricardo reformed that theory with his "comparative advantage theory." That theory has become the backbone of modern international trade.

In 1818, Ricardo was elected to the Parliament, and he spent his remaining years devoted to public service. The last work he wrote while serving in Parliament was *Plan for a National Bank*. The work concerned itself with the operation of the existing banks with a common policy about the issuance of currency. Ricardo's ideas got wider publicity through two of his admirers and disciples, J. R. McCulloch and John Stuart Mill, the son of his best friend James Mill. In 1814, after amassing a large fortune, Ricardo had retired from business life. In the same year he obtained an estate in Gloucestershire. It was there at Gatcomb Park, on September 11, 1823, that David Ricardo died.

Analysis of Ricardo's Major Economic Thoughts

Ricardo accepted labor as a commodity that can be bought and sold at market prices. Hence he arrived at two wages, the market wage and the natural wage. In defining the natural wage, Ricardo did not differ much from Smith and Malthus. He defined natural wage as the wage necessary to enable the laborer to subsist and perpetuate his species without increasing or decreasing in number. He did not accept the quantity of money the laborer got as the natural wage but how much that money could buy in the form of food and other necessities of life.

The market price of labor is the money paid for labor based on supply and demand of labor. Like all other commodities, wages increase or decrease depending on the law of supply and demand. When the market price of labor exceeds the natural price of labor, the wage earners enjoy prosperity. When the natural price of labor exceeds the market price, the wage earners experience famine, disease, and so on. In better days, the affluence of the laborers will lead to population increase, which in turn will depress the wage level to a minimum. That will cut back the population naturally. Similarly capital increase and decrease also will reflect on the wage level. If investments increase faster than population, wages rise and vice versa. Adam Smith considered technology a way to higher wages. Ricardo did not accept that theory totally. He thought that higher productivity would decrease the price of the object produced which in turn would decrease wages because the demand for labor would decrease and the supply of labor would remain constant. He failed to see that higher productivity would decrease prices so that more people could consume the product which in return would create a new demand on labor, thus boosting the wage level.

Inflation

Ricardo visualized inflation as the ratio of paper currency to the existing market price of gold (the commodity theory). The overprinting of bank notes and drafts made it impossible to redeem these notes, especially in the crisis of bankruptcies. Ricardo's book, *High Price of Bullion*, identified inflation in England due to this cause, i.e., too much money was made available to the public, and the first step of "demand-pull" inflation had to appear. He recommended a gold bullion standard that would watch over the quantity of bank notes by itself. He did not look at the other side while proposing this. Can an economy be tied to a limited amount of gold? The real things of value are goods and services, and the money supply should necessarily be tied to the real things of value. Gold is of value because of scarcity and popular consensus. In the eighteenth century it would have been hard to base the quantity of money on any other value than gold.

Taxation

Ricardo's explanation of taxation is not very clear. To him, the government was a consuming agent. The ability to consume should come from (1) increase in productivity; or (2) decrease in consumption of the consumers and business. The government stood for the private citizen and business, hence they had the burden of supporting the government. The revenue of the state from other sources was not to be tampered with. Therefore, the working expenses of the government must be met by annual contributions from the consuming public and business. If annual production failed, then the burden of tax would fall on the rate of consumption which in turn would impoverish the nation. One can see that Ricardo did not have a clear perception of the law of taxation.

International Trade

A product can be valued on the basis of labor hours involved in its production or according to the market value offered by the consumers. Ricardo used the example of wine and clothes. England could produce wine and clothes, but to produce wine it took 120 labor hours while clothes took only 100 labor hours. Portugal could also produce wine and clothes. But in Portugal wine could be produced with 100 labor hours while clothes needed 120 labor hours. Thus, England had a comparative advantage in clothes production and Portugal had a comparative advantage in wine production. Ricardo recommended that England specialize in clothes and Portugal in wine so that both countries could benefit by trade. If at the same time Spain could produce both wine and clothes in fewer man hours than England and Portugal, it would be better for England and Portugal to extend capital to Spain so that all production could be done in Spain. This idea encouraged the mobility of capital from one state to another.

Specie Flow

Ricardo noted two things about specie flow caused by trade. First,

the gold flow between countries always enriched one and impoverished the other. In order to perpetuate trade, therefore, it is
important to create a bilateral trade so that the specie flow can be
brought into balance. Secondly, he said that improvement in
manufacturing in one country would tend to alter the distribution of
valuable metals among the nations of the world, since exporting
nations would sift the world gold into their coffers.

Summary

Ricardo's basic economic assumptions can be summed up as
follows:
1. Increase in wages does not raise prices.
2. Profits can be raised only by decreasing wages.
3. Profit is the whole progress of the society.
4. Bank notes should be in proportion to the quantity of gold a
nation hoards.
5. Currency should be monometallic.
6. Nations should defray their expenses from income rather than
loans.
7. Trade between nations should be based on comparative
advantage.
Based on some of these assumptions Ricardo recommended a
system of distribution of agricultural products among landlords,
farmers, and laborers. He was apprehensive about population growth
like Malthus, but he saw no correlation between overpopulation and
unemployment. Indeed, he found no reason for sustained unemployment.

Footnotes

1. Hoselitz, Bert F. *Theories of Economic Growth*, New York: The Free Press,
1960, p. 75.

JOHN STUART MILL

On May 20, 1806, John Stuart Mill was born in Pentonville, London. His father James Mill was a highly respected economist who associated with the greatest economists of that era, like Adam Smith, David Ricardo, and Thomas Malthus. James Mill planned an educational program for John under the direction of Jeremy Bentham and according to the intensified educational program of Helvetius. This plan was a pressurized and enigmatic system that would give the entire depth of a university course when John reached his thirteenth year of age. The elder Mill acted as the junior's tutor and constant companion. In fact they worked together in James' office and went playing, hiking and horseback riding together. At the time James was writing for the Encyclopedia Britannica and another work, *History of India*. John delved into the numerous volumes that adorned his father's library and culled materials relevant to the scholarly work his father was involved in. This experience trained John to be on his own later while pursuing his scholarly works.

Mill's education began at the age of three. At eight years of age he mastered six dialogues of Plato and a good part of World History, especially Greek, Roman, and English. He studied Euclid and algebra with the same ease. Greek and Latin poets enchanted him and his love of poetry led him to the English poets, but of course some of the great treasures of English classical literature were not yet written. John's love for history prompted him to write an account of the long-admired Roman system of government. James Mill did not forget to familiarize his son with political economy, which was the normal area of specialization for the aristocracy of England. All studies were only stepping stones to that pinnacle of education. This prepared a student for jobs with the government or in the business world in which England enjoyed primacy. John studied law under Austin and economics under Ricardo, and Bentham's School of Jurisprudence gave John an overview of "legislation."

At the age of 17, John accepted a position with the East India Company. He started as a clerk but was soon promoted to "examiner" of the company, which is like an auditor of company accounts. He kept that position until the company was nationalized by the British government in 1836. He became chief negotiator with the Indian states in furthering the company's interest and thus achieved a field for exercising the diplomacy learned under Austin and Bentham. His father and his friends organized a school of "philosophical radicals," which was later called the School of Utilitarianism. John followed his father's lead and became the number two man in that system, number one, of course, being his teacher, Bentham. The Reform Bill of 1832 was enacted by Parliament because of the power exerted by the "philosophical radicals." John was also a member of the editorial board of the famous *Westminister Review*. In that capacity he wrote impressive editorials, went into debating groups, and shared in the contemporary intellectual and social life of the time.

One may wonder how one man can get involved with so many activities of different natures. This is where the division of labor becomes operative. A person who wants to work can always find time. Some are blessed with speed and intellectual power in whatever they encounter so that whatever they touch becomes a masterpiece. Thus they really live many lives in the span of a human life. John was among these privileged ones. He edited Bentham's *Rationale of the Judicial Evidence* in 1843. He wrote a book of his own, *The Principles of Political Economy*, which was published in 1848. This book was a revision of many essays he had written and published earlier in the *Westminister Review* or had debated in front of debating societies with which he was associated. These essays had been published under the title, *Essays on Some Unsettled Questions in Political Economy*.

In 1851 he married Harriet Taylor, a lifelong companion and a woman of great erudition. She helped him in his literary pursuits and encouraged him in his radicalism that attracted public attention. One can see that their first seven years of married life were less productive in publications. Still that shortage was in quantity rather than quality. His mature works like, *Essay on Liberty, Thoughts on Parliamentary Reform, Representative Government, and Utilitarianism* were the brain children of those seven years. He also led the fight for Women Suffrage and in 1865 became a member of the Parliament. After a very fruitful life, Mill died on May 8, 1873.[1]

Mill falls under the category of Classical Economists. He believed in the rights of private property, free enterprise, and government of the people. He also believed that a certain amount of government direction in the private enterprise system was needed to protect a free competitive economy. Like Adam Smith, he believed in an invisible hand that determines what to produce, for whom to produce, and when to produce. If the economy were left alone, by the sheer forces of supply and demand the market system would operate freely for the best interest of all concerned. If democracy in government is the best form of government for achieving the common good, Mill stated, a democracy in the market system should be the best form of economic system to impart the highest happiness to all. He wanted free allocation of resources and a free distribution of final products in order to maximize the happiness of all.

Classical economic theory is not always infallible. In logic there are two categories, one categoric and the other syncategoric. The categoric assumptions take into account real life; syncategoric assumptions have no foundation in real life. Hence there is the distinction between idealism and realism. The classical theories are a mixture of idealism and realism. The pure competition that the classical economists believed in has become a dead piece of ideology. The flow of pure competition is hampered by outside forces of vested interests or government. The classical economists assumed that man was a rational being and would always operate for the best interests of the society. Man may be rational, but he seldom operates for the common good, he operates for his private good. If all people try to maximize the private good, there could be an overlap of interests and final dissipation of total goods through frictional waste. The classical theory accepted the flexibility of wages upward or downward according to the business cycles. The workers and producers do not always follow this law. The full employment theory is also untenable because of its impracticality. All of these reasons made Mill differ from the classical economists and pursue his own ideology as contained in the Utilitarianism followed by his teachers and his venerated father. Even in that philosophy Mill took a detour into a new system called *eclecticism*. This system permits taking the good from any school of thought without accepting or identifying with any one of them. Mill's strength and weakness comes from this system; strength because of its widespread popularity and weakness because of its inconsistencies and apparent contradictions.

In some ways, Mill was caught between the reverence he gave to his father and the respect he gave to his teacher Bentham. Mill tried to take a middle approach between his father and his teacher, and that way made a rough journey. Augustus Comte, his instructor in law also exercised great influence on Mill. This situation hampered him in criticizing their works and denied the freedom required for a person of his originality.

The Economic Man

Mill did not use the term *economic man*, but he used the method of abstraction to depict this being. The economic man is "solely a being who desires to possess wealth and who is capable of judging the comparative efficiency of means for obtaining that end. It predicts only such of the phenomena of the social state as take place in consequence of the pursuit of wealth."[2]

Political economy considers mankind to be occupied solely in acquiring and consuming wealth.[3] This is where the utilitarian principles were concentrated. Then is the purpose of human life only to acquire and amass wealth so that one can enjoy material happiness unreservedly? What about the finer and nobler values a person enjoys? Since those values are not lit with dollar signs, are they nonexistent? Like all other utilitarians, Mill failed to answer many questions of such paramount importance.

Free Trade

Mill is accepted even today as giving a systematic direction for free trade. Free trade demanded eliminating the barriers to trade so that goods could flow from one nation to another. Customs and tariffs were restraints on free trade. When colonization came to a standstill because there were no more lands to conquer, the spirit of parochialism arose, leading to petty subdivisions of markets and territories. Each nation built up barriers to trade denying the free trade policies evolved by Mill.

Laissez-Faire

The classical economists spoke for a free trade and against any monopoly of business or government. In *The Principles of Political Economy*, Mill upheld the teachings of Ricardo and Malthus in the freedom of private enterprise. The private enterprise philosophy is based on the principle of specialization. That is, each person is blessed with a certain gift. In order to maximize his satisfaction, he should be free to pursue the field in which nature has blessed him with talents. When a government determines what occupation a person must follow, the idea of natural talents is ignored. The classical economists sought to improve the national wealth. They understood wealth consists of the goods and services the nation can produce. And they believed a free enterprise system would lead to the highest production of goods and services. That is why Mill prompted the laissez-faire philosophy.

Mill said that production required the application of labor to natural resources and capital. He did not think that capital should come from capitalists alone. He wrote: "Distribution of wealth is not inalterable, but differs in different ages and countries and is a matter of human institution, solely." He said that the job of the economist was not to discover universal natural laws in the distribution of wealth, but to analyze the practical consequences that would flow from any existing system of distribution.

The concept of production was broadened by the inclusion of several men and elements: the inventor; the pure scientist who is not, in reality, involved with the application of his scientific inventions to commercial pursuits; the philosopher who guides the value system, even though he is not in direct operations of production or distribution; the statesman who protects the society by upholding the rights of individuals and business; and even conducive elements that form a background for production.

Mill thought that "the natural resources are not just minerals and raw materials, but also power to do the work or the modern term "skill." With skill man possesses a command over natural forces immeasurably more powerful than themselves; a command which great as it is already, is without doubt destined to become infinitely greater." This statement made in *The Principles of Political Economy* in the nineteenth century, is indeed prophetic, as the modern day attests. Mill criticized the socialistic and communistic writings of his time. He found virtues and defects in their treatise. He foresaw the possibility of the creation of socialistic states. He rejected their theory that under capitalism the worker's condition cannot be improved. He also suggested the restriction of the population growth. He suggested improvement in the productive skill to advance profits and thereby increase the wages of the working class. The existence of a leisure class and a working class was repugnant to his thinking. He expected all people to work, but he insisted that they should be free to choose the areas of their specialization.

Mill pointed out that the goal of society should be technical progress that would enlarge "leisure for improving the art of living." Today when people talk of thirty-five-hour workweeks, are we not dealing with "improving the art of living"?

Mill expected cooperation between producers and consumers. He rejected monopolies of producers that exploit consumers. A free competition would satisfy both producers and consumers. When the United States enacted the Sherman Act of 1890, it was not existing monopolies that prompted the act, but fear of monopolies as depicted by the classical economists. It may have been premature, but it discouraged the potential monopolies that could have come into the picture.

Mill's writing became extremely popular in England and the United States. Most of his writings were directly against the existing systems and were branded as radical. Time changed that outlook. Contemporary radical and revolutionary themes often seem very conservative to the next generation. Mill wrote of practical things and so he is called, pragmatic, expedient, and utilitarian. Let the student be "eclectic"—able to cull out the good and leave the bad like a colt that eats the oats and leaves the pebbles deliberately added by the farmer to slow the eating process.

Footnotes

1. His important writings are: (1) *Logic* (1832), (2) *Utilitarianism* (1834), (3) *On Liberty* (1852), (4) *Examination of Sir William Hamilton's Philosophy* (1865), (5) *A Treatise on the Subjection of Women* (1861, but not published until 1869), and (6) three posthumous essays on *Nature, The Utility of Religion*, and *Theism*.

2. Cohen, Marshall, ed. *John Stuart Mill*, New York: Harcourt, Brace & World, 1961, p. 301.

3. Leslie, W. C. *Criticism of John Stuart Mill*, London: Howell Soskin, 1949, pp. 13, 15, 19.

SOCIALISM

Socialism is both a movement and a theory and takes different forms against different social and historical backgrounds. It aims at creating a classless society based on the socialization or nationalization of all private property—in some cases of all essential instruments of production, in other cases of only the key industries. From the beginning of man's history, there has existed a class of people who were exploited by some who possessed better minds or bodies. As time went on, the exploited number increased while the exploiters decreased, so that a cleavage between man and man broadened and a class system developed. The oppressed class dreams of a day when the world will undergo a reorganization with wealth being taken from the class that controls it and made available to all on the basis of need and ability.

The Development of the Principle of Socialism

Socialism is a reaction against existing ideologies concerning private property. The ownership of property leads to a class system based on differences in wealth or to a caste system based on differences of culture and social stratification. Adam Smith proposed the "classical liberalism," which is based on the implicit belief in the efficiency of a free market supported by unrestrained competition and enterprise free from government intervention. In order to maximize the common good of all, the classical liberal argued that there should be free markets—a policy of laissez-faire. To them, this was the only way to harmonize the various classes and free all from exploitations of the monopolists. Even though individuals are intensely selfish, by seeking to maximize individual pleasure, under the invisible hand of a free market, exploitation is supposed to decrease and the common good of all will increase.

This view was applied to all aspects of human life. Two areas were specifically noted—the realm of ideas and the realm of economics. The liberals contended that all should be free to think as they wished and even to uphold doctrines opposing time-honored views. They coined the word, "the marketplace of ideas," which underlies the notions of freedom of speech and writing. Freethinking should lead to freedom in all areas of everyday life. Thus free ideas and free commerce originate almost at the same time. One can safely say that liberalism was the ideology of the commercial and industrial middle class of the eighteenth and nineteenth centuries.

Liberalism argued that the best use of resources can be effected only with an unhampered operation of the market. Each individual should be free to buy as cheaply as possible and sell as dearly as possible to foster his own interests. Artificial restraints like government intervention with imposition of tariffs, customs, quotas, interest rates and licenses, and the like interfered with the competitive process. The classical liberals demanded that all restraints be lifted to allow people freedom of action. This was fundamentally a revolutionary doctrine contrary to traditionally conservative principles. Advanced countries in Europe and the United States were very receptive to such a cogent and persuasive doctrine. Intellectually assessing the liberal ideas, no one can find any social heresy in them.

Liberalism triumphed as the intelligentsia embraced its ideology without reserve. Colleges and universities taught it as the birth of a new era. The disciples of the new doctrine gained prominence in economics and politics and the middle class gained unusual stature in society. Free trade opened the way to maximum profits, minimum costs and increased productive efficiency. But, in the process, workers in the mines and factories were called on to perform duties far beyond human capability. England, especially, enacted laws to regulate the working class. Many of these laws were to protect the interests of industry and commerce and were detrimental to the interests of the workers. Out of the dissatisfactions of the working class, the doctrine of socialism began to be generated.

Socialism and Human Nature

Private ownership of the means of production and distribution by one class led to the disregard of the interests of all other classes. That made people think of a new system where all the means of production and distribution could be owned by the whole society. They thought that the system of private property had destroyed the natural harmony of society by creating distrust and enmity between the haves and the have-nots. They believed that mankind has an obligation of reconstituting nature to its pristine condition, with nature for man and man for nature. Men had built walls between themselves, creating classes and castes. Thus, rich and poor needed to work for the reorganization of society to do away with distinctions, discriminations, and higher and lower levels of society. Equality, liberty, and fraternity were the ideals, and they had tremendous appeal to all but the rich, who enjoyed the fruits of the earth at the expense of the poor. Implementing socialistic doctrine was not and is not easy. Socialists themselves differed about the best method to establish socialistic principles in all phases of life.

Anarchy versus Bureaucracy

The Fabian socialists, Beatrice and Sidney Webb classified people into two broad groups: A's and B's, anarchists and bureaucratists, or bureaucrats. The B's stress the need to concentrate power in the hands of the state, while the A's want a wide diffusion of power among the numerous groups that constitute the state. The A's want the people to do things for themselves and for each other; the B's want the state to do things for the common good of all. Anarchism rejects the power of the state; the bureaucrats believe that concentration of the power in the hands of the state is the most effective means for operating with a common plan, coordinating various activities and attaining the efficiency of a single command.

Since the main goal of the socialist is to escape from oppression from any force, the anarchists fear that the state could become an unchallengable oppressor, and they refuse to yield all power into the hands of the state. Karl Marx and Frederick Engels said that the ultimate end of socialism is to "wither away the state" and the government over people would ultimately lead to the government of the individual over himself. Some socialistic anarchists like M. A. Bakunin and P. A. Kropotkin advocated immediate overthrow of the state to bring about government of the people over themselves. Today most socialists have accepted the bureaucratic model of concentration of power in the hands of the state. They want the state to control the means of production and distribution, in order to guarantee greater freedom to the citizens as producers and consumers.

Between the A's and B's, there are some other differences also. One difference has to do with collectivism versus syndicalism. The collectivists advocate the nationalization of industries. They are not apprehensive about the inequalities of power of administration that may arise from state monopolies. Syndicalists or, as they are sometimes called, guild-socialists, want to see all industries controlled by the workers who labor in those industries. They hope for what they call industrial democracy. Another difference can be identified as partial versus total socialization. The totalists demand that all factors of production and distribution be controlled by the state, completely denying the right of private property and private enterprise. The partialists want socialization of only the key industries.

Some other groups split over the question of revolution versus evolution. Although all socialists ultimately demand a classless society, not all accept the notion of evolution from democracy to socialism as explained by Marx and Engels in their theory of inevitable economic evolution. The revolutionists believe bloody revolution is the most effective way of reaching their goal. Herein lies the real distinction between communism and socialism. The former believes in bloody revolution while the latter believes in a democratic evolution of society. Strategy is the main distinction between them.

Before the publication of the *Communist Manifesto*, socialism stood for various ideologies, especially the most prevalent, Utopian Socialism. This doctrine emphasized reeducating the rich to mend their ways and work for a classless society. Engels termed such a system, "house-trained socialism." The *Communist Manifesto* urged the working class, "workers of the world arise, you have nothing to lose but your fetters"—a call for unity and the overthrow of the upper class through bloody revolution. Socialism preached the brotherhood of man, while communism demanded the solidarity of the class.

In the present interpretation given by the Soviet literature socialism and communism are two different stages of the same ideology. They point out that under socialism goods are distributed only according to each man's productivity or "according to ability" and that under communism the same goods are distributed according to need, which is a finer form of distributive justice. The utopia they envision has goods in plenty and each one can help himself freely Work is compulsory but pleasant enough to create its own motivation and incentive. Greed for money is replaced by a sense of fulfillment. Vladimir I. Lenin gave the name "communism" to the movement whose objective is to establish the dictatorship of the proletariat or the rule of a classless society.

The Major Systems of the Socialist Thought

Socialist philosophy, the doctrine of the road to power, the methods of industrial development, and the political machinery of the socialistic state are areas we must interpret still further.

Utopian Socialism

Francois Fourier, Claude Saint-Simon, Robert Owen, Horace Greenley, Charles A. Dana and many others wanted changes in the social structure but wanted it through the "conversion of the rich." They did not understand the evolutionary or revolutionary forces that work in economic society. They thought that the realization of truth and the working of the moral laws would change the discrepancies of wealth.

Utopian socialism was followed by Marxist socialism as described in *Das Kapital* by Marx and the *Communist Manifesto* by Marx and Engels. In those works Marx and Engels held that the history of a nation—its culture or philosophy—consisted in the methods by which men and women owned, produced, and distributed goods and services. They said that economic changes depended on the class conflicts between the capitalists and the workers.

Revisionism

Marx and Engels initiated the revolt in 1848, but it was ruthlessly suppressed and its leaders went into exile. To stop any recurrence of such agitations the capitalists enacted one factory legislation after another. Workers got better wages, better working conditions, and better working hours. These changes were not up to the standards one sees in the twentieth century, but the workers got a better standard of living and better education, and they began to lean on the democratic process and legal channels to attain their demands.

Under these circumstances, new social thoughts came to the surface. The important writings came from Eduard Bernstein, a German journalist who described himself as a "revisionist." Later a new sect of socialists appeared led by Beatrice and Sidney Webb under the name, "Fabian Socialists." George Bernard Shaw, Graham Wallace, and American revisionists joined this group. Bismark exiled Eduard Bernstein, who then lived in Zurich and London respectively. The revisionists challenged the socialism initiated by Marx and Engels and especially their indictment of capitalism as evil.

Fabian Socialism

Bernstein owed most socialistic ideas to his close contact with the English socialists during his sojourn in London. The Fabian Society was organized in 1884, and it was founded on the natural opposition of people to the exploitation of the monopolies, mergers, and cartels. Expansion of municipal and national ownership resulted in a new interpretation of social morality and of the individual's responsibility to the Commonwealth.

The Fabian Society accepted as their motto, "For the right moment, you must wait, as Fabius did most patiently, when warring against Hannibal, though many censured his delays; but when the time comes you must strike hard as Fabius did, or your waiting will be in vain and fruitless."

Guild Socialism

Immediately before and after World War I, another school of social thought appeared on the European scene. Guild socialism, a movement led by Samuel George Hobson, G.D.H. Cole, and other prominent British writers and economists, was also called syndicalism. It emphasized the rights of the producer and warned that the national and municipal monopolies controlled by the state would bring on a "servile state" and a universal "craftsmen's challenge." The guild socialists urged that everything be done to meet the demands of the workers, but that they should achieve their demands through democratic processes rather than violence and revolution. They demanded that the operation of individual factories should be left to the workers themselves, to create labor factories such as were later recommended in the immortal *Rerum Novarum* of Leo XIII. The guild socialists did not care whether the *ownership* of factories was left with individuals, municipalities, or the state, but they wanted the *management* of the factories to be free from the regimentation of the state. They stated that since a factory needs every type of worker—skilled, semiskilled, and unskilled—these three groups should organize a board representing them fully, and this board should have the power of administering each factory through democratic methods. Right after World War I, this movement collapsed because of the global depression, which ended in dire unemployment and the dissipation of unions for some time.

Democratic Socialism

It became perfectly clear by 1900 that capitalism was not deteriorating into the monstrous disparities between classes that Marx had predicted. The lot of the working class in the progressive nations was improving rather than becoming worse. Furthermore, the menacing condition of the rich becoming richer and the poor becoming poorer was not happening at all. The rich and poor alike benefited from the gradual elimination of the lower class. Economic thinkers could see that industrial peace could be achieved by the democratic processes of collective bargaining between management and labor.

There were two broad alternatives left for the socialists of the world to follow under these circumstances. They could follow the revolutionary course propounded by Marx to achieve their goals, or they could abandon the revolutionary ideas and implement Marxist goals by a peaceful approach. Labor conditions were different in different places. Some overpopulated areas with fewer industries took the revolutionary course. But in other places, where labor found that most of its grievances were somewhat resolved, a peaceful approach of mediation, arbitration, and conciliation was taken. Those who remained faithful to the Marxist principles of revolution, were soon dominated by the Russian Bolshevik movement, and are now properly called "communists."

The socialists who accepted the peaceful approach to attaining labor demands are called "revisionists." Many followed the German writer Eduard Bernstein (1850-1932) in his work entitled *Evolutionary Socialism*, 1899. In England the revisionists followed the Fabian Society. The revisionists abandoned the Marxist principle for "the inevitability of gradualism." They believed any goal set by anyone could be achieved by "eternal vigilance." Problems could be solved by striking at the most propitious moment.

Role of Socialist Economics

Objectivity demands that economic principles can be true or false regardless of the political system that sponsors them. If a principle is true, it is true universally and does not depend on political creed. But in the area of value judgments there can be room for misunderstanding. The Marxist rejects the view that social science is neutral and that theory and practice can be separated. Liberal economists accept the existing legal and political framework and study the price and income within that framework. Socialists study the framework itself.

Labor Theory of Value

The pre-Marxian society set as its goal a good society. Private property hindered the laborer from getting his due share. Socialists accept the idea that labor alone is valuable. The difference between what the laborer created and what was given him for subsistence went to the owner of the productive factors like machines and materials, but under the theory that labor alone is valuable, they deserved nothing from the output of the laborer.

Economic Planning

Socialists believed that the economic reorganization of the society could be effected by deliberate planning, so that step by step goals could be reached. Marx ridiculed such planning, saying that it would be ineffective before the revolution and unnecessary after the revolution. The democratic planners suggested (1) redistribution of income, (2) the socialization of capital investment, (3) monetary reform of banking and credit, (4) restrictive practices on monopoly, (5) consumer and producer cooperatives, and (6) the achievement of these goals by persuasion rather than revolution.

The Socialist International of 1951 adopted various courses of action:

> Socialism seeks to replace capitalism by a system in which public interests take precedence over the interest of private profit . . . in order to achieve these ends production must be planned in the interests of the people . . . Democratic Socialism therefore stands in sharp contradiction both to capitalist planning and to every form of totalitarian planning. . . .

Conclusion

The socialists believe in society acting through its political institutions and taking over the economic processes of production and distribution. Although socialism and communism are half-brothers, their relations are rather those of Cain and Abel: They have been the bitterest of enemies for many decades. The specific characteristic of modern socialism is its commitment to the gradual realization of its goals through the use of democratic techniques. Democracy and socialism are complementary rather than antithetical, since democracy also stands for the preservation of freedom.

MARX, ENGELS, AND LENIN

Karl Marx

Karl Marx came from a radical or liberal family background. He was born on May 5, 1818, in Trier, Germany. His father embraced Christianity a short time after the birth of Karl, so that the discrimination against him as a Jew could be lessened in his legal practice. The young Karl read extensively the works of Hegel, Voltaire, Locke, and Diderot and joined a group called Young Hegelians that debated daring questions like atheism and pure theoretical communism. Soon he accepted the editorship of *Rheinische Zeitung*, a small liberal newspaper. He was censured later for writing a bitter denunciation of a law that would have prevented peasants from collecting dead wood in the forest. Marx then went to Paris to take over the editorship of another liberal paper, but that paper was quite short lived. Later he edited a radical magazine and offended the Prussian Government with his scathing editorials, for which he was expelled from Prussia. He was married to Jenny von Westphalen, the daughter of a Prussian aristocrat.

For four years Marx lived in Brussels as an exile but that stay was also terminated because the Belgian king started rounding up the radicals and Marx had to flee to Germany. In 1849, Marx moved to London. Marx got into extreme financial trouble, but a stockbroker with an acutely radical mind named Frederick Engels supported the Marxes with a steady stream of money and checks. Marx was so poor at that time that he had to pawn his coat and shoes for a piece of bread. In fact, he could not even buy the postage stamps to send his works to the publishers. In 1881, after the deaths of her three children, Jenny herself died.

Marxist Philosophy

Marx was an empiricist who contended that everything is in a state of change. Reality is the creation of change. "The dialectic method of Karl Marx is a way of dealing with what is both constant and variable in every situation."[1] The dialectical method is opposed to the universal scientific method, yet one can see that Marx borrowed heavily from scientific methods.

The scientific method accepts only things that can be measured. Marx goes farther: "There are other realms of experience, such as the arts and practical affairs, in which qualities and activities are the fundamental organizing concepts and not quantities." Marx accepted three primary concepts: the state, the society, and the government. To Marx society is any group of human beings living together for the satisfaction of their fundamental economic needs.[2] Government, according to Marx, is the administrative mechanism by which these economic needs are controlled and furthered. The more primitive the society, the more rudimentary the form of government. The state is a specially organized public power of coercion, which exists to enforce the decisions of any group or class that controls government. Marx underwent punishment himself through banishment and the many restraints put on him while editing his papers and journals. He knew that for example, the Andamann islanders . . . lose power, social standing and are socially ostracized—which is regarded as a severe form of punishment.[3]

Marx thought that the state through its intervention tries to monopolize the total economic system and caters directly to the interests of the vested aristocracy. He says that, "the state conceals its injustice under the euphemism of social services." Marx expected that the goal of state or society should be the security of its citizens rather than distributive justice. Hence he stood for the overthrow of the state. Benedetto describes this phenomenon in his *Essays on Marx and Russia*: "If Marx's analysis of the state is valid, then it follows that no fundamental change in the control of the instruments of social production is possible without the overthrow of the state."[4]

Marx ran into two separate oppositions while vindicating his philosophy of revolution. One was the opposition of the existing ruling class or bourgeoisie. Going back into the origin of the ruling class one can see that they took over with revolution and they made certain that no other revolution would spring up in their territory. The other force that stood against Marxist revolution was the strong stance of the Christian Socialists. This group opposed all forms of violence and hoped to attain their goals by peaceful means. "For Marx the use of force in a revolutionary situation was no more a moral problem than the use of fire in ordinary life; it was only the intelligent use of force that constituted a problem."[5] Marx stated again, "It is to force that in due time the workers will have to appeal if the dominion of labor is at long last to be established."[6]

Marx understood well that revolution might not be an effective weapon for establishing socialism in all countries of the world. However, he thought that the countries in which he lived—Germany, Belgium, France, and England—were ripe for revolution and that only violence could succeed in that revolution. Marx could also see the possibility of dictatorship after a revolution has been successfully implemented. He felt that, "the dictatorship itself is only a transition to the ultimate abolition of all classes and a society without classes."[7]

Marx did not concede that bourgeois dictatorship is the rule of the majority. "Only the dictatorship of the proletariat can bring a rule of majority. Bourgeois dictatorship is by a minority of population—a minority defined not by the number of votes cast, but by the number of those who own the instruments of social production."[8] If the banks, factories and markets should be tightened due to political pressures then the citizen is victimized and has virtually no say in the matter of policies enacted in the parliaments or congress. The common man has a voice at election time but none in the enactments in the legislature. Moreover the common man is unable to exercise his right of free election because the power groups and vested interests either intimidate or buy off his right of franchise. The proletariat dictatorship, according to Marx, is also based on force: "The first task the proletariat dictatorship must accomplish is to crush all actual or incipient counter-revolutionary movements." The problem of economics and education are the most important job of the government of the proletariat. The capitalist system has to be transformed into a socialist system.

Marx was not consistent in his thinking when he demanded the suppression of counterrevolution. He did not say whether the counterrevolution of which he spoke also stood for the creation of the real socialist state. If both aim at the same end through two distinct ideologies and approaches, which should get priority and precedence? In other words, of the two types of revolution against capitalists, which one should be endorsed by the public at large? "What distinguishes Marx's economic analysis is its infusion of the historical and analytical moments of capitalistic production in the interest of a practical program of revolutionary activity."[9] It is evident that the central theme of Marx's writing is only revolution; there is no room for peaceful evolution.

Marx had his own version of capital: "Capital is not a thing, but a social relation between persons, established by the instrumentality of things."[10] Marx also had his own ideas of supply and demand. He did not say that prices varied according to the forces of supply and demand. He watched the directions in which prices fluctuated. Then he tried to analyze the causes of these fluctuations. He decided that supply and demand are the basic causes of disorder in the price mechanism and that the control of these factors was necessary to create a stable economy.

Labor Theory of Value

Marx delved into the economists of the past in distinguishing two types of values, namely, value in use and value in exchange. He accepted the labor time involved in the creation of a product as that which establishes the value of an object. He defined a commodity as anything that is produced for exchange rather than for the use of the producer. Its exchange value is then the outward manifestation of the social relationship between producers. The exchange of commodities becomes an exchange of labor between two producers. The determinant factor between two products is labor. Therefore, abstract labor becomes the common denominator in the human activity of production.

Now all labor was counted as the base for value. Only labor that could be characterized as "socially desirable" counted for value. "The labor time socially necessary is that time required to produce an article under the normal conditions of production, and with the average degree of skill and intensity prevalent at the time."[11]

Commodity production itself is not the base of capitalism. On the other hand, it gives capitalism a terrific power as the only buyer of labor. The capitalist hires a person for a day and pays him a wage equal to the value of the worker's means for subsistence, when in fact, the worker's productivity is worth many times what is paid him for subsistence. This difference between the value of the productivity and the real wage is called the surplus value. In other words, the surplus value is the amount the capitalist exploits from the worker as the profit or reward for employing the worker. This theory is reduced to an algebraic form by Marx—$C = c + v$, where C stands for total capital, c for constant capital, and v for variable capital the total value of which can be increased. The variable capital is labor. By forcing the worker to work longer hours the capitalist can maximize his profit. It seems obvious that if a certain number of workers, raw material inputs, machines, and plants are required to produce a certain number of shoes in a day, all these components become productive. It is not labor alone that contributes to the production. Marx knew that the other factors also contribute to productivity. In a socialistic society where property is owned by workers, the total product will still exceed wages to allow for: (1) depreciation, (2) capital replacement and addition, and (3) social economies that are not linked to earnings. These three components should be equivalent to the surplus value. The German socialist and writer Rosa Luxemburg discussed this point very clearly when treating surplus value as a common factor in socialism and capitalism.

Theory of Employment

Marx's theory of employment was that while capital accumulated and the working population increased, employment would be limited because of the limitations of plant and equipment. If capital accumulated beyond the available labor force, then labor would become dear, real wages would increase and profits would fall. This would check the process of capital accumulation and restore the surplus of labor, the "reserve army of the unemployed." It is hard to find a relationship between the falling profits and increasing wages Normally, profits and wages travel in the same direction. The rate of profit is determined by the same factors that determined the surplus value. Thus the capitalist who employs technology and whose workers are more productive will have a higher rate of return.

Marx accepts in the *Theory of the Law* that profits can fall. If the rate of surplus remains the same and the other factors of capital increase, then the rate of profit decreases. Marx and Engels talked about the "increasing organic composition" of capital because of the inverse ratio of capital to profit. The fall in profit can be checked by (1) raising the intensity of exploitation (e.g., increasing the working hours); (2) depressing wages to cut back the unit cost of the product; (3) exploiting the reserve of overpopulation; and (4) foreign trade.

Price Determination

Marx asserted that the values of commodities are measured by the value of the labor time required for their production. How can we translate that value into price? Marx maintained that every society is built on an economic base; it is ultimately grounded in the hard reality of human beings who have organized their activities in order to clothe and feed and house themselves.[12] However, in whatever form men organize to solve their basic economic problems, society requires a whole superstructure of noneconomic activity and thought, which needs to be bound by laws, supervised by a government, and inspired by philosophy and religion. This is what Marx forgot to include.

Das Kapital

Das Kapital was started in 1851 and completed in 1865. It was a bundle of illegible manuscripts that took two years to edit and publish. Marx died in 1883 and two volumes remained unpublished. *Das Kapital* was an attempt to find the goals of the capitalistic system. If the purest form of capitalism is headed for a total crash, then any form will have the same fate sooner or later. That is why Marx treated pure capitalism. In this system the capitalist is an owner-manager engaged in an endless race against his fellow entrepreneurs. He must strive to accumulate, otherwise a stronger competitor will swallow him.

Marx distinguished three classes: capitalists, landlords, and wage earners. It is presupposed that these classes are split into hostile groups—the bourgeoisie and the proletariat. This class struggle is caused by the excessive exploitation of the working class. [13]

The second principle contained in *Das Kapital* is the idea of revolution. Class struggle was the beginning of this revolution. "If the people are exploited enough and find that they can no longer sustain themselves, this could serve as the catalyst upon which the revolution could foster. Only through class struggle can a change in property relationships (i.e., social revolution) be achieved." [14]

Finally the class struggle would end in the reorganization of the political government. A revolution would overthrow the ruling party, which would be replaced by another group, those who led the revolution. In other words, the class struggle causes revolution, which in turn opens the door to the socialistic state, or the rule of the proletariat. This was the final goal of all Marxist philosophies.

The Essence of Das Kapital

In the first volume (Critique of Political Economy) Marx considered the wealth of a capitalist nation as commodities laid out for sale. The value of a commodity depends on its ability to attract owners of other commodities so that an exchange may take place. Marx did not say that this exchange is a direct barter, but with the aid of the medium of money, the products move from the producer to the consumer. Every commodity has a surplus value so that it can be sold to a consumer. This consumer surplus is the amount exploited from the laborers by the capitalist. The price of a product is established at the point of supply and demand where the consumer surplus becomes zero. Wages are seldom higher than prices. This makes the never-ending process of profit maximization and exploitation of the working class. Marx said, "by transforming money into commodities . . . and by incorporating living labour power with their dead substance the capitalist transforms value into capital . . . as if love were breeding into his body."[15]

In the second volume, Marx raised the question of economic crisis. Capitalism, according to Marx, is in constant danger of being thrown out of equilibrium. The forces of production are not dependent on the forces of consumption and for the survival of capitalism both production and consumption should go hand in hand. The consumer is king in capitalism, and he cannot be told what to do by the producers. The power tool of capitalism will turn against itself to destroy it. There are many forms of crises that happen in the capitalistic system. Marx thinks that every cause that created a crisis evolves into the effect of another crisis, thus making them a chain of disturbing forces in capitalism. Hence there is no easy remedy or way out when economic turbulence occurs.

Friedrich Engels

Revolutionary ideas are usually associated with adverse experiences one undergoes in the environment of origin or business or working conditions. In the case of Marx, the discriminations imposed on him by the establishments made him a revolutionary. Lenin and Stalin had the same kinds of experiences, which forced them to the ruthless life style they accepted.

Friedrich Engels, on the other hand, was born into a very rich family where poverty was only a word. His parents were very religious and extremely hardworking. Engels rebelled against the extreme religious overtone of his parents' life and the unwanted imposition of the same spirit on him. Engels was a gifted child with unusual taste for poetry and literature, but one day his father packed his suitcase and sent him to Germany to learn export trade under a famous teacher at Bremen. His father really wanted him to be a cleric and forced him to live with a cleric at Bremen. Religion and money-making were the unctions of the human soul, according to Engels senior!

Engels did not waste his educational opportunity in Germany. He dutifully applied himself to the type of education that was offered. Yet he could not find any meaning in the education he struggled to internalize. Money-making was never a challenge to him or an aspiration of his young heart. He found a cleavage widening between his father's goals and his. He often spent his evenings at the harbor watching the boats sail in and out. He saw the captain's cabin, "in mahogony ornamented with gold," while on the deck, "people packed in like paving stones in the street." This disparity of the lives of people made him think deeply about the social problems of the time. This spirit of concern for others started dawning in him in a new form. He read avidly every book he could find that discussed the social problems and recommended remedies.

Germany at that time was going through a "youth rebellion." The government opposed every form of free speech or discussion of radical ideas. Besides, the government suppressed any attempt at formation of any new political party. There was open misuse of authority both in church and state. Important literary writings of the time questioned the social imbalance and condemned the "establishments" for being responsible for such inequalities.

Engels was young and energetic and wanted to be "involved," so he joined the clandestine groups that fought the government and the church. He accepted worship of human society over the worship of God and became one of the leaders of the underground rebel organization. He knew rhetoric and literature; he converted legions of youth with his oratory; his versatile pen wrote scathing criticisms of the king's policy of oppression and brutal retaliation against critics. As history attests, no rebel plans a violent revolution. Each hopes for a peaceful settlement of differences, but usually little is accomplished by peaceful means. This state of affairs leads a rebel to resort to violence. This happened to Engels—he was goaded to advocate violence as a means of redressing social ills. He was 22 by now; he knew for sure that freedom cannot be obtained through peaceful bargains; he accepted "communism" which at that time did not have any real concrete definition, other than as a system that did not accept the right of private property.

The king was hunting down the underground rebels one by one and so Engels returned to Manchester to join his father in his textile mill. There he saw the same dichotomy and boiling animosity between rich and poor in Manchester that he had noted in Germany.

Even the streets were zoned so that the poor were not permitted in certain areas considered exclusively for the pleasure of the rich. The rich had no idea how the poor eked out an existence in penury, filth, and disease. *The Conditions of the Working Class in England*, Engels' first book, described the terrible conditions under which the working class lived in England.

Engels became a respected writer after the publication of his book. Soon his articles appeared all throughout England. Still he saw tremendous strides in the technological progress and economic conditions of the upper class, while the lower class lived in the same abject conditions. He attacked the classical school that stressed the accumulation of wealth through the operation of the market system. The upper class of England found it the perfect ideology for their advantage and the perfect theoretical justification to oppose any factory law that demanded amelioration of the conditions of the working class.

Engels called on the government to remedy the social disadvantages of the working class to no avail. As a last resort, he called the workers to demand the changes they needed. He offered his services for organizing the working class. Other socialists of the time joined him to carry the banner for the working class.

By this time Karl Marx was exiled from Prussia and had found his haven in England. Engels recruited the services of Marx and supported him from his own pocket during his lifetime. Marx and Engels became the perfect complement to each other and together they laid the foundations for world communism. Together they molded the communist movement into an effective political philosophy. They wrote a paper, *German Ideology* and made themselves the leaders of the German Communist Party. They needed a written set of bylaws during the Second Congress of the Communist League Convention, so they coauthored the famous *Communist Manifesto*. It bears the personal traits of Marx's ability and genius to put his thoughts in words effectively. One can still see in the *Manifesto* the many personal thoughts Engels expressed in his articles before its publication. It may be safe to say that the *Manifesto* shows the ideas of Engels and the eloquence of Marx.

The *Manifesto* points out that "the history of all hitherto existing society is the history of class struggles." It accused the contemporary feudalistic system of exploiting the labor class to perpetuate the ascendency of the upper class. "Not only had the bourgeoisie forged the weapons that bring death upon itself; it had also called into existence the men who had to wield those weapons, the proletarians," stated the *Manifesto*.

Marx and Engels predicted the demise of capitalism out of which would come a classless society. They said political power was a bourgeois contrivance to set one class against another for their mutual destruction.

Engels left England to join the revolution that took place at Baden, Germany. At the failure of the insurrection, he returned to England. He joined his father's business as a clerk and shared his income with Marx. His father died in 1860, leaving Engels heir to his wealth. He signed a partnership with the firm in 1864 and also married Mary Burns, his companion and secretary throughout his revolutionary life. In 1869, he sold his partnership and left for London, where he lived with Marx until the latter's death in 1883. Together they worked on *Das Kapital* and after Marx's death, Engels completed the unfinished volumes. Friedrich Engels died in 1895, after seeing his movement take root firmly in Europe.

Lenin and Communism

Lenin did not follow Marx or Engels in building his philosophy of Bolshevik socialism. He eliminated the historic tieup with the class system and reorganized his followers according to their ideals of life and dedication to their conviction. Russia was known for its "Narodniki"—groups of people very dedicated to some public causes — but the new breed under Lenin was imbued with Marxist ideologies and techniques. Some Marxists did not approve Lenin's ways and accused him of "Jacobinism and Blanquism." Lenin's strategy was to attribute all his abilities to Marx and nothing to himself. Marx had a mystic faith in the power of the proletariat but Lenin knew that this is meaningless unless a leader can use the power to his advantage. Lenin called himself a socialist but in reality he was an autocrat who shared very little authority with anyone else.

Lenin did not follow Marxist metaphysics because it was totally impractical in revolutionary circumstances. Marx said that his mission was to "bring the working class a consciousness of its destiny," an idea which Lenin refused to accept. He made himself the artisan who could mold this dormant power of the masses to subdue the age-old power of the upper class. Lenin failed to see that the material elements of the world are spontaneously evolving into socialism as Hegel and Marx repeatedly taught. "The elemental development of the workers' movement," he said, "goes straight toward subjection to the bourgeois ideology . . . for the elemental worker's movement is trade unionism . . . and trade unionism means just exactly the intellectual enslavement of the workers by the bourgeoisie."[16] Lenin believed that the world was and is an ordered movement of matter and that our knowledge is the highest product of nature.

Footnotes

1. Hook, Sidney. *Toward the Understanding of Karl Marx*, New York: John Day Co., 1933.
2. Tucker, Robert C. *The Marxian Revolutionary Idea*, New York: W. W. Norton, 1969, p. 54.
3. Lokowitz, Nicholas. *Marx and the Western World*, South Bend: University of Notre Dame Press, 1967, p. 217.
4. Croce, Benedetto. *Essays on Marx and Russia*, New York: P. Unger Publishers, 1966, p. 141.
5. Korsch, Karl. *Karl Marx*, New York: John Wiley & Sons, 1938, p. 203.
6. Berlin, Sir Isaiah. *Karl Marx: His Life and Environment*, New York: McGraw-Hill, 1963, p. 84.
7. Baer, Max. *Life and Teaching of Karl Marx*, Boston: Small, Maynard & Co., 1924, p. 220.
8. Garaudy, Roger. *Karl Marx: The Evolution of His Thought*, New York: International Publishers, 1967, p. 61.
9. Speigel, Henry Williams. *The Development of Economic Thought*, New York: John Wiley & Sons, 1952, p. 241.
10. Horwitz, David. *Marx and Modern Economics*, New York: Modern Reader Paperbacks, 1968, p. 99.
11. Sweezy, Paul M. *The Theory of Capitalist Development*, New York: Monthly Review Press, 1956, pp. 94, 17, 42.
12. Stachey, John. *Contemporary Capitalism*, New York: Random House, 1956, p. 103.
13. Mehring, Franz. *Karl Marx: The Story of His Life*, London: John Lane, Inc., 1936, p. 85.
14. Taylor, Overton. *A History of Economic Thought*, New York: McGraw-Hill, 1960, p. 97.
15. Mattick, Paul. *Marx and Keynes*, New York: Extending Horizon Books, 1969, p. 27.
16. Lenin, Vladimir. *What Is to Be Done: Burning Questions of Our Movement*, New York: International Publishers Co., 1969.

References

Wilson, Edmund. "The Young man From Manchester," *The New York Republic*, August 13, 1938.
Wilson, Edmund. "Marx and Engels: Grinding the Laws," *The New Republic*, September 7, 1939.
"Engels: Man With a Mission," *Saturday Review*, December 20, 1952.

WILLIAM STANLEY JEVONS

William Jevons was born in Liverpool, England, on September 1, 1835. He registered at the University College in 1851, to pursue studies in Social Science. Because of unforeseen family problems, he had to terminate his studies. After six years absence from academic life, he returned to college to resume his studies and in 1863 he became the proud recipient of a master's degree.

Even while Jevons was away from college, he did not waste his time. He accepted a job as an assayer in Australia. He worked for a mine in Sydney, and that practical experience was very useful to him later. While doing his graduate studies, he published two papers that won him great admiration. *General Mathematical Theory of Political Economy* and *A Serious Fall in the Value of Gold* were the two works that secured his acceptance among the economists. In fact, in the first paper he outlined the marginal utility theory of value, an area never before explored by the economists. The discovery of gold in California and Australia happened at the same time, which had its effect on the market price of gold. He analyzed the price fluctuation caused by the sudden supply of gold in a mathematical way. His approach to this analysis opened a new method called the "Index Method" in analyzing economic problems.

In 1865 Jevons wrote another essay, *The Coal Question*, which was a powerful warning to England about the fast depletion of its coal reserves. In 1866, Jevons was offered a chair at the Owens College in Manchester. Ten years later, he was invited by the college that taught him to accept a chair at the University College.

While at the University College, Jevons wrote his important work, *Theory of Political Economy*, in which he expatiated on the term he had introduced, "marginal utility of value." History does not say that Jevons was the first to construct the marginal utility of value

111

theory. In Germany Herman Heinrich Gosen developed the same theory at the same time. One can see some similarities but more differences in the way both economists presented the marginal utility theory.

Jevons wrote another book, *The State in Relation to Labor*, which became an important topic for labor management dialogues of that time. In the book Jevons made a strong plea to the government to direct the life of the working class through appropriate labor legislation. Unfortunately this was to be the last of Jevons publications; he drowned near Hastings, England on August 13, 1882, at the age of 46.

Marginal Economics

The industrial revolution created many social problems that had never existed before. The people migrated en masse to the cities hoping to find new jobs and share the prosperity they heard about in the cities. The supply of labor was beyond demand, and consequently the employers exploited the helpless situation of the masses looking for jobs. Unfair wages and miserable working conditions became the thorns of the working class. In order to combat this social injustice, many movements took shape in England, of which three deserve mention: Most important was the spirit of socialism taking root among the workingmen. The second was trade unionism. Many unions did not last long, yet trade unions, the legal mandate to serve as collective bargaining agents became a powerful force in England. The third was the government's increasing interference with private enterprise. The marginalist school was founded to combat government interference in the private sector. The same school fought against both the trade unions and the maltreatment accorded to the working class by the employers. In fact, the marginalists were against the three predominant movements.

Jevons was the leader of the marginalist school. The following are the basic premises of the marginalists.

1. That they would concentrate on margin—the point of change —where decisions are made to implement the economic phenomena.

2. That their method would be abstract and deductive.

3. That the economic system must be based on pure competition.

4. That price is determined solely by demand.

5. That income and expenditure must be emphasized, rather than production and distribution.

Marginalism was also known as conservatism and thus opposed all changes regardless of other aims and purposes. The marginalists defended the landowners and blamed unemployment on high wages. In essence, this was a school of the wealthy, who did not want high taxes or the redistribution of income.

Jevons and Utility

According to Jevons, our wants are constantly changing in quality and quantity. "Human wants tend toward variety; each separate want when satisfied, other wants begin to be felt."[1] Senior called this theory, "The Law of Variety." Jevons thought that there is a coherent pattern in which our wants increase. It is very close to the "hierarchy of needs" theory. Jevons set up a hierarchy of wants, but one can easily see that there is no upper limit for wants. The amount of utility that one draws from these wants depends on the usefulness derived from each of them. Jevons illustrated this by making a comparison between diamonds and water. All people can live without diamonds, but no one can live without water. Yet diamonds are priced far above water. In this case, the usefulness is not the measuring stick; it is the scarcity of diamonds that prices them above water. Jevons sums up his argument, "water is useful when and where we want it, in such quantity as we want it, and not otherwise."[2] In summary, utility as Jevons sees it, depends on the usefulness of wealth. He continues: "All wealth is produced in order that it may be consumed when it best fulfills its purpose, that is when it is most useful."[3]

Jevons defines wealth as "all that man desires as useful or delightful." He identifies three factors of production that contribute to the formation of wealth: land, labor, and capital. We apply labor to the land and give capital to the laborer so that he willfully applies the labor to the land. The laborer must have capital to maintain his livelihood and to procure the necessary tools to work on the land. Land without labor remains sterile. Land or nature can beget new wealth, but to get the specific product, labor has to be invested according to the farmer's plan. A piece of land can naturally produce clover, but if the farmer wants to produce tobacco, he will have to remove the clover and plant tobacco.

Land and labor cannot bring in the desired crop without the necessary capital. Seed, fertilizer, irrigation, farm equipment, and necessary protection from outside incursion require capital. The lack of capital diminishes and often nullifies the expected return from the land. So the role of capital in the production of wealth cannot be underestimated.

Jevons stated that if a man owned the most fertile land and possessed the greatest amount of capital but failed to apply any labor to the land, the production from the land would be zero. So he said, "the amount of wealth people can obtain depends far more upon their activity and skill in laboring than upon the abundance of material around them."[4]

Jevons thought that the greatest amount of capital, the best fertile land, and the most skilled labor were still not enough to bring about the highest productivity. Each of these three factors should be combined together in the right proportion to yield the highest return. Every productive element has its right ratio to the other productive element. So the amount of labor on a specific acre of land may not be the most desirable amount of labor on another acre. The secret of maximization of productivity depends on the formula in which the three factors of production are combined together.

One can see that Jevons was aiming for a fourth factor of production which he did not bring out clearly in any of his writings. Presently, all economists would admit that there are four factors of production, not just three. The fourth factor of production is "entrepreneurship" or management. Without using the word *management*, Jevons talked about the fourth factor. Since he described the total exploitation of the factors of production as the way of maximizing wealth, indirectly he was referring to the increasing return, decreasing return, constant return, and negative return as treated in microeconomics. The combination of land, labor, and capital under the sagacious plan of the entrepreneur can result in an increasing return, without lowering the marginal rate of output.

Like Jeremy Bentham, Jevons used the pain-pleasure theory of marginal output. It is a graphic demonstration of the intensity of the work over a given period of time. The intensity of the work is different at different times. Suppose that a farmer plows the ground when the ground is still moist or rather wet. The intensity of work will be different because of the state of the soil. Similarly, let one measure the intensity of work on a regular working day and on a work day before a national holiday. The work is the same but the intensity is different. Or within a day, let one measure the intensity of work at eight o'clock on Monday morning and the intensity of work on Tuesday at eight o'clock. One is sure to find the difference as Frederick Taylor did in his time and motion studies.

Jevons had internalized these phenomena long before they became major issues of business science. He said, "Amount of labor will be a quantity of two dimensions, the product of intensity and time, when the intensity is uniform, or the sum represented by the area of curve when the intensity is variable."[5] If the labor is extended upon a long period of time, it becomes more and more painful. A few hours of work may be desirable, but if the same work is extended to a longer period of time, exhaustion, monotony, and psychological resistance against the surroundings (however beautiful they may be), will slow down the intensity of work and cause a loss in productivity. There is a certain distance between the point of incipient effort and the point of painful toleration. As the point of painful toleration is approached, there comes a sense of resistance offered by an opposing medium. The rate of productivity, then, is the balance between the natural quota of production and the opposing force.

Government Intervention

The marginalists demand that the government keep out of the private sector. The government's primary functions are to defend the rights of the people and to safeguard them from foreign invasions. In the Western nations, where a desirable level of progress has been accomplished, the government should not enter the commercial sphere with wares pitted against the commodities offered by the private enterprises. Jevons did not consider the conditions of the underdeveloped nations where the government's capital and its blessings are necessary for the smooth running of any business enterprise. Of course, in Jevons' time, all the underdeveloped countries were colonies of the big powers. Jevons supported government intervention in certain industries, where the public welfare and common good took precedence over profit, like railroads, communications, public health, utilities, and the like.

Conclusion

Jevons was an ardent believer in the laissez faire or free enterprise system. He believed that socialism had invaded the educated class. Therefore, since government officials were drawn from the educated class, the executive branch of the government would be controlled by people imbued with the socialist philosophy. When this happened, Jevons believed the government would tend to appropriate many functions once controlled by the private sector. In other words, under the guise of safeguarding the common good, the government would invade the free enterprise system. This kind of government intervention was the object of marginalists' opposition.

HISTORY OF ECONOMIC THOUGHT

Footnotes

1. Jevons, William Stanley. *Political Economy*, New York: Kelley, 1965, p. 16.
2. Ibid., p. 17.
3. Ibid.
4. Ibid., p. 27.
5. Ibid., p. 170.

References

O'Connor, Peter A., et al. *American Encyclopedia*, New York: McGraw-Hill, 1967, vol. 15.

Oser, Jacob. *The Evolution of Economic Thought*, New York: Harcourt Brace and World, 1970.

JOHN CLARK

Although John Bates Clark is not considered as a very outstanding economist, he played an important role in developing the economic thoughts of today in American economic circles. Therefore, many economists refer to Clark as "the Dean of American Economists."

Clark was born in Providence, Rhode Island on January 26, 1847.[1] He attended Brown University and Amherst College. Later he went to Europe and attended Heidelberg University and Zurich University. His overseas education made him closer to the German historical school, and his economic thinking was greatly influenced by the writings of Heinrich Pesch, Joseph Schumpeter, and Alfred Marshall. The German historical school accepted the intimate relationship of economics with politics and sociology. Thus the main stream of thought was "partial equilibrium" that dominates the rise and fall of economic growth.

Clark returned from Europe to resume his research under the new frame of thinking he had internalized during his European schooling. He taught at Carleton College, then at Smith College, and later at his alma mater, Amherst College. During his tenure at Amherst, he became a spokesman for the American economists. His reputation as an economist spread, not only in the United States but also in England and Germany. Columbia University invited Clark to accept a professorship in economics. From 1895 to 1923 he served Columbia University. In 1911 he was made the director of the Division of Economics and History of the Carnegie Endowment, which job he held concurrently with his professorship at Columbia. He retired from Columbia in 1923, and for 15 years he spent his time writing. He died in New York City on March 21, 1938.

Clark wrote his most prominent work, *The Distribution of Wealth*, in 1899. The book was an extension of an earlier work, *The*

Philosophy of Wealth, which was published in 1885. Clark wrote as a philosopher in the earlier work. His primary investigation concerned the methods of acquiring wealth—interest, profit, and wages—and the purpose of wealth. While writing *The Distribution of Wealth*, he concerned himself with the class system and the ownership of means of production. He looked into the rights of the entrepreneur and of the employee. He also analyzed profit and asserted that profit should be distributed rather than kept as the sole prerogative of the entrepreneur.

Clark's third major work was *The Control of Trusts*. This was written in 1912 and dealt with the abuses of monopolies. The antitrust act of 1890 was already viewed as an illegal intervention in the free enterprise system. Woodrow Wilson, however, was campaigning for the presidency with the promise that he would enforce the antitrust laws if elected. *The Control of Trusts* served some purpose in the election of Wilson, but beyond that the book did not enjoy lasting influence. There are some minor works worth mentioning, e.g., *Capital and its Earning* (1888), *The Problem of Monopoly* (1904), and *The Essentials of Economic Theory* (1907).

Clark's philosophical ideas had two distinct phases. His earlier writings were highly influenced by the German historical school, especially the main trend exhibited at Zurich. *The Philosophy of Wealth* is obviously the product of the Zurich philosophy. But every innovator has to chisel off the old establishment, in this case the existing classical theory of political economy. It is the job of the innovator to find fault with the existing system as a reason for the new system. Any student can see Clark locking horns with the political economy of Smith, Ricardo, Malthus, and Mill. Clark advocated the rejection of competition as an equalizer of wealth. He substituted for competition the "effective utility theory of comparative values." If Clark proposed the elimination of competition as a major factor for the distribution of wealth, how could he advocate elimination of monopoly? A state bereft of competition is monopoly. If monopoly and competition are eliminated, what would be left within the economic process? Clark tried to solve this paradox with his effective utility theory. Thus, while fighting against the "establishments of pre-recorded economic writings," Clark depended deeply on Bentham and Mill in the expatiation of his new approach.

The second phase of Clark's philosophy began with the writing of *The Distribution of Wealth*. He divorced himself from the German schools and exhibited his independent analysis of economic events. He rejected the categories of factors of production accepted by the old school, and he came up with the "specific agents of production" as the underlying reasons for distribution. Someone may ask what actually distinguishes the factors of production from the specific agents of production. He did not explain the difference; one has to infer the difference from the value theory, the history of wealth, and, most important, his marginal productivity theory of wages and income.

The functional distribution of income is founded on the marginal productivity theory. Clark defined the marginal theory as "simply the amount of wages paid to the last worker should equal the value of the additional product attributable to the marginal worker." [2] An additional worker is capable of producing a certain number of outputs. If those outputs are sold in the market, that would bring the marginal revenue product. The last worker's output is called the marginal physical product. The wages are determined by the relationship between the marginal physical product (MPP) and the marginal revenue product (MRP). If the system is operating under competition, the employer can keep hiring until the MPP is equal to the MRP. If the MRP is less than the MPP, the employer will lose money in hiring the last worker, since his cost will exceed his revenue. On the contrary, if the MPP is smaller than the MRP, that will force wages to rise, because other manufacturers will attract the workers away from the employment. In order to keep the factors of production within the firm, the employer has to increase the wage and prices of raw materials so that the suppliers will keep supplying. The growth of wages will come to an end when the MPP rises all the way up to MRP. The basic premise for this theory is, "productivity is what makes the cost factors useful and determines their income."[3]

Clark's theories of value and wealth are predicated on the marginal productivity theory. This theory is not totally foolproof; there are some practical limitations. The first of these is the task of identifying the cost of hiring, training, and finally paying the last worker. In the modern big business there are tools to measure these intangibles, yet to come to an accurate measurement is far from feasible computation. Many questions arise that show the hardship involved in determining the real cost due to the addition of a new worker. The variable costs due a marginal worker, especially in an assembly line type of production method, are not easily discernible. The second problem is to determine the marginal product due the marginal worker. As it was difficult to find the marginal cost, it is equally difficult to find the marginal product. Any industry that uses varied skills to produce an end product goes through problems of high productivity in one area compared with bottlenecks in other areas. The skill or lack of skill that contributes to the marginal output can be lost in the stream of total output. This is especially manifest in the construction industry and other mass-production industries. Clark understood the road blocks in the marginal theory, and provided some major guidelines for assessing the marginal cost and marginal revenue in the employment of an additional worker.

From the marginal theory, Clark moved to the theory of wealth and income distribution. As treated above, the value of MPP converted into MRP determines the marginal income. The rate of productivity is the major basis of the rate of wages offered to a worker. Different workers have different rates of productivity depending on the type of industry they are in. Each industry produces outputs with varied price structures and margins of profit. This inequality in industry is the reason for unequal wages and unequal distribution of wealth. The total goods produced in a nation become the wealth of the nation or the gross national product. The net national income is the "pie" to be divided among the factors of production. The contribution to the pie is the basis of the distribution of income. The relationship between incomes and productivity is summarized in the statement—made in reference to Clark's theory—"income distribution is . . . determined by the marginal products of the factors of production."

Marginal theory, when used to explain the theory of value, is the relationship of labor to productivity. The same theory, when used to define the national wealth, is based on the participation of factors of production to the net national income. In order to measure these intangible shares of production and income, Clark used some mental gymnastics. He thought everything was measurable if one took the trouble of going through the right steps. If three factors of production are kept constant and we subtract one unit of the factor of production in the fourth, then empirically one can arrive at the rate of productivity of that factor. This experiment can be repeated by changing another unit and keeping all others constant. Even this type of laboratory exercise meets with some stumbling blocks because of the indivisibility of the factors of production.

Clark came up with his idea of "manner of application of the theory of facts."[4] He prepared for his approach by assuming natural order, pure competition, profit maximization, and coherent harmony of interests. "All things being equal," a phrase all economists use to hide a multitude of sins, never happens in the real world. Offering a theory that has no room for practical application is futile. The laws in a static economy cannot be equated with the laws prevailing in an economy of continuous adjustments and flux. Clark thought that the classical economists did not have any solutions to the changing nature of modern economy. He said, "the effectiveness of the natural laws of the imaginary static society was limited by the operation of natural laws of change in the real world of men."

A German economist named Eugene von Boehm-Bawerk was Clark's loudest critic. He questioned even Clark's basic idea of capital: the "permanent abiding fund which is embodied in the capital goods."[5] Boehm-Bawerk said that Clark's definition of capital was unreal, Clark's main error, he said, was his inability to distinguish between productive capital and enterprise capital. He also objected to Clark's conception "of true capital functioning to synchronize input and output, so far as to eliminate the need for the consumer worker to have to wait for production of consumer products." Clark thought that there would be enough goods to satisfy the immediate needs of the consumer and that no one had to wait for production to be over with in order to satisfy consumer wants. If capital controlled production, it could create a rationing system to limit the volume of production artificially and place the consumers at the mercy of production to satisfy their needs. Boehm-Bawerk pointed out that the necessity of production and the replacement of capital goods would necessarily create a shortage of goods and the market system would always run with a shortage of consumer goods instead of having a surplus of consumer goods. Boehm-Bawerk did not attack the marginal theory in depth.

Other critics questioned the reality of marginal theory in the operation of business enterprises. George Soule saw marginal theory as an extreme "mechanistic abstraction." In practical life, according to Soule, no producer or consumer paid any attention to the last man's productivity that influences the price or wage. Prices and wages are settled according to the comparable price and comparable wage theories. If General Motors can produce a car for $1,200, and Ford can produce a comparable car for $1,600, and Chrysler can produce a similar car for $1,800, all of them will sell for $2,800 more or less, so the cost of production has very little effect on the price. Pricing is done by the market system existing or artificially created by high-powered advertising. The concept of marginalism does not play any role in this world of reality. Soule also questioned the tools of testing to be accepted as an empirical theory. He thought that marginalism was an abstraction without definite use, yet it had some distant influence on economic theory like the "invisible hand" idea, created by Adam Smith.[6]

Clark's marginal theory has some validity. In measuring productivity, is there any alternative to marginalism? Today's microeconomics have no use if the idea of marginalism is totally ignored. Clark did establish a means of determining the relative values of productive factors. The value theory and the theory of wealth are extensions of that production theory. In the mass production industries marginalism can become abstract, but in the small enterprises, every additional man or additional factor of production means the very existence of that enterprise. Clearly, marginalism is not a phantasm or pure abstraction as the critics say. Clark's three theories are used implicitly by big and small business; they are the guidelines of wages, interests, and price. From this viewpoint it is no wonder that Clark is called the "Dean of American Economists."

Footnotes

1. Moffet, James E. "John Bates Clark," in *Collier Encyclopedia*, vol. 6 (1962), p. 562.

2. Pearlman, Richard. *Wage Determination*, Boston: D. C. Heath & Co., 1964, p. 1.

3. Hermann, Edward. *History of Economic Doctrines*, New York: Oxford University Press, 1964, p. 197.

4. Goleb, Eugene O. *The ISMS*, New York: Harper & Row, 1954, p. 37.

5. Rogin, Leo. *The Meaning and Validity of Economic Theory*, New York: Harper & Row, 1956, p. 543.

6. Soule, George. *Ideas of the Great Economists*, New York: The Viking Press, 1953, p. 138.

ALFRED MARSHALL

Alfred Marshall is one of the luminaries among the makers of contemporary economics. His economic thought was clearly expressed in one of the most widely used textbooks published, *Principles of Economics*. In fact, the innumerable textbooks written on economics on both sides of the Atlantic are all based on the format and contents laid out by Marshall. William R. Scott writes, "His influence was enormous, so much so that the first 25 years of twentieth century economics may be described as the age of Marshall and subsequent developments as extensions of and counter movements to his influence."[1]

Marshall was born in Clapham, England in 1842. His father, John Marshall, was a cashier in the Bank of England. He belonged to the middle class of the time, enjoying the respect of society and the modest comfort that can be expected of the position he held. The Victorian era was a period of conservatism. Education was accounted the real wealth of a household. Parents strove to impart the best education to their children so that when grown up they could make a comfortable living of their own. John Marshall was deeply religious by nature and expected a high degree of moral values in his home life. Alfred was brought up under this severe value system. His education was supervised by his father and was geared to prepare Alfred to be ordained a priest in the Anglican Church. He was expected to study classics at Oxford. A brilliant performance at Oxford could win a fellowship to the School of Theology and thus the blueprint of a future career as minister was laid out by his father. But a life in the ministry was not what Alfred wanted. He had his own plans for attending St. John's in Cambridge and pursuing a secular education. The result of this conflict was estrangement between father and son. Alfred borrowed some funds from a wealthy

123

uncle and left for St. John's. There he read mathematics and became one of the best mathematicians ever to come from the college.

After graduation Marshall accepted a fellowship in mathematics and became a member of a group of social thinkers concerned with the social problems of the time. The group was disturbed because industrialization was widening the gap between the classes, especially between business and labor.

Philosophy and ethics were the topmost social science disciplines in England. Mathematics alone did not receive the highest respect from the elite. So Marshall devoted a few years to philosophy and ethics. He found that economic conditions, especially poverty and the maldistribution of wealth, were root causes of the social problems of England and the world. This conviction led him to the study of economics. He later wrote in his work, *Principles of Economics*, "the sutdy of the causes of poverty is the study of the causes of the degeneration of a large part of mankind."[2]

In 1877 Marshall married Mary Paley, who was the first woman to be admitted to Cambridge and was also one of Marshall's students. In those "good old days" the Fellows of a college were not permitted to marry before the end of the educational span. So Marshall was forced to resign for having broken two of the existing academic regulations: (1) marrying while holding a fellowship and (2) marrying one's student.

Marshall found a new position as principal and professor of the University College of Bristol. There he displayed his innate capabilities as a scholar and an administrator. He was liked and respected by all because of his didactic superiority. By that time his fame had reached other parts of England. In 1883, Baliol College invited him to join their staff as a Fellow, and the following year the same institution that expelled him because of his marriage invited him to return to the Chair of the Political Economy Division. He stayed in that capacity until 1908, when his own disciple, A. C. Pigou, succeeded him.

Marshall wrote and published many books. Some are *The Pure Theory of Foreign Trade* and *Pure Theory of Domestic Values* (1879); *Principles of Economics* (1890); *Industry and Trade* (1919); *Money, Credit and Commerce* (1923); and *The Economics of Industry* (1879). With his wife Mary he published several articles that were reprinted in 1925 in the *Memorials of Alfred Marshall*. He also had many reports and papers submitted to the Royal Commission, which are still kept in the archives.

Contemporary economics frequently used Marshallian models in the analysis of economic problems. These methods are not a specific set of hypotheses or models proposed by Marshall, "but represent ways of setting up a problem or partitioning it so that it can be solved."[3] Any big problem can be subdivided into smaller parts that can be solved separately. If all these parts are solved one by one, the remaining problem will be to synthesize these various solutions into one. Marshall's main goal was to arrive at a general equilibrium in the solution of the total problem. By compartmentalizing the problem, Marshall thought an economist could reach partial equilibrium. Then in one further step, he could reach a general equilibrium. Of course, this method is not foolproof, since the solutions of individual parts may not always blend together into a single mosaic whole or, as he called it, a general equilibrium.

In the preface of his work, *Principles of Economics*, he wrote, "The main concern of economics is . . . with human beings who are impelled, for good and evil, to change and progress. Fragmentary statistical hypotheses are used as temporary auxiliaries to dynamic — or rather biological — conceptions: but the central idea of economics, even when its foundations alone are under discussion, must be that of living force and movement."[4]

Marshall introduced a new form or model called static equilibrium. He applied a time-period concept to develop static equilibrium into a dynamic equilibrium analysis. For instance, he thought price derived not from a sudden jump in supply and demand but from a process of many adjustments within a span reaching the equilibrium price. These adjustments are inevitable because the seller would like to get the highest price and the buyer would like the lowest price. Hence there are many stages in which these buyers and sellers revise their stance of offer and acceptance before reaching a specific price. This essential market mechanism was overlooked by many other economists. Marshall warned that the period of adjustments should not be measured by a clock but by operational changes or cycles, since market conditions differ with different industries.

Marshall divided the time into short periods and long periods. The market period is usually fixed since producers control the supply. But if the sellers have a reserve price other than the quoted price in the market, then the market is not cleared automatically, because of the wedge forced in by the reserve price. The market should be cleared to reach equilibrium. In the short run, the capital investment is predetermined and as such the supply cannot be increased at will. So short time equilibrium is reached because of the inflexibility of supply. Even if a limited increase in supply is still possible because of better use of existing capabilities, partial equilibrium has reserve room for a small adaption to supply. In production theory, the modern economists use the law of "variable proportions," but it is not clear whether Marshall treated the variable proportions law clearly. Similarly modern microeconomics uses the law of return to scale in the forms of increasing return, constant return, diminishing return, and negative return to scale. It is debatable whether Marshall held a clear understanding of these concepts. Moreover, the modern concept of short run in which the factors of production are not adjusted to the desired level of output is difficult to find with clarity in Marshall.

"The Marshallian long period allows for optimal capital stock adjustment. The market is cleared within the framework in which supply can be considered to be fully adaptable, because all factors have adjusted to the situation."[5] In the long run, one can see, Marshall accepted a process of "differential adjustment" of market through the supply and demand framework. Thinking in this line led Marshall to his prime theory of value. If there is no more innovation in this long run, full equilibrium or a "stationary state" would be reached. Marshall's central contribution to economic theory was the working out of the stationary state. Marshall did not consider the stationary state as the ultimate goal of economics. If the population does not grow any more, and people become complacent in their living standards, and there is no more desire to grow, then a stationary state would be useful. But human nature does not incline to such lulls, and thus a stationary state is not an end but only a starting point for a new cycle.

Marshall held that the wages are determined by the marginal productivity of labor. The supply and demand for labor also determine the wage rate. If there is an increase in the labor supply without proportionate growth in the other factors of production, then, "the marginal productivity of labor and wage will fall. If the supply of labor is reduced, the marginal productivity of labor will increase, and wages will rise."[6] However, the marginal productivity of labor is not the only criterion for wage determination. It may be more reasonable to say that if one considers a specific group of laborers working under the same conditions, wages will shift in the same direction as the shift of the marginal productivity of labor.

In short, the argument that wages can be raised permanently by stinting labor, rests on the assumption that there is a permanent fixed work-fund, i.e., a certain amount of work which has to be done whatever the price of labor. And for this assumption, there is no foundation. On the contrary, the demand for work comes from the national dividend; that is, it comes from work. The less work there is of one kind, the less demand there is for work of other kinds; and if labor were scarce, fewer enterprises would be undertaken.[7]

Talking about agriculture, Marshall made some interesting observations. To begin with, a farmer who has extensive farms enjoys a great deal of prestige in society. The prestige factor takes this farmer into important political positions opening the way for participation in the legislative or executive functions of the government. The same farmer may be able to use modern scientific farming devices to increase his productivity. Marshall wrote about the diminishing returns operating in farming also. Addition of more land and more workers in the field would gradually usher in the laws of dinimishing returns. As a consequence the output of farms becomes hardly sufficient to meet the operation of the farms. The farmer then is forced to sell out most of his farms to others who are in the process of increasing the farmholdings to achieve economic and political power. This cycle repeats, opening the door for rotation of farm lands among the people.

Like the classical economists, Marshall distinguished value in two ways; value in use and value in exchange. Value in exchange leads to the idea of consumer surplus. Every buyer feels that he got a thing below cost. He could identify an area of consumer surplus in the commodity which prompted him to buy that product. The sale of a product ends when the value of the product is equal to zero consumer surplus.

Marshall accepted interest as the price of distributing capital. The borrowers would borrow more when the interest is low and vice versa. The interest cannot be more than the marginal utility of plant or equipment. If wages are above the marginal revenue product of labor, then no more workers will be hired by the employers. So also is the marginal utility of plant and equipment above the interest rate; then not one more dollar will be borrowed by investors. Hence the interest rate does not really depend on the supply of money but the marginal utility of plant and equipment or productive factors.

Saving function does not entirely depend upon the interest rate. Saving depends upon the size of the family, the value of the earner, job security, and family affection.

Monetary Theory

The monetary laws govern the value theory laws, according to Marshall. The value of money depends on the supply and demand for money. "The value of each metal is determined by the relation in which the supply of it stands to the demand for it."[8]

Marshall based his theory on "the incentives to liquidity." He said, "a large command of resources in the form of currency," made the convenience factor. A store of precious metals offers the advantage of speculation or ability to buy on favorable bases. The liquidity preference for money entails some disadvantages also, like loss of interest and even theft or fire hazards.

Marshall's predecessors and contemporaries influenced him to arrive at the internal value of money. Ricardo, Senior, and Mill wrote about the liquidity preference for money before Marshall formed his money value theory. Dealing on "cash balance theory" Marshall confessed that Locke and Cantillion measured quantity of money in terms of rent, wages, weekly expenses, and trade.[9]

The technical development in the quantity theory of money was already visible at Cambridge when Marshall lectured about it as a new idea. Others had already treated the component parts of money, like money velocity and income velocity compared to transaction velocity and other technical analyses. The quantity theory of money evolved into the study of price change at various levels of employment and fluctuations in the levels of investment.

Marshall wrote about the establishment of exchange rates between two countries or many currencies of various nations. First he compared the exchange rate of two countries, enjoying a currency system based on identical metallic hoardings. Assuming both countries are on gold standard, he said, "trade tends to adjust the supply of gold relatively to the demand for gold in two countries, as to bring about gold prices at seaboards of the country to equality, allowances being made for carriage." Secondly he concerned himself with two countries having two different metals as the base of their currency. For example, if India is on silver standard and England is on gold standard, "the value of each metal is determined by the relation in which the supply of it stands to the demand for it."

If a country bases its currency on metal and another country is based on paper currency, then the exchange rate between the two currencies will depend on the productivity of each currency or the work it can turn out in the creation of its gross national product. The value of each currency will be determined by the effectiveness it enjoys in domestic transactions.

One can see that Marshall based his value theory of money on the "purchasing power parity" of different currencies. In addition he performed a useful function in developing and clarifying the classical theory of exchange. He delved into the analysis of the price index numbers in the purchasing power parity theory. He also made an important contribution with the analysis of short term and long term equilibrium. Marshall introduced a new technique of analyzing exchange problems by using "income analysis" and "saving and investment technique" analysis. Under certain conditions, the purchasing power parity theory can provide some indications of the probable change in the balance of payments position. His theory was a warning to nations that upheld an inflexible exchange rate, yet permitted changes in wages and prices in domestic and foreign trade.

Utility Theory

Marshall developed his utility theory for two reasons: "first to place restrictions on demand functions, and second, to create what he hoped would be powerful tools of welfare economics." [10]

Demand is defined as a schedule of quantity asked by the buyers, at a given price, time, market. But Marshall had his own definition of demand. Demand, to him, was a relationship of "unit of time to its own price." It is hard to decipher what Marshall meant other than the common definition of demand. In the relationship of time to price, Marshall held, other prices and incomes are held constant. Marshall's "Law of Demand" was that the price of a good and the quantity demanded are inversely related. In the Appendix to *Principles*, Marshall has a mathematical formula to measure the utility function. The restriction of demand function is rooted in the utility function of a commodity. He built up the idea of cardinal utility and ordinal utility functions in his analysis of utility. To him, some utilities were measurable and others immeasurable. Human evaluation of value depends on the affectations of an individual. This makes some values out of reach for measurement. The total utility derived from the consumption of various goods and services is the sum of individual utilities derived from the consumption of each good or service.

The basic restriction given by the additive nature of the function is that interrelationships between goods are excluded. Further, the law of diminishing marginal utility operates with respect to each good; this means that the extra units consumed of a given commodity will increase total utility at a decreasing rate. Thus the addition to total utility induced by the Nth unit of a commodity will be less than the increase in utility induced by the (N-1) unit. [11]

It is a natural phenomenon for the consumer to maximize his utility at given incomes and prices. In order to maximize utility, the consumer uses substitutes occasionally. By substitution the consumer can climb higher in the difference curve. The consumer tries to maximize utility by lining up his isocost and isoquant curves. The maximizing utility can be subjected to two different restraints namely, budget restraint and substitution restraint. Marshall brought out this idea in an algebraic formula:

$$\frac{MLa}{MUa} \text{ equals } \frac{Pa}{Pb}$$

$$\frac{MUa}{Pa} \text{ equals } \frac{MUb}{Pb}$$

Here the P represents the price of the commodity. This formula excludes the idea of income of a price change. Marshall uses a constant marginal utility of income.

Strictly speaking, a partial analysis demand curve requires that real income be held constant as price changes, so as to eliminate from the analysis the income effect of the price change. Holding money income constant is insufficient, since the real value of money income is its command over commodities and if commodity prices change, this changes also. [12]

Marshall brought out this formula in reference to money income. He also accepted small changes in the prices of goods and services that make up the total demand of the consumer. The error of using the money income as a base is in some way lessened by accepting the small change in the price of goods and services. "The real cost" of a product is not only the cost of paying the factors of production so that these factors of production can be supplied when needed, but also the cost involved in the change in the intrinsic value of money due to inflationary effects, and the cost of transporting the products to the market. It seems that while Marshall wanted to incorporate all the details involved in the cost, he failed to see the various other costs involved in marketing the product. By singling out inflation and transportation, he did not add significantly to the marketing theories of today. Marketing is the cost of delivering the product from the manufacturer to the ultimate consumer. Inflation and transportation are only two of a whole series of additional costs involved in this transit of the product from the manufacturer to the ultimate consumer.

Marshall brought out the idea of the principle of substitution. Suppose an electric fan can be manufactured with aluminum or with both steel and aluminum, by the process of substitution, the manufacturer can arrive at the lowest possible cost. The manufacturer substitutes at the margin to arrive at the lowest possible cost without losing the efficiency of the product.

Economists question Marshall's comprehension of the production law. He used variable proportions and the law of return to scale. He called increasing return, decreasing return, and vice versa. While discussing the increasing return, he brought out the internal economies and external economies that further led to the economies of scale and diseconomies of scale. "Internal economies are those dependent on the resources of the individual house of business in an industry, while external economies are dependent on the general development of the industry." [13] Internal or external diseconomies raise the cost curve and internal or external economies lower the cost curve. This falling of the cost curve can be influential in lowering price by one firm and thus affect the total competition. When one firm alone is able to monopolize technology and thus lower the cost of production, that firm may cut prices to attain a monopoly. This is harmful to the total economy. Marshall used his "life cycle theory of entrepreneurship" as a partial explanation for the survival of competition.

Marshall formulated a mythical business organization called the "representative firm." This representative firm enjoys internal economies, because it has a falling marginal cost as a special asset. Yet, it does not strive to be a monopoly. There is legislation which prohibits underpricing. More than that, no firm really wants to be indicted as a monopoly. There can be consumer resistance, searching for substitute products, or governmental intervention can act against this "representative firm."

Marshall's life cycle theory includes birth, growth, decay, and death of a firm. Marshall did not think that a firm would expand indefinitely to prolong the life cycle. The modern empire-building trends of business question the validity of Marshall's assumption. "For Marshall, however, the continual searcher for the dynamic solutions, this answer was inadequate." [14] The economists of the time taught that the life cycle of a firm was extended by the ability to keep constant cost concurrent with average variable cost as long as possible. If this is possible, there is no reason for the decay and death of a firm. But as experience attests, few businesses are able to make the average variable cost and marginal cost run on the same scale.

Marshall's theory of distribution is worth examining. He worked on the theory of joint demand and derived demand. "The demand schedule for any factor of production of a commodity can be derived from that of the commodity by subtracting from the demand price of each separate amount of the commodity the sum of the supply prices for corresponding amounts of the other factors." [15]

Rent plays an important role in the Marshallian distribution theory. The classical economists used rent as payment for the use of land. But they had nothing to denote any payment for plant and equipment. Marshall used the word, "quasi-rent" to define a reward for the use of plant and equipment.

Through lack of caution, Marshall's analysis of welfare economics developed a number of contradictions. He went along with the classical economists in saying that a free market system maximizes the welfare of the common people. In order to explain the maximization of welfare he wanted every micromarket to maximize its surplus. If the economy is controlled by monopolies, then the sum of surpluses will be lessened. What Marshall considered as surpluses were both consumer surplus and producer surplus. In the usual intersecting supply and demand diagram, any area above the equilibrium on the demand curve is the consumer surplus and any area below the equilibrium on the supply line is the producer surplus. In some way Marshall accepted Bernoulli's theorem—any increase in income decreases the marginal utility of money. The utility of the last dollar of the high income earner has less marginal utility than the last dollar of a low income earner.

If the government could tax the profit takers and subsidize the marginal industries, a higher consumer and producer surplus could be created, which in turn would increase welfare. Although Marshall based his welfare economic theory on the slope of the supply alone (with all the weakness of such a treatise), one can say that Marshall built up the theory of externalities and divergences between private and social welfare. Modern welfare economics still uses the tools developed by Marshall.

Some accuse Marshall of not going deep enough into his monetary analysis. This may not be a justifiable accusation. The *Principles* has an adequate monetary analysis. Moreover, his work, *Money, Credit and Commerce* discusses the importance of money. Another source of monetary analysis is his *Official Papers*, which consists of many papers submitted to the royal commission. Marshall was a great teacher. He trained students all throughout his life, and they in turn trained thousands of economic professors all over the world.

To many of his contemporaries it seemed that Marshall had solved the most fundamental problems of economic theory by demonstrating the mutual relations of cost, utility and value; that he had measured economics against psychological and ethical criticism by basing his analysis upon money measures of the force of motives, which remain valid on any interpretation of the motives themselves; and that his engine for discovery can be applied to whatever new problems economics may encounter in the future.[16]

Footnotes

1. Scott, William R. *Alfred Marshall*, London: British Academy, 1958, p. 3.

2. Eprime, Eshang. *From Marshall to Keynes*, Oxford: B. Blackwell Co., 1963, p. 45.

3. Viner, Jacob. *Readings in Price Theory*, Chicago: University of Chicago Press, 1952, p. 84.

4. Eprime. op. cit., p. 68.

5. Stegler, George J. *Production and Distribution Theories*, New York: Macmillan, 1941, p. 86.

6. Marshall, Alfred. *Principles of Economics*, 8th Ed., London: Macmillan, 1920, p. 697.

7. Oser, Jacob. *The Evolution of Economic Thought*, New York: Harcourt Brace, 1970, p. 239.

8. Marshall, Alfred. *Official Papers*, London: 1922, p. 177.

9. Ibid, p. 22.

10. Parsons, Talcott. "Wants and Activities of Marshall," *Quarterly Journal of Economics*, 39 (1924-25): 507.

11. Homan, Paul T. *Contemporary Economic Thought*, New York: Books for Library Press, 1968, p. 49.

12. Scott, William R. *Alfred Marshall*, London: British Academy, 1958, p. 35.

13. Viner, op. cit., p. 76.

14. Stigler, George J. *Production and Distribution Theories*, New York: Macmillan, 1941, p. 139.

15. Homan. op. cit., p. 189.

16. Pigou, A. C. *Economics of Welfare*, London: Macmillan, 1952, p. 89.

AUGUSTIN COURNOT

Antoine Augustin Cournot (1801-1877) is not known to many as one of the builders of economic philosophy. He attended the École Normale Supérieure in France where he distinguished himself as a gifted student, born leader, and public speaker. After graduation, he was appointed a professor at Lyons in 1834. Later he was made rector (president) of the Academy of Grenoble in 1835. He manifested his talents as an effective administrator at the academy. The French government appointed him Inspector General of Studies, a director of public instruction for the nation in 1838. He left the public service in 1854 to become the president of the Academy of Dijon in 1854.

Cournot's mathematical training led him to the analysis of supply and demand functions, the backbone of economic analysis. The demand curve describes the phenomenon of change of quantity bought due to the lowering of prices. He also found the relationship between the rate of prices and the rate of change of quantity purchased, which now is called the coefficient of elasticity. He brought to light the difference between elastic demand, inelastic demand, and unit demand. Cournot did not relate his finding of demand and supply to the utility analysis that came later with Jeremy Bentham and Alfred Marshall's conception of the marginal utility theory.

Cournot published one of his researches under the caption, *Researches into the Mathematical Principles of the Theory of Wealth*. Cournot considered all competition to be pure competition in which no buyer or seller has any control of price. He recommended that production be continued ad infinitum when the firm is facing continuous decreasing marginal cost. The time to decrease production is when the market has reached the point of saturation, showing noticeable slowness in inventory turnover. He warned that larger firms would capitalize on decreasing cost and increasing demand, so that one day most small firms would be devoured by the big firms, ending finally in the creation of monopolies.

Cournot considered monopolies diametrically opposed to pure competition. He thought the evil of monopoly was its power to set its own price, since in a monopoly, industry is firm, and vice versa. Even monopolists, however, have to consider their production costs and the elasticity of demand before they attempt the total exploitation of the consumer or the maximization of profits. The marginal theory was in some form expressed by Cournot but not the way the marginalists formed their analysis. He accepted the idea that profit is the difference between total cost and total revenue. This difference can be maximized when the additional revenue associated with the increment in production or output reaches the point where the extra cost equals the extra revenue. Cournot did not use the terms marginal revenue and marginal cost, but he still proved that profits are maximized when the firm reaches the point of MC equals MR. Cournot brought this idea to the public in 1838. The idea was lost in oblivion until Alfred Marshall picked it up and presented it as the credo of the marginalist school.

Cournot's analysis of duopoly (two sellers but in Cournot's analysis buyer's monopoly and seller's monopoly or what is today called bilateral monopolies)stated that buyers name their price and sellers adjust their output to meet with the buyer's offer. This theory rests on the assumption that the consumer is king and can dictate his price for anything he buys. This is not natural at all. Cournot said that the quantity the buyers would buy is predetermined and the duopolists merely adjust the quantity offered accordingly. Suppose the quantity required is 3000 units and A and B are involved in production. In the first round A produces half of 3000, or 1500 units and B sees the market demand as 1500 and produces 1250; in the second round A sees the market demand as 1750 and produces half of that, or 875; B at the same time sees the market as 3000 minus 875, or 2125, and produces half of that unit. In this way A and B alternate the quantity produced until they reach more or less the same quota of production. Of course, this type of analysis has no more effectiveness since markets are wide open and products are offered from all over the world, disturbing the theory's natural progress. Moreover, no economy can predict the consumption function of society or predetermine a consumption quota. Economics is built on the disclaimer "all things being equal or, as the Romans would say, ceteris paribus," and under this qualification Cournot's analysis has its merit.

Jacob Oser in his work, *Evolution of Economic Thought* asserts that, "Cournot was the first to visualize the general interdependence of all economic quantities, and he developed a system of equations to depict general equilibrium." However, J. A. Schumpeter and M. Blaug are not quite so willing to ascribe that credit to Cournot. Schumpeter says, "I do not think it historically correct to attribute to him (Cournot) more than a vague and nonoperational idea of general equilibrium." Blaug says, "for a complete and precise solution of the partial problems of economic system, it is inevitable that one must consider the system as a whole" and that is where Cournot fails to be the author of the general equilibrium theory. According to Blaug, Walras was the author who used mathematics to arrive at the general equilibrium theory. Most historians, however, would say that Cournot was a better mathematician than Walras.

Mathematics needs empirical data to prove the assertions it makes. Otherwise, the pure theory cannot have proofs to convince its critics. When Cournot expressed his theories in mathematics, the world was not ready to accept most of them, since the theories transcended the vision of most of his public. Some critics of Cournot think that the monopoly profit maximization theory he proffered failed to include the discriminatory pricing technique used by monopolists. The marginal revenue analysis is meaningful only if the market is the same and prices are what is offered in the same market. If markets are diverse because of the discriminatory practices of the monopolists, then the whole theory loses its flair due to the lack of a common denominator.

It is safe to summarize Cournot's theory as follows:

1. Cournot should be given the credit for his analysis of past economic theories and his ability to graft them to the newer ideas he originated.

2. He did preliminary groundwork for the supply and demand analysis that has become the fulcrum of economic science.

3. His theories of monopoly and duopoly are laudable attempts to bring them under predictable bases so that businessmen can have some blueprint for market research and forecasting. He should be given credit at least for opening new trains of thought, which his followers later explored in depth.

4. Cournot used his mathematical knowledge to express economic phenomena. This is not easy since mathematics is an exact science while economics is only an approximate science. Time has witnessed

Cournot's efforts and found them the best means available to perform a difficult task. Today, econometrics has gained a lofty position in the science of economics. Cournot laid the ground work for this branch of science.

References

Blaug, M. *Economic Theory in Retrospect*, Homewood, Ill.: Richard Irwin, 1967.
Oser, Jacob. *The Evolution of Economic Thought*, New York: Harcourt, Brace and World, 1970.
Rima, I. H. *Development of Economic Analysis*, Homewood, Ill.: Richard Irwin, 1962.
Schumpeter, Joseph A. *History of Economic Analysis*, New York: Oxford University Press, 1954.

MAX WEBER

Max Weber was born at Erfurt, Germany in 1864, and was educated at the University of Heidelberg, the University of Berlin, and the Göttingen Institute. Weber's important writings are: *Ancient Judaism, The Religion of China, The Theory of Social and Political Organization,* and *The Protestant Ethic and the Spirit of Capitalism.* The last one mentioned gained Weber a worldwide reputation and acceptance as an economist. Writing about this book, William J. Goode wrote: "Unfortunately, this was a comparative study, trying to show how various ethical-philosophical factors impeded modern capitalism from developing under Hinduism, Buddhism, Confucianism, Taoism and ancient Judaism, even when many material factors were to be found in each."[1]

Much of Weber's work had something to do with Marxism, either refuting or concurring. Weber extolled the bureaucratic framework of capitalism and the institutionalization of its gradual development. A society, according to Weber, is worth its means of production. Although Marx found the very institution of capitalism to be a reason for its final decay, Weber felt that capitalism would triumph because of the strength of that institution.

Weber built his theories on the findings of the great German sociologist Max Offenbacher who analyzed the Grand Duchy of Baden for sociological reasons. Offenbacher found that the Protestants of the Grand Duchy owned a disproportionate share of the landed properties of that Duchy, which had 60 percent Catholics. In fact the Protestants held more skilled jobs, academic positions, and political seats. Weber used this study as the base of his immortal work, *The Protestant Ethic.* Calvin taught that economic success was a visible sign of God's predilection for certain of his children and an assurance of eternal salvation. The Protestants were successful not

139

only in economic activities, but in every field imaginable. Weber's conclusion that Calvin's teaching for material success was the only reason for the economic growth of Europe and America in the last two centuries seems unconvincing. In fact other minorities, like Jews, made a greater success in financial matters. They never followed Calvin, hence Weber's juxtaposition of religious teaching and financial success is not completely successful.

Weber wrote the essay, *On the History of Medieval Trading Companies* in 1889. At that time many limited and unlimited partnerships were formed for the sake of developing foreign trade with colonies. Weber compared the two types of partnerships that originated then with the Genoese partnerships for foreign trade and Florentine partnerships for family craft trade. In his studies, Weber found that the overseas trade partnership concentrated on limiting responsibilities, whereas, household partnerships combined the higher responsibilities offered by both capitalism and communism.

Alfred Heuss called Weber's *The Economic Theory of Antiquity* "the most original, daring and persuasive analysis ever."[2] Weber tried to relate the ancient economies to their contemporary political structures. He saw that ancient civilization flourished near sea coasts and river beds. This was for trade facilities and protection from enemy invasions. He found that slavery was an economic rather than social factor.

In another study he conducted, he deplored the impersonality and debased ethics of the marketplace. The market served as the only tie between people and races. Freedom of movement of goods from afar destroyed the local monopolies of the guilds and consumers benefitted by the open trade policy. "Yet the very success of the free market led to new monopolies based on alliances or sheer superiority. Thus religious and political groups moved in to protect monopolies."[3]

The Agricultural Organization and Agrarian Communism

The idea of agrarian communism was first developed from the German economic organization by Hanssen and von Maurer. Some of the ideas came from Russia and Asia, in particular, India.[4]

Land was the source of value for the physiocrats, and the distribution of land was a matter of continuous debate throughout medieval history. The Romans accepted the policy of distributing land according to the seignorial method to create a dependent establishment of small towns. Russia used the collective farm system to further the interests of the state. In India, laborers are not paid for their work, but share according to the size of the harvest. In the primitive agricultural life, the so-called, "hoe-culture" took precedence. Max Weber wrote about the stock market and commodity market systems of the early 19th century. The stock exchanges and commodity exchanges are merely market centers in the purchase and sale of manufacturing companies and commodities harvested during the current year. The commodity market was designed to spread out a seasonal agricultural product into a year-round market. The perishable nature of commodities gained a big lift by the introduction of commodity markets.

Manorism was a subdivision of the feudalism that existed in the 18th century. The lord had three types of power: (1) landholding or territorial power; (2) possession of men or slavery; (3) appropriation of political rights or power to participate in the political governance by voting etc. The large household of the lord and the small households of the peasants existed side by side. The peasants depended on the lord for land to till and the lord depended on the peasants for a regular royalty from the yearly harvest. Later on money was introduced so that the lord could pay the tenants in wages and take over the entire crop. The tenant was free to move away, if he was able to find another lord to 'adopt' him and his family.

Social Stratification

Weber is renowned for the sociological term, "social stratification." He saw the gradual rising of the middle class and slow disappearance of the lower class. Like Marx, he recognized the importance of the changes in the class structure. Marx addressed himself to the ownership of the factors of production, but Weber concerned himself with the metamorphosis of the marketplace. While Marx discussed the exploitation of the working class, Weber dealt with the inability of the working class to compete with the more educated and sophisticated of the capitalists. Weber found that social stratification was a mere economic factor, aiding or impeding the economic future of each class.

Weber also found that although political power was not an automatic consequence of economic power, stratification was the basis for the distribution of political power. Stratification was not only a prestige factor but, in a true sense, the life style of the class.

The interaction cf the social and political variables really constitutes the difference between the old and new schools of thought. Weber's study of social stratification will remain for a long time the guiding light for any one researching in that field.

In *The Protestant Ethic*, Weber showed that the Calvinist traditions constituted the motive power for the growth of capitalism. He confessed that the drive for profit was not a unique feature of capitalism, but the cycle of saving to invest and investing to save is in fact something unique with capitalism. Still Weber said that Protestantism did not produce capitalism alone, but given the prerequisites for capitalism, the religion contributed the impetus and motivation for this strenuous endeavor.

Max Weber possessed unusual dynamism and an almost preternatural charismatic power to inspire his students and the audience that flocked from all over Europe to hear his lectures. Weber was a sickly person from childhood, but his magnetic personality hid his true life from the people who flocked around him. He was in some cases a stoic, fanatic, and cynic when dealing with controversies and academic criticisms. Some people consider Weber and Freud to be the only true social scientists of this era. Weber is known for his objectivity in all his writings. To him it meant the necessary conformity to a scientific method that reflected the just means of achieving uniformity between the seemingly conflicting ideologies of the world. Marx wrote to bring about a classless society; Weber wrote to bring about a class society in which the chasms between classes could be bridged with an equitable income for all.

Weber found the following relationships between law and economics:

1. Laws go beyond economic interests.

2. Law can remain unchanged in certain circumstances, while economics is undergoing radical changes all the time.

3. Any legal guaranty is directly at the service of economic interest to a very large and meaningful extent.

4. Only a limited measure of success can be obtained through the threat of coercion supporting the legal order.

5. Legal status of matter may be basically different according to the point of view of the legal system from which it is considered.

Footnotes

1. Goode, William J. "Max Weber," in *Collier's Encyclopedia*, New York: 1969, vol. 23, p. 376.

2. Weber, Max. *l nomy and Society*, ed. Guenther Ross and Clause Wittich, New York: Bedminster Press, 1968, p. 39.
3. Lowenstein, Karl. *Max Weber's Political Ideas in the Perspective of Our Times: A Criticism of Max Weber and His School*, Cambridge: Cambridge University Press, 1933, p. 211.
4. Gerth, H.H. "Max Weber," in *Essays in Sociolgoy*, New York: Oxford University Press, 1958, p. 374.

References

Bendix, Reinhard. *Max Weber: An Intellectual Portrait*, Garden City, New York: Doubleday, 1960.

Freund, Julian. *The Sociology of Max Weber*, New York: Pantheon Books, 1968.

Fusfield, Daniel R. *The Age of the Economists*, New York: Scott, Foresman & Co. 1966.

Heiman, Edward. *History of Economic Doctrines*, London: Oxford University Press, 1964.

Janowitz, Morris. *On Charisma and Institution Building*, Chicago: Chicago University Press, 1968.

Marshall, Howard D. *The Great Economists*, New York: Pitman Publishing, 1967.

Miller, S. M. *Max Weber*, New York: Thomas Y. Crowell Co., 1963.

Robertson, George R. *Aspects of the Rise of Economic Individualism: A Criticism Of Max Weber and His School*, Cambridge University Press, 1933.

Roth, Guenther. *Economy and Society*, New York: Bedminster Press, 1927.

Schutz, Alfred. *The Phenomenology of the Social World*, Evanston, Ill: Northwestern University Press, 1967.

Weber, Max. *General Economic History*, London: Greenberg, 1927.

Wrong, Dennis. *Max Weber*, Englewood Cliffs, N.J.: Prentice-Hall, 1970.

THORSTEIN BUNDE VEBLEN

On July 30, 1857, Thorstein Bunde Veblen was born to Thomas and Carol Bunde Veblen in Cato Township, Wisconsin. Veblen's parents had been important farmers in Norway, and they pursued the same trade in the rich dairy land of Wisconsin. Thomas Veblen had some reverses of fortune when he started in Cato, but that did not discourage him. He knew that failures are the reasons a man should work harder. He acquired another farm and employed modern technology on that farm.

When Veblen was eight, his parents bought a bigger farm in Minnesota. Veblen attended the Congressional Carleton Academy at Northfield, Minnesota. This school was primarily for those who entered the Lutheran ministry. In 1880 Veblen graduated from Carleton with a major in philosophy. He did not want to pursue the ministry as his parents had designed for him. He took a teaching job at a parochial school at Monona Academy in Madison, Wisconsin. The teaching did not interest him, and he joined Johns Hopkins University where his older brother Andrew was considered a prominent mathematician. Veblen's restless mind did not find what he was searching for, and after one semester he left Hopkins for Yale. He studied philosophy under Noah Porter, the president of Yale, and sociology under William Graham Sumner, who was famous for his adherence to Darwinism. He received a doctoral degree from Yale for a masterpiece of a dissertation on the *Ethical Grounds of a Doctrine of Retribution*. Under Sumner, Veblen became a confirmed agnostic, and that eliminated the possiblity of a teaching position with Yale.

Veblen married Ellen Rolfe and settled on the farm without really finding a suitable job or even trying to get one. He read much and wrote a little. In 1891, he joined Cornell University as a student in economics under J. Laurence Laughlin. The University of Chicago was founded in 1890 and required a few professors, so Veblen secured a teaching position there in 1892. Veblen could not stick to any place for any length of time. In 1906 he joined the faculty of Stanford, and in 1911 he joined the University of Missouri. He was only an associate professor, and the highest salary he received was $3,000. Economic pressure made him a teacher although he had no natural instinct to be an effective teacher. In the ideal university Veblen conceived there would be no students, only research assistants. In spite of his personal failings as a teacher, a good number of dedicated students sought him.

While teaching at Chicago, Veblen wrote essays for the *Journal of Political Economy* and the *American Journal of Sociology*. Veblen's life moved from one tragedy to another. His first wife divorced him, and he then married a student from Chicago University. He received a government position and moved to Washington, but that did not last. He turned down a job offered by one of his students to edit *The Dial*. His wife had a mental collapse at the same time and died two years later in a sanitarium. It is important to know these difficulties in his life, to understand fully why he turned out to be a dismal philosopher and economist later on. By 1925, Veblen had to abandon all work because of his poor health. He retired to Palo Alto, penniless, solitary, and dejected in mind and body. Veblen died on August 3, 1929.[1]

Veblen's Publications

The Theory of the Leisure Class: An Economic Study of Institutions —1899.
The Theory of Business Enterprise—1904
The Instinct for Workmanship and the State of the Industrial Arts—1914
Imperial Germany and the Industrial Revolution—1915
An Inquiry into the Nature of Peace and the Terms of Its Perpetuation—1917
The Higher Learning in America: A Memorandum on the Conduct of Universities by Business Men—1918
The Vested Interests and the Common Man—1919
The Place of Science in Modern Civilization and Other Essays — 1919
The Engineers and the Price System—1921
Absentee Ownership and Business Enterprise in Recent Times: The Case of America—1923
The Laxdœla Saga—1925
Essays in Our Changing Order—(published in 1934)

From this list, one can see that Veblen spent quite a bit of his time on writing. These writings give vent to his philosophical thinking on economics, business enterprise, and sociology. Only the economic thoughts are culled for analysis in this biography.

Theory of the Leisure Class

This book is primarily composed of Veblen's thoughts on sociology and anthropology, dealing with three fundamental bases, the leisure class, conspicuous consumption, and pecuniary emulation. He believed that "exemption from industrial employment" was the first requisite for membership in the leisure class. Veblen somehow felt that supervision is not real work, since supervisors do not produce. The supervisors attach themselves like leeches to the workers who are producing and the consumers who are paying for the product. Business leaders are the primary leisure class while military, religious, and political leaders belong to the secondary leisure class. The student can see some affinity between Marx and Veblen in defining production.

He thought that although businessmen were only a minority of the population, they wielded the total political power. In order to perpetuate their ulterior motives, they subsidized governments and social institutions like churches, schools, etc., who in return protected the businessmen. Under the influences of patriotism and religion, the working class stayed obedient to this tyranny and never attempted to revise the social structure.

Veblen compared the interaction between the aims and objectives of business enterprise and the inroads of business technology. The liberty of the individual and the identity of his labor are robbed by technical innovations and the mass transportation of goods within and without the producing nation. On the other hand, the efficiency of a business is increased by standardized products, automatic and continuous production, and large-scale plants and equipment.

Veblen's core ideas are strikingly similar to those of Marx. Veblen emphasized the class concept; questioned the private property right; and pointed out a tension between business owners and industrial producers. He called the modern state "an executive committee for businessmen." Finally, he thought the states were bound to be involved in wars.

Veblen's Ethics

In 1904, Veblen condemned the use of inside information on the

stock market to amass wealth in stock market transactions. Only
large corporations and banks can get this inside information and
these are already wealthy. Use of such devices destroys the free
competitive system. The large profit earned in some exceptional
years becomes the "normal profit" for business in the normal years.
The scrambling for higher profits by big enterprises destroys weaker
competitors and opens the way for oligopolies and monopolies.
When the nation is controlled by monopolies and oligopolies,
depression looms. This is how Veblen treated the business cycle
theory. The rich then spend their time in "patterns of conspicuous
consumption" and "pecuniary emulation." When a society is
controlled by the rich, it becomes wasteful, predatory, and reaction-
ary. Veblen often pointed to the acceptance of private property and
national sovereignty as the triumph of "imbecile institutions."

Veblen termed himself a neoclassical economist and criticized the
classical economists. He came up with a new definition of essentials
through the process of abstraction from the common bases like the
nature and function of economic and legal institutions and the
process of social change. He called the contemporary neoclassical
economists mere "marginal utility economists." *The Representative
Firm* describes an entrepreneur, well-informed about the technique
of production and market conditions, who refrains from asserting
any influence to alter the course of the free market. This happens
when the business cycle is in favor of the representative firm. Veblen
found that the same businessman is totally lost when the economy is
plagued by tight competition, the workmen threaten with strikes,
consumers reject the products on the market, outside competition
strives to outmode the domestic production, and there are general
signs of depression on the horizon. The renowned management
wizards become helpless and ineffective in crisis. Veblen thought that
business shrewdness and acumen were merely imputed epithets, not
innate qualities. The growth of a firm usually depends on external
economic factors, either domestic or foreign. Right after Veblen's
death in 1929, the great depression started and, in fact, not even the
shrewdest businessmen could do anything effective to combat or
even survive it.

Veblen was disturbed about the growth of Nazi power in
Germany. He called it "the prime disturber of peace," and he felt
somewhat the same about the military buildup in Japan. In his
Nature of Peace he outlined the necessity of defeating Germany
completely and establishing a democracy of the common man. He
accused Germany of "aggressive propensities to advanced technol-

ogies, coupled with a nationalistic, militaristic attitude, preserved from the primitive time." He traced the growth of Germany's power to the establishment of custom unions and facilitation of modern transportation. As a consequence, Germany was able to broaden her markets; the heavy industries provided raw materials for rapid industrialization and military strength; and interlocking corporations, banks, and cartels unified her economic strength. The scarce resources were located at the periphery of Germany, which induced many foreigners to interfere with the peace of Germany. In order to protect the scarce materials, Germany had to be prepared for a war at all times. Veblen felt that Germany should be forced to abandon its economic and military concentration.

Economics was one of the liberal arts in Vebeblen's times and was studied together with sociology. Veblen hoped to liberate economics from the clutches of the social sciences and make it an independent discipline as it is today. The job of the economist, he thought was (1) to use the technology available at the right place at the right time; (2) to shape human behavior so that one's actions may be in tune with the "economic man"; (3) to reform the social psychology of man within the framework of production and consumption; and (4) to allow the interaction of all these to raise the quality of life with a higher standard of living.

Veblen modified the Marxist analysis of machine-age society. The key factor of the modern business is its profit-seeking ownership and its demand for maximum productivity from the workers. Since business has become very selfish, it restricts its production to attain higher prices regardless of what happens to the workers who are laid off because of the cutback in production. These rising prices with rising unemployment are the causes of depression. In other words, the modern entrepreneur is the cause of the business cycle, especially with depressions.

Veblen did not develop any organized economic theories. He was concerned with the social milieu and the consequences of economic factors affecting it. In his work, *The Vested Interests and the Common Man* he exposed the various methods of exploitation used by the businessman. His leading ideas on social change, business versus industry, nationalism, and other burning problems are succinctly treated in this booklet.

Even though Veblen wrote a book almost every year, the only work that became popular was *The Theory of the Leisure Class*. "It was a savage attack on the business class and their pecuniary values, half concealed behind an elaborate screenwork of irony, mystifi-

cation, and polysyllabic learning."[2]   Was Veblen jealous of business?
His practical life was a total failure. His education did not bring him
even modest comfort, and his teaching experience was a collosal
failure. How could he forgive the businessman who, with little or no
education, hauled in fortunes in every enterprise and then lived in
the splendor of "conspicuous consumption and pecuniary emulation"?

Veblen believed the privilege of the rich would dig its own grave.
He thought that the real threat to the profit-oriented business would
be from its own coworkers, the impersonal, skeptical, twentieth-
century machines. The use of technology would erode the institutions necessary to business, such as nationalism, religion, and private
ownership. The institutional bonds of employers and employees,
producers and consumers, and corporation owners and administrators would become weaker as technology gained momentum, and
that would expedite the disintegration of the system.

It is not enough to point out the pitfalls of the social structure
without offering solutions to bad conditions. Did Veblen give any
constructive ideas to improve the socioeconomic conditions of his
fellowmen? It seems he had some optimistic thoughts when he said
that the triumph of the machines would supersede the profit motive
of the businessmen and the common good would be maximized by
the conquest of machines over crafty businessmen. The second
answer is given in a pessimistic tone in his work, *Absentee
Ownership*. There he said that the continued supremacy of business
nationalism would lead to servile despotism and there would be a
reenactment of the medieval rule of the upper class.[3]

Veblen's Influence on Modern Economics

Veblen did not found a school of thought, but many of his
students were highly influenced by him because of his total
eccentricity. The students sought him out precisely because of his
odd, negative philosophy, which placed him outside the academic
society. Hence, the students differed from the teacher both inside
and outside the classroom. His students, among whom were H. J.
Davenport, Joseph Dorfman, Walter Stewart, W. C. Mitchell, Robert
Hoxie, and J. R. Commons, constituted a large portion of the
intellectual leaders of the United States for two generations. Some
writers have grouped Veblen, Mitchell, and Commons as "institutional economists." When the New School for Social Research was
formed in 1919, Veblen, John Dewey, Mitchell, and Robinson as the

four most noted social scientists of the time, lectured there during its early years.

Footnotes

1. Lerner, Max. *"Thorstein Bunde Veblen,"* in *Dictionary of American Biography*, New York: Charles Scribners & Sons, 1936, pp. 241-24; Dorfman, Joseph. "Thorstein Veblen," in *Thorstein Veblen and His America*, New York: Viking Press, 1934, pp. 188-189.

2. Homan, Paul T. "Thorstein Veblen," in *The American Masters of Social Science*, ed. Howard W. Odum, New York: Henry Holt & Co., 1927, pp. 256-57.

3. Dorfman, Joseph, "Thorstein Veblen," in *Thorstein Veblen and His America*, New York: The Viking Press, 1934, p. 134.

ARTHUR CECIL PIGOU

Although Alfred Marshall was the father of the neoclassical school of economics, Arthur Cecil Pigou (1877-1959), a devoted disciple of Marshall, raised the neoclassical school to the prestigious position it enjoys today. Marshall held the chair of political economy at the University of Cambridge when Pigou studied under him, and when Marshall retired in 1908, it was Pigou who succeeded his master in that position.

Among the distinguished members of the neoclassical school with whom Pigou worked were R. F. Khan, Piero Sraffa, and Joan Robinson. In 1939 by the publication of *Foundations of Welfare Economics*, J. R. Hicks joined the same school. This was followed by Melvin Warren Reder with his book, *Studies in the Theory of Welfare Economics*, Ian Malcolm David Little with *A Critique of Welfare Economics*, and Kenneth Joseph Arrow, with *Social Choice and Individual Values*.

Pigou published his first book, *Wealth and Welfare*, in 1912. He expanded and revised the same book and republished it in 1920 under the name, *Economics of Welfare*. Another important writing, *Industrial Fluctuations,* appeared in 1927. It was followed by *A Study in Public Finance* in 1928.

The identifiable aspect of neoclassical economics is its concern for the poor and underprivileged. The classical economists rationalized ways and means to increase the wealth of the nation as a whole. They did not take into account the real welfare of the individual, but presumed that the economic growth of a nation would automatically upgrade the standard of living of all its citizens. One thing they possibly forgot was that there can be hunger amidst prosperity even in the richest of nations. They were strangers to the idea that hunger is evil and must be eliminated, or as Cardinal Wright once wrote,

"Poverty anywhere is a threat to prosperity everywhere." Neoclassical economists professed as their goal the elimination of poverty through governmental action. They believed that poverty could be fought successfully by initiating a new technique of distributing of wealth.

Welfare economics studies the welfare of the individual in relation to the total economic welfare of the nation. Professor Lorenz explained the same phenomenon with the aid of the "Lorenz curve." When some privileged groups are far away from the "line of equality" which he drew connecting the opposite corners of a rectangle, he showed the disparity of various income groups. When the departure from the line of equality is lessened by the use of a graduated income tax, the social welfare is increased. In other words, any transference of income from a relatively rich man to a relatively poor man of similar temperament, since it enables more intense wants to be satisfied at the expense of less intense wants, must increase the aggregate sum of satisfaction.[1] Thus, the welfare economists do not just talk about the dire conditions of the poor; they present alternative solutions to the problems.

There are some who think that welfare can be maximized by increasing the productivity of labor. Here Pigou considered the marginal cost and marginal benefit that can accrue by increasing the productivity of labor. Marginal cost in this case is the labor put into the last unit of product; marginal benefit is the use gained by the last unit produced. If the labor is overworked or their standard of life is well supported by a reasonable wage scale, the marginal benefit can be smaller than the marginal cost of labor, since cost would be greater than revenue.

Pigou offered a theoretical basis on which the government might operate to redress the poverty of low income groups. He defined welfare economics as "that part of social welfare that can be brought directly into the measuring rod of money." He believed that the function of economics is to help social attainments. Welfare is a term that includes a whole galaxy of human wants. Economic welfare is a little different from the term welfare, since the economic welfare should be measurable in money. Social welfare takes into account the sum total of all welfare enjoyed by all people of a nation.

Pigou based his dissertation on welfare on two other economic terms, *economies of scale* and *diseconomies of scale*. If a farmer plants his corn in the valley between two hills and two other farmers plant their corn on the elevation of the same hills, then the first farmer enjoys the economies of scale. The other two farmers have to fertilize and irrigate their fields. In doing so they are helping the farm in the valley, since one rain brings most of the fertilizers down to the farm in the valley, and by cutoff and runoff most of the irrigation water reaches the farm in the valley.

Diseconomies of scale operate by reverse action. The steel mills that puff out soot and smoke damage the roofs and paint of neighboring buildings. The problem of pollution has become the biggest example of diseconomies of scale at the present time. Pigou used these illustrations in examining the social welfare analysis. His thesis was maximum happiness for all, not just the total happiness without reference to the individuals involved.

Pigou did not find any measurable meaning in advertising. There are two types of advertising according to him. One is intended only to sell more products; the other, besides selling products, educates the public with useful information. He condoned the second type of advertising because of the public service it renders. Many may not go along with Pigou's opinion of advertising. Any firm will maximize profits if its production can be brought to a point where marginal cost equals marginal revenue. The intersection of MR and MC is the least-cost combination of the production function. When the firm can produce at the lowest cost per unit, it can also sell at the lowest possible price. Suppose General Motors can sell 10,000 Cadillacs at $10,000 per unit without advertising. If 10,000 units comprise the use of only a fraction of the capacity, the company is really wasting factors of production. This waste adds to the price. If by advertising the firm can sell 100,000 units instead of 10,000 units and sell each unit at $7,000, no one can find fault with advertising expenditures. Advertising helps firms to bring their output to the least-cost combination of production function. Thus the social gain of advertising far surpasses the advertising costs involved in selling. This may not be all true in some cases where innocent consumers are misled in buying goods without measurable social benefits.

Pigou did not think that the successes of business were usually for the public good. He thought that if private costs of firms became too low, the situation would lend itself to the creation of monopolies. Moreover, society would be inundated with goods that have less public usefulness to promote the welfare of the people. On the other hand, consider the case of industries in which private costs are too big. Even though the product or services they render may have higher contribution to public welfare, the higher costs can curtail their expansion or keep them frozen at a survival standard. The amount of public good or welfare created depends on the type of goods produced rather than the quantity of goods produced. Schools, hospitals, etc., which have high private costs, remain always at the borderlines of survival although the service they render is unique and necessary. At the same time, industires oriented to low private costs but less public benefit may amass huge profits and build themselves into monopolies with command over credit and capital. The factors of production are relatively limited. If more goes for guns, then less is available for butter. If industries with less social benefits monopolize resources, that will lead to the decline of industries with greater social benefits. This is why Pigou insists on governmental intervention to bring the economic swing into a healthy equilibrium where public benefits are maximized by planned allocation of resources.

Pigou treated the saving and consumption function as a means of maximizing the social welfare. He identified three stages of time for an income earner to spend his money: present, immediate future, or remote future. In the appreciation of values, spending at present is better than immediate future spending, and immediate future spending is better than remote future spending. Yet present spending may not bring the maximum social benefit in the long run. According to Pigou, most consumers expend their income on present needs that have low benefits, depriving the total social welfare.

One can see the operation of the principle of saving and consumption coming to dismal practical conclusions in the life style of some ethnic groups. Even those who earn a decent wage live a life of poverty. Pigou believed this situation existed because of inability to budget. Ability to budget one's income is a science in itself, and ignorance of this science leads people to exaggerate the benefits of spending on current needs and devaluate the favorable aspects of saving a share of income for precautionary or speculative needs of the future. Pigou felt that it was imperative to impart at least a rudimentary knowledge of sound budgeting.

A nation can also be blind in budgeting its resources. The world will last after this generation and a new set of people will inhabit this universe. Each generation that succeeds will inherit fewer assets and more liabilities. Pigou pleaded for caution and discretion in the use of natural resources, and his plea should be heeded.

Plato discussed the idea of social contract. He professed that everyone is born into a society refined by centuries of culture and civilization. The standard of civilization one inherits at the point of birth is a gift from the past generation to the newborn. In receiving this gift, the newborn should undertake to leave the world what he

received together with an additional dividend of personal contribution to the betterment of society. If each person bears in mind this
social contract, there will be progress generation by generation. Each
individual should give more than he received. Pigou thought that
spending on current needs without regard to future needs could
lessen the overall welfare of the nation.

Hobson thought that consumption was the key to economic
growth. Consumption should lead to full employment; full employment to greater purchasing power; and higher purchasing power to
more consumption. Pigou differed from Hobson's views. He felt
saving was the key to economic growth. It is an accepted principle in
economics that all savings become investment. Pigou came up with
the principles of acceleration, which means replacement, and
expansion spending. To keep the economy in progress, adequate
replacement and expansion should occur. This is the function of
investment. There can be no investment without commensurate
saving. In addition the labor force increases every day. A steady
stream of investment should be available to absorb the addition in
the labor force. While emphasizing the role of saving, Pigou did not
condone excessive saving or hoarding. Joseph Schumpeter had
already warned about the ill effects of underconsumption, a
dominant cause for recession and depression.

Pigou contended that economic welfare is a product of self-
esteem. Each person should have a goal in life and a plan to
accomplish his goal. In a competitive society the gifted will be
chosen over the average and the skilled over the unskilled. Self-
esteem will prompt the individual to educate himself for his goal and
achievement will enhance his self-esteem.

Pigou wanted the government to step into the impregnable
laissez-faire system of capitalism to prevent the private benefit of the
strong from depressing the public benefits of the weak. In other
words, besides the affluent upper class and middle class, there will be
always a lower economic class. This lower class needs the government's help to share the bounty of nature around them. The role of
the government is to supplement the welfare of the downtrodden.
Only the government can do this herculean task. Hence Pigou
advocated the "cutting the hills to fill up the valley" idea involved in
the graduated income tax.

There will always be disparity between income earners in sharing
the wealth of the nation. Philosophically all are created equal, but in
the real world there is no equality. If the government does not
interfere, the society can grow into a caste system with no room for

mobility. That can lead to an avowed enmity between haves and have-nots. Such a situation might pit poor against rich, employees against employer, and hemisphere against hemisphere. Total welfare is wasted by the growth of diametrically opposite factions in society. The government has the dominant right to step into the stream of private enterprise to bridge the gap as far as possible and safeguard the social welfare.

Footnotes

1. Dudley, Dillard. *The Economics of John Maynard Keynes*, New York: Prentice-Hall, 1964, pp. 17, 18, 24, 30, 32, 48-50.

SAMUEL GOMPERS

Was Samuel Gompers an economist? He had no formal education in economics, and never wrote a word about economics. Then how can he be included in a collection of economic thought, together with Adam Smith and Paul Samuelson? Gompers practiced economic philosophy although he has no writings of his own. He built up the labor philosophy practiced by 15 to 20 million workers who are the members of the AFL-CIO. Millions more all over the world have accepted his philosophy because of the values he imparted to the labor unions of the world. Samuel Gompers came to the United States as an immigrant worker. Born in the East End of London in 1850, he came to the United States at the age of 13 and lived on the East Side of New York.

Europe had seen the beginning of the industrial revolution in 1776, but it was 100 years before its impact was felt in the United States. The class struggles between the haves and the have-nots were felt primarily between the employers and employees. The United States was slow to accept a labor union as a legal entity. The union efforts initiated by the Knights of Labor faded away by 1880. America was not industrialized enough to support a formal union. But long working hours, unhealthy working conditions, and poor pay created discontent among workers. The labor movement was the creation of the working class to realize their normal aspirations for a better life. Samuel Gompers came into the labor group as a born leader demanding "more, more, more now."[1]

Before 1900, Gompers held the view that the working class was involved in a class struggle. The only philosophy that was prevalent at the time was the philosophy of socialism. In that sense Gompers started as an astute socialist. Testifying before the United States Industrial Commission he said, "I believe that as time goes on the

wage earners will continue to become larger sharers per dollar of
wealth produced. There is a struggle between the wealth possessors
and those who produce wealth. . . . That struggle has continued to
date and will continue so long as there are divergent interests
between the two."[2]

Gompers was a socialist, but he could not understand the methods
of accomplishing goals through the socialist tactics. He gave up
socialism for trade unionism. The skilled workers of the United
States did not want to align with socialism; they wanted reform
through unionism. Gompers joined them and later took over the
leadership.

In Europe there was a class system that did not allow for mobility
from one class to another. The class system of the States was very
different. That is why the class struggle suggested by socialism could
not work in the States. The employer-employee relationship was
somewhat based on class lines but they were not inflexible. There
were visible conflicting interests between the employer and employees, still there was also a visible identity of interests between them.
Labor-management cooperation seemed to to be the best way of
achieving the betterment of both. "Trade unionism, attention to
immediate gains, indifference to ultimate ends, action on the
economic field, craft autonomy, these constituted the formula for
meeting the difficulties besetting the use of the labor movement in
this country."[3]

Social legislation in Europe depended on group activities. Gompers
wanted individual action more than group endeavors to attain labor
goals. Building up a strong government based on socialism and then
passing legislation to achieve working class aims could not function
under the prevailing economic conditions in the United States. He
said:

Without egotism and, I hope, little if any vanity, I will say, I came to the
conclusion, many years ago that it is our duty to live our lives as workers in the
society in which we live, and not to work for the downfall or the destruction, or
the overthrow of that society, but for its fuller development and evolution.[4]

Gompers did not challenge the existing order. He accepted the
cardinal principle of private property and said that private property
was a necessary agency for securing opportunity for individual
independence and resourcefulness. He thought if private property
were simply held for individual aggrandizement or to establish
autocracy, then the right of private property should be challenged.
He clarified his position on private property, and the ideology of the

trade union movement was "to bring property into such relationship to human life that it shall serve, not injure."[5]

Gompers had his own interpretation of interest and profit. He thought that interest was a legitimate payment for the use of money and profit a legitimate reward to the entrepreneur for the risk he accepted by going into business. Gompers thought that the profits of production are sometimes shared by agencies that have no right to a share. He outlined the legitimate group in sharing the profit. "The legitimate factors are superintendence, the creation of wants, administration, return for investment . . . as long as they are not watered stocks or inflated holdings."[6]

He did not condone the practice of distributing the entire profit to stockholders. When talking about the unfair portion of profits, Gompers did not specify what constitutes that unfair portion. He said that the increase in the wage level diminishes the unfair portion and promotes industrial peace. This comes close to the "surplus value" theory of Marx. When the profit reaches the point when the stockholders receive the due share of return, there is no room for exploitation of labor. If instead, the wage level is kept depressed to increase the return on investment, there is room for exploitation. The wage-earning class should share an equitable portion of the difference between the total revenue and the total cost. He thought that labor has a right to demand, fight for, and secure a large share of the product of industry.

Gompers was a brilliant person but not an intellectual. He tried to keep intellectuals out, because his world was a practical one and did not need theory and hair-splitting arguments. He was suspicious that intellectuals might creep into trade unionism and undermine the movement for the benefit of the employer class.

The labor unions should be guarded not only against enemies, but its misguided friends. It is a movement of wage earners, by wage earners, and it may not be amiss to warn the well-intentioned, the so-called intellectuals or the savior of labor, who would dominate the labor movement with their panaceas or destroy it, that they had better watch out. [7]

Trade unions give the workers a sense of strength based on number and economic status, not in owning economic power, but in the ability to control economic power. Gompers believed in economic power only. Whoever controls economic power controls the nation. Political power cannot be attained without economic power. Beyond certain limits, political power cannot control economic power.

In 1914, the labor movement got a boost from the enactment of

the Clayton Act, which was hailed as the "Magna Carta" of labor.
The labor union was accepted as a legitimate bargaining agent. This
achievement made Gompers change his ideas and attitudes. From a
radical labor leader and organizer, he became a conservative labor
administrator. Gompers thought that the industrial peace could be
real and permanent if only labor had participation in the control and
management of industry. He wanted the industries to subordinate
profits to social goals. Gompers found that the industries are not
run so scientifically that profits and continuity of operation are
assured. The bankruptcy of a firm causes the workers to suffer more
than the firm itself. He thought that the industry was at the mercy of
the market, which is usually in imbalance because of unfair
competition between the producers. If social welfare is taken into
primary consideration and profits are relegated to a secondary
position, there can be a coordination of the various firms within the
industry and all parties would benefit from the arrangement. At the
annual convention of the American Federation of Labor in 1923,
Gompers said, "The functional elements in our national life must fit
themselves to work out their own problems, eradicate their causes
and furnish America with an ever increasing flood of commodities
. . . Industry must organize to govern itself, to impose tasks and roles
and to bring order into its own house."[8]

Gomper's social philosophy motivated his actions and statements.
He believed in individualism, within organized groups. He did not
feel, as the socialists did, that public ownership of industry has
nothing to contribute to the growth of a nation or to its citizens'
standard of living. He believed that private ownership instills the
sense of dignity and incentive necessary for the higher productivity.
That is why he demanded participation in operation rather than
sharing of ownership. He thought a few basic principles were
important for the development of a business operation. He believed
in:

1. Functional organization as an essential factor for growth;
2. The voluntary association of groups into a national industrial
council;
3. The development of skill in negotiating all agreements.

Gompers desired mutual trust and responsibility between unions,
management, and workers. With this kind of trust, he believed a
system of government could be developed in which all three units
benefited. He did not talk about the hierarchical status within the
government of laborers, unions, and management or how far each
group should share the power of decisionmaking. His intention was

to pose the question so that future growth of unions could be directed along those lines. At the grass roots, there is a possible conflict of interests between workers and employers. The union was to make matters acceptable to both parties and to serve as a catalyst to resolve the problems arising for the employer or employee. Harmony between employer and employee will generate the primary goal of a social system, namely the public welfare. The profit motive is necessary for greater investments. Greater investments are necessary to keep a full employment economy. Full employment leads to a better life for the working class. Yet, "profits must be kept in bounds; they must constitute a reward for service, instead of reward for specialization, chicanery, exploitation, and automatic domination."[9]

Gompers thought that the industries should escape from the sole motivation of profits. More capital investments would bring in more demand for profits. If there could be a break between finance and industry, then profit could be made secondary to business goals. It is the profit emphasis that causes industrial conflicts between management and workers. But Gompers failed to show an alternative to finance. He felt that finance could be reduced by increasing the labor factor. There are labor intensive industries and capital intensive industries. Wherever technology becomes more costly, labor can be added to replace technology. But today technology is the core of industrial success, and the implementation of technology requires capital.

Gompers thought the political government was incompetent, because congressmen and senators are not chosen according to ability but according to their financial ability to defray the cost of election. He had very scathing statements on this matter, "The legislators have no understanding of industry, of its needs and of the laws of its development." Only low caliber people seek politics; the better ones go into industry. "The gulf between politics and industry is as wide as the seven seas and as deep." He thought that politics bred demagogues, emotionalists, flatterers, and masters of cajolery, while industry bred masters of knowledge.[10]

Gompers never pretended that he was a philosopher. He was an organizer and leader. He entered labor unions at the beginning of an epoch and laid the foundation of the trade union movement. The capitalist economy depends on the cooperation of employers and employees. That is why the little immigrant laborer from the East Side became a big spokesman of the economic thought of modern times.

Footnotes

1. Reed, Louis S. *The Labor Philosophy of Samuel Gompers*, Port Washington, N.Y.: Kennikat Press, 1930, p. 12.
2. U. S. Industrial Commission of 1899. *Report of the Relationship of Capital and Labor*, vol. 7, p. 64.
3. Harvey, Rowland. *Samuel Gompers*, Stanford University Press, 1922, p. 176.
4. Ibid., p. 21.
5. Ibid.
6. Gompers, Samuel. *The American Labor Movement, Its Makeup, Achievements and Aspiration*, AFL pamphlet, 1914, p. 20.
7. Gompers. Editorial, *American Federationist*, November, 1915, p. 974.
8. American Federation of Labor. *Convention Proceedings*, 1923.
9. Gompers, Samuel. Article in *American Federationist*, September 30, 1922.
10. Reed, op. cit., p. 48.

EDUARD BERNSTEIN

Eduard Bernstein was born on January 6, 1850, in Berlin. His parents were of the lower-middle class, and his formal education was very limited. At the age of 16 he became an apprentice in a bank, something like a messenger boy. He watched the bank operations and discovered a new interest in life. In fact, after a few years he was promoted to the position of clerk, and he held that job until 1878, when he left for Switzerland. On the job, he had long hours, small pay, and really no opportunity for growth. He read many books dealing with wealth, money, credit, and distribution of money. Karl Marx's *Das Kapital* had gained wide acceptance by this time. Many new organizations sprang up under the socialistic ideology. The most prominent were the Lassallean Socialistic group and the Eisenacher Socialistic group. They followed Marxian philosophies, yet each had its own version of the socialistic society they wanted to create. In 1875 the Lassallean and Eisenacher groups merged and formed the German Social Democratic Party. Bernstein was a member of the Eisenacher group even before the merger.

Bismark was in power in Germany. He openly attacked the Social Democrats and was able to outlaw any socialistic group in Germany. The party moved its headquarters to Switzerland, and when Bernstein, who was a leader of the socialist party, was sought by Bismark's police, he also fled to Switzerland. There he accepted the editorship of a paper published by the exiled German Social Democratic Party. The socialist party was able to distribute their publications in Germany through their underground network. The paper criticized in uncompromising terms the many anti-socialist laws Bismark enacted and enforced in Germany. Bismark exerted pressure on the Swiss government, and Bernstein's paper was outlawed and all the leading members of the party were exiled from

Switzerland. Bernstein left Switzerland for London, which was an open forum where most of the German socialists found a haven. There he met Frederick Engels who worked with Karl Marx and financially supported him in his times of penury. Bernstein became a close collaborator with Engels. In fact their friendship was so close that Bernstein was named the "executor" of the will of Marx and Engels. That made him almost the heir apparent to the leadership of the socialist party, once held by Marx and Engels. All the literary works of Marx and Engels were left with Kautsky and Bernstein under joint control.

Bernstein had his own view of the socialist society Marx and Engels espoused. During the lifetime of Marx and Engels, it was difficult to interpret their thinking. But after their deaths, Bernstein came out with his own version of the socialistic philosophy. By 1890 Bernstein openly expressed his view of future socialism. Fundamentally, Bernstein was a follower of Marx. Yet he could see the repugnant aspects of the theories of Marx. Marx stressed the idea of the corruption and vitiation of capitalism and dwelt on the inevitable economic evolution and class struggle that would end finally in the classless society or the Supreme Soviet Republic of the Proletariats. Bernstein could not see how this metamorphosis could happen. Even if Marx's theory were true, it would take hundreds or even thousands of years for the completion of the social evolution.

Bernstein demanded that socialism should start from municipalities to cities and then to the parliaments. The spirit of nationalization of all private properties should be accomplished from the lowest levels of government, rather than waiting for it to come from above. He criticized Marx's dogma of

(1) The doctrine of the rapidly growing industrial concentration. (He could see the formation of corporations that diffused the ownership among all classes, which could make the establishment of socialism all the more difficult.)

(2) The doctrine of increasing misery. (Industrialization was increasing the income of the workers and raising their standard of living, which also could make socialism unwanted.)

(3) The doctrine that the class struggle was ever sharpening. (There was more industrial peace, and relationships were improving between landowners and peasants.)

The three foundations on which socialism rests became the target of Bernstein's criticism. Since the final crisis Marx predicted seemed too distant, Bernstein proposed a piecemeal reform. *Die Neue Zeit* was the official periodical of the socialist party. Bernstein used the same channel to disseminate his revisionist ideas. He wrote a series of articles on the problems of socialism. The German Social Democratic Party was shocked at Bernstein's independent radical thinking on Marxian socialism. It was heresy coming from the heir apparent of the two teachers. To appease the opposition, Bernstein proposed the practical approach of a mixed economy rather than jumping right from capitalism into socialism.

Revisionism

Bernstein can be considered the father of revisionism in socialist thinking. When someone detours from the accepted dogmas of religion, he is called a heretic or schismatic according to the extent of his departure from the original view. Revisionism is apparently a detour from the social dogmas handed down by the two masters— Marx and Engels. Socialism split into different versions as time passed by. Some forms of socialism changed the goals of the philosophy; others the means of the system; and others, both the means and the goals of the system. Revisionism mainly changed the means rather than the ends of socialism. That is why it is only a schism rather than a heresy. The pre-World War I socialist movements were very much influenced by Bernstein's writing and teaching. After World War II there was some neorevisionism in the communist philosophy as one can see in the differences between Tito, Mao, Castro, Albania, and Russia. One can see the same ideology getting mixed with nationalism, thus disproving the possibility envisioned in the "blueprint of world conquest." Revisionism is a term of abuse to orthodox socialists. They find in it the element of betrayal and apostasy.

Bernstein called himself a revisionist in spite of the contempt of orthodox socialists. Without breaking off from the philosophies of Marx and Engels, he pointed out some of the impracticalities and subsequent meaninglessness of his teachers' theories. He invited his colleagues to join him in approaching the ideals of their teachers with a scientific mind and reorganizing the theories on a better intellectual basis. He pointed out that the teachers wrote their dogma under pressure and restraints and could not always concatenate their thinking scientifically. Hence he said that his approach was not mutiny but an obligation that all socialists were bound to perform, if they took pride in their beliefs. He thus made revisionism an intellectual necessity. Although Bernstein tried to exonerate himself for his action under scientific reasoning, there were not too many converts from the orthodox German Social Democrats. The opposition venomously attacked his prestige and personality. They claimed that Bernstein was unaware of the real mass movement happening in the world as Marx had predicted and of the imminent inception of socialistic states on all continents.

Socialism had many capitalist enemies who used Bernstein's arguments to thwart the socialistic expansion in their strongholds. This made the orthodox Marxians more bitter against Bernstein. The German Social Democrats ousted him from the party and called for a total boycott of his new thoughts. In fact, friends and foes interpreted his writings to suit their own purposes, and poor Bernstein stood in the middle of the controversy, unable to defend his position. He could see misrepresentation of his writings right before his eyes, but no one cared about his protestations. Some affixed Kant's thinking and others, Blanqui's theories to Bernstein's revisionist writings. In fact, the word revisionism became an epithet of little honor. Even Bernstein's friends wrote "apologia" for him instead of supporting him.

In fact, revisionism continues all the time. The United States Constitution is only a small booklet, but the interpretations of it can fill a library. So it is with Marx's writings. Some can see Freud in Marx; others think that he was an oriental with a Buddhist overview; others think that he was a true Christian and what he said was only what was spoken by Christ; others say that he is the father of existentialism. Yet none of these writers call or dare to call themselves revisionists.

Bernstein concerned himself with the truths advocated by Marx and in that sense he cannot be called a revisionist. He could not brand any of Marx's judgments false. He refined some of them and credited it to Marx out of a false loyalty to the teacher. He wanted Marx's thoughts to be immune to discredit.

Bernstein's Three Major Dissents

Marx predicted the collapse of capitalism. This is supposed to happen because of the inherent weakness of the capitalistic system, such as the increasing misery of the working class, the rise of the working class against the upper class ending in bloody revolution, the destruction of all private properties, the creation of a collective state ownership, and finally the nationalization of all means of production and distribution. Bernstein argued that the collapse of capitalism was not as imminent as predicted by the teacher. Marx said that under capitalism the rich would become richer and the poor would become poorer. This prediction has not materialized. Under capitalism both the rich and the poor prosper. If that be the case, the process of revolution and class struggle would be more a myth than a reality. Bernstein said that Marx had a distorted view of the operation of a free enterprise system. Moreover, Marx did not understand that the wealth of a nation does not consist of land, gold, silver, and precious stones but of its capacity to produce goods and services. The poverty of a nation is predicated on its inability to expand the production of goods and services. Of course this mistake is a common denominator of most classical theorists all the way from Ricardo and Malthus.

Bernstein conceived of socialism as a true fulfillment of the theory and practice of democracy. He found evils in democracy because of its ineptness in bringing theories into practice. He held the adage given by Tertullian in the eighth century, "Universal franchise is a universal lie." Bernstein thought that only in true socialism does democracy truly transpire. He wanted the abolition of all class privileges and the elimination of all inequalities in human relationships. Socialism draws the majority of its membership from the workers, yet this majority should implement laws best suited to all people, not monopolize power to attain their ends only. According to Bernstein, it is important to abolish all private enterprises, because these enterprises have no interest in the common good or human welfare. He also wanted to suppress some of the freedoms men claim as inherent right, since the exercise of those freedoms retard the pursuance of the common good. However, he demanded a strict, legal, and constitutional method to implement the goals set by socialism. Hence he did not favor totalitarianism and dictatorship within the rank and file of communist rulers.

Bernstein wanted to purge Marxism of its apparent focus on utopianism. The socialist society Marx conceived was an earthly paradise, but Bernstein felt that that fallacy needed dispelling. He saw the socialist state composed of ordinary people with ordinary talents and individual differences. To build a social state, the ruler has to impose strict rules and laws, and members must employ themselves in some gainful vocation. Fulfillment of this dream would demand work and in fact hard work of all members. It won't be a state of inertia but attainment of the common good with the cooperation of all. Human nature being what it is, the state has to impose a higher quota to finally reap a part of it in reality. This is where the notion of utopia fails. The socialist state will be a land of hard work not a lazy paradise. Bernstein's opponents did not like this depiction of the true nature of socialism, which they felt could discourage many followers.

Effect of Revisionism

The German revisionists and the English Fabian Socialists left some lasting effects on the economic thoughts of the 19th century. First of all, their willingness to differ from Marxian dogmas made many others study Marx under critical standards. The fame of a philosopher can sometimes force his followers to accept his ideologies blindly. Even Lenin and Stalin in later years found it was impossible to follow Marx verbatim and incorporated changes as they deemed best. Krushchev, in modern times, even had appreciation of the capitalistic system and tried to incorporate some of its salient features in the operation of Russian socialism. Deviations from the Marxist dogmas are no longer considered heretical and odious. In many socialist states, the principles of private properties and private enterprise are reintroduced to increase efficiency and productivity. Some capitalist states are gradually introducing some governmental controls on private property and private enterprise and moving more and more to socialization. One can see the spirit of revisionism working on both ends, socialism and capitalism.

Summary of Bernstein's Economic Philosophy

1. Generous provisions for social welfare;
2. Equitable distribution of wealth and income through higher taxation;
3. A higher allocation of resources to the public sector for roads, houses, schools, hospitals, parks, theatres, museums, etc.;
4. Town and city planning;
5. Measures against monopolies, excessive advertising, and consumer exploitations;
6. Promotion of higher investment and establishment of a full-employment economy; and
7. Balance between consumer goods and capital goods and between defense spending and welfare spending.

HEINRICH PESCH

Heinrich Pesch was born in Cologne on September 17, 1854. He attended the University of Bonn, where he did his studies in social science. In 1876, he entered the Society of Jesus and underwent training in classical literature, mathematics, natural science, and all the special sciences involved in the training of a student to the Holy Order in the Roman Catholic Church. During his studies, he was sent to England for four years. There he saw the hardships of the laboring class at Lancashire which prompted him to dedicate his entire life to upgrading the conditions of the working class. After his ordination to the priesthood in 1888, he became involved in writing and teaching. He died at Valkenburg, Holland on April 1, 1926.

His first article, *Zinsgrund und Zinsgrenze* (Theory of Interest) appeared in 1888.[1] It was a discussion of the ethics of interest rather than an economic analysis. The biblical condemnation of interest has been a topic of discussion from the very beginning of Christianity to today. Capital has been accepted as a factor of production, inseparable from land, labor, and entrepreneurship. Interest is a payment for the use of capital, as rent is a payment for the use of land and equipment. Some people have not accepted the role of capital as a factor of production. For a short while Pesch associated with the *Stimmen der Zeit* a German periodical, and wrote many articles on the problems of economics and society. Pesch received an invitation to lecture at Turmitz in North Bohemia from Count Silva Tarouca, who became the last minister of agriculture in the Austrian Empire. At that time, a well-known socialist, Rudolph Meyer, was also lecturing at Turmitz University. Pesch challenged him to an intellectual duel, but Rudolph refused. Pesch took this as a personal insult and left Turmitz for Vienna, where he had been invited to lecture.[2]

171

He became the spiritual director of a seminary while in Vienna, yet continued with his writings and lecturing. He gradually grew popular throughout Germany. He joined the German Catholic Center Party and affiliated himself with Munchen-Gladbach, an elite group of social-minded scholars of the French *Semaines* and *Rheims*. At this time he wrote two volumes on *Liberalism, Socialism and Christianity*. He took the views of the great Bishop von Ketteler, well known for his social works in Germany, and used his directions as the guidelines for his writings.

Pesch knew that his mastery of economics as a science was only peripheral. So at the age of 47 he took economics as his new area of exploration. A number of celebrated economists were teaching at the Berlin University. Pesch spent two years under Gustav Schmoller, Max Sering, and Adolph Wagner. After completing his studies at Berlin, he came back to spend the rest of his life in writing and lecturing on economic issues. His most celebrated work, *The Text Book of Economics*, was the product of about 23 years of effort.[3] He established himself at the Jesuit *House of Writers* in Luxemburg, where most of the economic works in English, French, German, and Spanish were kept in the house library. Pesch preferred articles written in professional journals rather than lengthy treatises in book form. He said, "Science makes its progress through the journals."[4]

In 1905, Pesch published the first volume of the *Text Book*. It took such enormous effort to reorganize the manuscripts he had written at random and revise them for a specific technical volume that he fell seriously ill. He was asked by his doctors to rest for a year. After one year he resumed work on the other volumes. During World War I, he wrote the very effective *Volkswirtschaft Aufgabe und Weltwirtschaft* (The Task of Political Economy in the World), and in 1918 he published *Ethik und Volkswirtschaft* (Ethics in the Political Economy), which stressed the need of ethics in economic activities.

The fifth and the last volume of the *Text Book* appeared in 1923. Between the first and last volumes, Pesch often suffered ill health and had to stop his work occasionally. His entire works filled over four thousand pages. Demand for his works came from all over the globe and many reprints were needed to satisfy the demand. The University of Cologne bestowed on him an honorary doctorate in economics at the close of his life. Pesch spent his life in research and writing. According to his biographer K. E. Nickel, he got many invitations from foreign universities, but declined because he had not completed the five volumes of his *Text Book*. In the book, *Principles of Political Economy*, he called economics, "Our Science." He lived to see all his writings published and left an enormous wealth of knowledge for all men who pursued "Our Science."

Economic Thoughts of Pesch

It is difficult to bring out all the positive contributions Pesch made. It is easier to pick up a negative set of contributions he made.

First of all, his work was intended as a refutation of "economic liberalism" that was in force through the works of the socialists and liberalists. There were many evils perpetrated under the name of laissez-faire and market economy. Pesch tried to point out that exaggerated market economy could depress the social welfare of the people. The proponents of laissez-faire failed to look into the havoc done to society by the profiteers of the business enterprises. Excessive profits clearly showed the existing trend of exploitation of workers, consumers, and society at large. Pesch aligned himself with the socialists in this matter. An unregulated market according to them could not solve the social evils and hence government interference was necessary in the areas of economics and finance. This opinion is diametrically opposed to a laissez-faire philosophy and a free market economy.

Pesch was a scholastic, and his social studies made him a social philosopher. This special characteristic became the unique foundation of his works. One can see that Pesch never deviated from the scholastic philosophy handed down by Thomas Aquinas. Pesch was the first theorist who constructed an integrated economic theory based on Aristotelian-Thomistic philosophy. He was considered one of the leading Catholic economists. Pesch understood the delicate position he was in. He said, "Catholicism gives to the world no economic system; it is committed to no economic position; is tied to no particular economic system."[5]

He claimed that he did not treat economics as he would treat theology or philosophy. The bases of both are different and no one can make economics part of pure science. Theology is based on faith and revelation. Economics is based on the material needs of man. One takes care of the soul; the other takes care of the body. Yet body and soul are intimately connected and coexist in life. A better economic understanding helps the soul to function in its own direction. Ignatius of Loyola had a dictum for his followers, "Healthy soul in a healthy body." Pesch who was a follower of Loyola could see the necessity of a priest's entering into the fields of economics as an apostolate. But his religious goals did not visibly influence his writings.

The tradition of Christianity is to turn away from economic problems. Economics was treated occasionally as a moral and ethical problem. Canon Law forbids the clergy to enter "commercial pursuits." If a priest or a cleric entered into the study of economics, it was looked down on. However, the two immortal encyclicals, *Rerum Novarum* (New Order) and *Quadragesimo Anno* (Fortieth Year), changed the Church's attitude toward the study of economics. Pesch became a commentator on the *Rerum Novarum*, and a source book for *Quadragesimo Anno*, of 1931. The latter encyclical is totally based on Pesch and in Pesch no one can find anything inconsistent with the teaching of the church in the social realm.

In the general history of social thought, Pesch was a strong proponent of "solidarism," which stresses the concept of group action. Solidarism stands against individualism, which is the basic note of capitalism. Some writers did not go along with Pesch's idea of solidarism. Pesch did not clarify the boundaries of solidarism he dealt with. So it can be construed as a part of socialism, state socialism, or universalism.[6] Socialism accepts the society as a homogenous mass, which the economy is intended to satisfy. Adolph Wagner, Pesch's beloved teacher, felt that property is the prerogative of the state not the individual. According to Wagner, any private person is only an officer of the state to take care of the state's property. In other words, he is a custodian for the state. Pesch did not say that society had homogeneity, only unity. He stood for private property and private enterprise as a part of the total economy. Total economy is intended to impart the common good of all as its primary goal. Pesch wanted to have groups established in the total economy, who would be self-governing and self-sufficient. The idea is something like a block system or the communes established in Russia and China where the groups look after the whole of the group members. When Chester Bowles was ambassador to India, he established the "community projects" on the same principle, i.e., the nation is divided into smaller parts, and each part strives to attain economic sufficiency providing food, clothing, housing, education, medical care, and other needs of the group. Every group operates on democratic principles of self-government. The group stands as a middle entity between the state and its citizens, safeguarding the rights and duties of both the state and the individual. By the turn of the 19th century, "solidarism" was a popular slogan, and many radical groups used the term in demanding a socialist type of government. Pesch did not go along with this version of the term.

Without depreciating the abundant and worthwhile material for thought, which particularly the French solidaristic teaching offers, we must regret that . . . our system is distinguished—prescinding that we do not place the cooperative society and especially that of the consumer onesidedly in the foreground, but assert that the whole regulative and constructive significance of the solidaristic principles for the ordering and shaping of that part of the politico-social which we call the national economy. 7

Pesch's notion of solidarism emphasizes the vocational group who are organized to work for the benefit of the whole group. The proper spirit is the acknowledgement of the welfare of the whole as the goal of the economic strivings of the individual.

Summary

Pesch was a welfare economist. He did not go along with the pure or positivistic economists. He gave sound philosophical foundations for many of the basic concepts of economics. He analyzed the nature of economics with its environments. The normative character of economic science is founded on the goals of the economists. Economists in general, differ in establishing the goal of the economic society. Each interprets production, distribution, and consumption according to the constructs of their own economic goals. In the study of comparative economic systems, there is a happy blending of the interests of the individual and the community through the labor theory offered by Pesch. In the study of the organization of the economy, the psychological factor of the "spirit" motivating the workers to maximize the common good of the group was emphasized by Pesch.

Pesch delved into most of the economic writers that existed and regardless of the school of thought to which they belonged, he culled the beneficial parts of their writing and incorporated them in his economic thoughts. He was able to incorporate these thoughts so agreeably that nobody frowned on the thoughts taken from economists of lesser reputation and objectionable identity. Pesch was able to conciliate the contending schools of subjective and objective value theory; he was also able to ameliorate the apparent conflicts between the interests of the individual and the interest of the community or state. Goetz called Pesch a pioneer in the field of socioeconomics. As a pioneer, Pesch knew that his works were not so definitive as to preclude further exploration in the same field. In his own words, "it would be presumptuous to assume that we have found the last, best incontestable solution for the many questions of the modern economy." 8

Footnotes

1. Pesch, Heinrich. "The Theory of Interest," Zeitschrift fur Katholische Theologie (Magazine for Catholic Thought and Theology), XII (Heft 1,3), p. 36.

2. Pesch, Heinrich. Volkswirtschaftslehre der Gegenwart (The Presence of Political Economy) F. Muner et al. eds., Leipzig: 1924, vol. 40, pp. 5-6.

3. Pesch, Heinrich. Lehrbuch der Nationalökonomie, Freiburg 1 Br. Herder 1905-1925; volume I-III, 2nd ed., 6th ed; 1924-1926.

4. Pesch. Presence of Political Economy, p. 8.

5. Pesch. Text Book of National Economy, vol. 3, p. 547.

6. Lechtape, Heinrich. "Heinrich Pesch," in Staatslexicon 4 (1931) col. 132.

7. Pesch. Text Book of National Economy, vol. 1, p. 444.

8. Goetz, Briefs. "Heinrich Pesch," in Encyclopedia of the Social Sciences, 12 (1937): 160.

JOHN MAYNARD KEYNES

John Maynard Keynes was born in Cambridge in 1883 of a father who was an economist of some repute. He won a scholarship to Eton while attending preparatory school. At Eton, John blossomed out as a profound thinker with originality. He won prizes for classics, mathematics, history, and English and wrote essays on contemporary problems. By the time he went to King's College in Cambridge in 1902, he had already gained a reputation as a speaker, writer and young man of great ability and sophistication.

After graduating from King's College, he took the Civil Service Examination. At this time he got interested in economics, read Marshall avidly, and became acquainted with Pigou. He was appointed to work at the India Office as a civil employee. After two years he returned to Cambridge as a lecturer and later became a Fellow of King's College, a position he retained the rest of his life. By 1921 he published his first book, *A Treatise on Probability.* Bertrand Russell spoke of this work as "one which it is impossible to praise too highly."

In 1913 he wrote a second book, *Indian Currency and Finance,* a very useful guideline for the imperial government to meet the problems of the financially plagued colonies. The publication of this book helped him to be appointed to the royal commission in charge of Indian currency. In that post he came in contact with Nevil Chamberlain and other political figures. He was consulted in ironing out the problems of abandoning the gold standard.

In 1915 Keynes was appointed to the Board, a branch of the Treasury Department to oversee the financing of the war. During the discussions of imposing a war debt on Germany, Keynes came up with a figure of 2,000 million pounds (the Bank of England arrived at the figure of 24,000 million pounds). Reparation payments, he

177

argued, "could not be made by signing a check; they must consist of goods produced in Germany and shipped abroad without payment." Keynes demanded that the German war reparation should be met by a loan from the United States, something like a Marshall Plan, so that the war debt would not remain just a book debt.

There are different schools of thought about Keynes' intervention in the Versailles Treaty. Some say that his stand helped to save Germany from becoming totally bankrupt. More than that, his position helped to appease the United States and to keep it in the European alliance.

He wrote a best seller, *The Economic Consequences of Peace*, which gained international acceptance, first because it dealt with the burning problems of peace and secondly because it was written with authority, perception and force. In 1923, Keynes published an economic classic, *A Tract on Monetary Reform*. He warned Britain against returning to the gold standard. Since England was determined to return to the gold standard, Keynes argued that at least they should not go back to prewar parity.

In 1930 he published *A Treatise on Money*, a massive work that was the skeleton on which he later developed his immortal *General Theory*. Keynes enjoyed vast experience in decisionmaking during the war, later in the economic crisis before and after the gold standard act, and as a member of the Macmillan Committee on Finance and Industry. The work that established him as an authority on economics and earned him the name, Father of Neoclassicalism, is the work, *The General Theory of Employment, Interest and Money* (1936).

Even the title of this book has great significance for he thought that he had devised a theory that dealt with the volume of employment at any level. Classical theory presupposed a full-employment economy. He thought that full employment or relatively full employment would prevail if government and private monopolies kept their hands off economic operations.

Keyne's General Theory can be summarized as follows:

1. Total income depends on the volume of total employment.

2. The amount of expenditure for consumption depends on the level of income and therefore on employment.

3. Total employment depends on the total effective demand that consists of (a) consumption expenditures and (b) investment expenditures.

4. When the economy is in equilibrium, the aggregate demand is equal to the aggregate supply. Therefore, aggregate supply exceeds

the effective demand for consumption by the amount of effective demand for investment.

5. In equilibrium, the aggregate demand is equal to the aggregate supply, and aggregate demand is determined by the propensity to consume and the volume of investment. Therefore the volume of employment depends on (a) the aggregate supply function, (b) the propensity to consume and (c) the volume of investment.

6. The aggregate supply function depends mainly on relatively stable physical conditions of supply and propensity to consume and, therefore, the functions in employment depend mainly on the volume of investment.

7. The volume of investment depends on (a) the marginal efficiency of capital, and (b) the interest rate.

8. The marginal efficiency of capital depends on (a) the expectation of profit yields and (b) the replacement cost of capital assets.

9. The rate of interest depends on (a) the quantity of money and (b) the state of the liquidity preference.[1]

Keynes introduced a vocabulary of his own that needs some explanation. The propensity to consume is the portion of the total income that is used for the purchase of consumer goods. It denotes the relation between the community income and its consumption. The term aggregate demand is the total demand, in other words, a schedule of the proceeds expected from the sale of output produced at various levels of employment. The point at which aggregate demand equals aggregate supply on the schedule determines the amount of employment. If the propensity to consume and the aggregate supply are relatively stable, the fluctuation of the investment amount must be responsible for the fluctuation in investment. This leads to the marginal efficiency of capital, interest rate, and the volume of investment.

The marginal efficiency of capital is the expected rate of return on investment. The investment would continue to rise as long as the rate of return is above the current interest rate. The marginal efficiency of capital is characterized by short-term instability and long-term stability. The deciding factor of investment, then, becomes the stability of the market price. Keynes in his *General Theory* stated:

The fundamental psychological law, upon which we are entitled to depend with great confidence both a priori from our knowledge of human nature and from the detailed facts of experience, is that men are disposed, as a rule on the average, to increase their consumption as their income increases; but not as much as their income increases.[2]

This study of human nature made him believe that consumption does not rise at the same rate as the rise in income. This study led him to the "principle of effective demand."

When employment increases, aggregate real income is increased. When aggregate real income is increased, aggregate consumption is increased, but not so much as income. Hence employers would make a loss if the whole of the increased employment were to be devoted to satisfying the increased demand for immediate consumption. Thus, to justify any given amount of employment there must be an amount of current investment sufficient to meet the increased employment.[3]

A necessary result of consumption function is what Keynes called the multiplier. Keynes defined the multiplier as the coefficient relating the increment of expenditures to an increment of income.[4]

When some expenditure of money is introduced into the economic system, a large portion of it is spent according to the marginal propensity to consume. These expenditures would eventually become income for the second group who spend according to the marginal propensity to consume. Every time money is spent, a portion of that total marginal income will be saved or held unspent. This is because the consumption function decreases and saving function increases every time this marginal amount injected in the economy makes its circuit. This cycle will naturally slow down and finally come to a halt when propensity to consume from the marginal income reaches zero. The multiplier is determined by the marginal propensity to consume. The higher the propensity to consume, the greater will be the multiplier.

The Theory of Interest and Prices

Keynes contended that the theory of interest held by the classical economists was in error on two counts. First, that a priori reasoning leads to the conclusion that a high rate of interest stimulates saving and a low rate reduces saving. Keynes asserted that "the influence of changes in the rate of interest on the amount actually saved is of paramount importance, but it is in the opposite direction to that usually supposed." A second disagreement arose, when Keynes advanced the idea of liquidity preference. The classical economist held that the interest would fall, if necessary to zero, to bring saving and investment into equilibirium. But Keynes held that those in possession of savings have a liquidity preference, and will not part with it unless the rate of interest is sufficiently high and attractive.

The rate of interest, which also has an effect on the volume of investment, is in turn determined by two things: the quantity of money and the state of liquidity preference. Keynes thought that the people would hold money without realization of a gain for three reasons: transaction motive, precautionary motive, and speculative motive.

Investment

Investment means the purchase of any income-yielding asset. In the economic theory it means expenditures for additional plants and equipment to produce other goods. In the words of Keynes, "addition to the productive activity of the period."

Production is carried on by the firms and so they are the only ones to invest. The firm receives payment only for the output, which is sold to consumers. All others are considered in addition to capital equipment. The value of the unsold portion of output added to the value of equipment is what Keynes understood as capital. Of course, investment depends on the marginal efficiency of capital and the rate of interest.

Keynes thought that investment is the unstable element in aggregate demand. If the rate of increase in income is greater than the increase in consumption, it creates a gap between total income and consumption. This gap should be bridged by investment expenditures. Whenever investment expenditures fail to fill the gap between income and consumption, there are violent fluctuations in the economy. In order to protect the economy, the government should be a major consumer.

Lawrence R. Klein sets forth the following guidelines: (1) The government should act as a balancing agent and should keep its own level of spending to offset the deflationary gap; (2) a method must be devised to raise income to the full-employment level; and (3) the government should exercise manipulation of the rate of interest. The third method was recommended by Keynes also. Keynesian economics holds that the saving schedule is highly unpredictable. Only by the stimulation of investment can an economy be kept in equilibrium.

Quantity Theory of Money

The quantity theory of money had many irrelevant contentions that needed correction. The total quantity of money is important because of its influence on price. There is an incontestable relationship between money and price. If the quantity of money increases, to be sure, the price level will likewise increase. Vice versa, a decrease in money supply will decrease the level of price also. This theory of classical economics was based on the principle that "all money is spent and economy is in full employment." Keynes found the above theory defective, since all money is not spent; some is saved. No country really operates on full employment, since investment and spending fluctuate so unpredictably. Price also can depend on economic fluctuations and expectations, besides the quantity of money supply in the economy. The classicists thought that the velocity of money was stable. Keynes did not accept a constant velocity. The classical theory of saving was to consider it not as a leakage from the consumption flow but as another form of spending, namely, investment. The saving and investment were brought together through the interest rate which made saving and investment operate by the law of supply and demand. Keynes did not accept so direct a relationship between saving and investment. His analysis concluded that savings and investment were not directly related; that is,

in a sense the amount of saving and that of investment are always equal; the equality between them is maintained not by control of the amount of investment but by that of saving, by the influence of the (independently determined) amount of investment spending on that of total spending and thus on the volume of income in the system, and thus on the abilities of the people to save, and the amount of saving.[5]

During the 18th century, Jean-Baptiste Say developed what was to be known as Say's Law of Markets, which contended that all that was produced is consumed. In other words, supply creates its own demand; people are interested in goods rather than money, so they would convert money for goods. Keynes saw several inconsistencies in Say's Law:

1. Assuming all money will be spent (none saved), it will not be spent fast enough to clear the market of all goods, which will result in market surplus.

2. Business suppliers according to its projected expectations, do not feel that everything that they produce will be sold. Many buying decisions are slow to be made and some money is often held in anticipation of lower prices or as an asset, thereby reducing the output, employment, and income.

Monetary Policy and Fiscal Policy

Keynes brought out the idea of fiscal policies to operate as a counter-cyclical measure to keep the economy in general equilibrium. This was not a new idea as pre-Keynesian economists dealt extensively with fiscal policy as a cure for monetary ills. Faith in the monetary policies had been badly shaken by the 1929 global depression. When Keynes appeared with his *General Theory* in 1936, it was hard for the world to accept his strong recommendations of fiscal policy as the neutralizing force of business cycles. During the depression there was a fiscal policy in operation, but it could do very little to remedy the malady. Keynes recommended the manipulation of legal reserve and discount rates, selective credit control, establishment of margin, and many other functions of the central banks as effective weapons to combat business fluctuations.

Today, one can see that the monetary policies enforced by the central banks have done little to combat inflation. A tight money policy is self-defeating at the growing rate of national debt. The element of human judgment also has to be considered in measuring the efficacy of monetary policies.

This leads the reader to Paul Samuelson, who writes, "Today few economists regard federal reserve monetary policy as a panacea for controlling the business cycle." As long as government debt is large and appropriations exceed revenues with a constant increase in public debt and a policy of deficit financing, the fiscal policies fail to create a general equilibrium as Keynes envisioned. W. H. Hutt's analysis of Keynesianism in his book, *Keynesianism: Retrospect and Prospect* is that the basic assumptions are still valid although the experience of the depression showed that the market did not automatically adjust to the imperfections in the system.

Employment and Unemployment

The classicist believed that the employment level and the real wage were determined by the intersection of the demand and supply of labor; and second, that saving is nothing more than spending for capital goods. Keynes used the term, *propensity to consume* as a relationship between total income and total consumption. Although it is not a real thing, it is used as a yardstick to measure the expected rate of domestic consumption and expected rate of foreign trade to make up the total gross national product. Keynes took another step forward from consumption function to the marginal propensity to consume function, which measures increase in consumption due to increase in income.

Inducement to investment depends on two factors, "the marginal efficiency of capital" and the "rate of interest." The rate of interest, according to Keynes, is solely determined by the quantity of money and the liquidity preference. He repeatedly warned, ". . . unless savings are invested, they are wasted."

Keynes discussed the "money wage rate" and "real wage rate," and found a negative correlation between the two. Money wage increase has a few drawbacks: (1) Marginal costs increase in the short run; (2) in a closed system, marginal cost and marginal wage become equal in the short run; and (3) prices are roughly governed by the marginal wage. Keynes found a correlation between increased wages and increased unemployment.

Keynes' Major Assertions

Many economists held the theory of overinvestment and under-consumption as the root causes of business cycles. Keynes disagreed with the authors of that theory, since he did not find reasons for a consumption lag, when producers of goods and services regularly pay wages and salaries under full employment to keep up consumption.

He thought that the rate of interest should be abolished altogether. Interest is a man-made device of building up artificial scarcity of money, although the *General Theory* is built on the marginal efficiency of capital and interest rate.

He thought that even in the most progressive economy, there will be a layer of unemployed people. This unemployment may be caused by the structural weakness of employment practices and should not be counted as altogether injurious to the total economy. The existence of a low level of unemployment serves as a buffer against inflation. Keynes believed in government intervention in business and society. A government control serves as a superstructure over the possible disorders due to the profit maximization efforts of individual business. If business is left alone under the pretext of laissez-faire, monopolies may be created and gradually liquidate all small enterprises. Government planning can leave room for all groups and sizes to compete on fair and ethical standards and serve the business and society equally. Keynes proposed two methods of government control, either complete control or just filling in gaps left by business negligence.

Keynes supported strong unionization. Unions are the coercive power for equitable distribution of consumer surplus, profits, and the benefits of technology. Yet he did not condone excessive demands of unions that threaten the very existence of a capitalistic system. In this situation he called the unions "once the oppressed, now the tyrants, whose selfish and sectional pretensions need to be bravely opposed."

He discussed the "paradox of thrift" as a possible way of diminishing the multiplier effect of investment and paralysis of economic growth. Thrift is a virtue in an individual case, but if a nation goes on consumption austerity, that can usher in cyclical fluctuation immediately. Man can improve his standard of living almost unlimitedly. Income is intended for spending either by consumption or saving that can be available to the economy. If the circular flow of the economy is hampered by reduced spending, inventories pile up and employment is reduced. Therefore, consumption is a national virtue.

In attacking the classical doctrine that the supply and demand of labor determine the employment level and real wages, Keynes made the following dissenting notes. The supply of labor is not a function of the real wage, since the workers do not normally withdraw from the labor force just because of a fall in the wage level:

A fall in real wage due to a rise in prices with money wages unaltered, does not, as a rule, cause the supply of labor on offer at the current wage to fall below the amount actually employed prior to the rise of prices. To suppose that it does, is to suppose that all those who are now unemployed, though willing to work at the current wage, will withdraw the offer of their labor in the event of a small rise in the cost of living.[6]

Keynes denied the idea that the workers are in a position to determine the real wage and with it the volume of employment they could bring under contract with their employers. Keynes thought that the workers cannot be independent of the general level of prices. He believed that the classical economists were so preoccupied with the idea that prices depended on the quantity of money that they failed to see the implication of the behavior of the business firm.

Keynes stated that there were three types of unemployment, whether caused by voluntary or involuntary factors. He notes structural, frictional and cyclical or depression unemployment in his treatise. Structural unemployment is based on the natural state of under-development of a country, lack of skill, discrimination and such other causes. Frictional unemployment is caused by the changing of jobs or the unsettled process of changing jobs. Strikes and lock-outs are also considered as frictional unemployment. Cyclical or depression unemployment is caused by the cycles of the economy.

Conclusion

Although Keynes was an ardent critic of classical theory, one

186 HISTORY OF ECONOMIC THOUGHT

should not conclude that Keynes rejected the whole of classical economics. Keynes explicitly accepted the validity of classical analysis in the area of price and distribution theory. He said:

If we suppose the volume of output to be given, i.e., to be determined by forces outside the classical scheme of thought, then there is no objection to be raised against the classical analysis of the manner in which private self-interest will determine what in particular is produced, in what proportion the factors of production will be combined to produce it, and how the value of the final product will be distributed among them.[7]

Keynes did not develop a totally new concept of economics, because his main concern was curing the irregularities of the classical system. He wanted to correct the classical notions of money "as a ticket obtained by selling goods or services and useful only for buying goods or services."

Keynes preferred his liquidity preference to that of the classicists. The General Theory is often ranked with Adam Smith's Wealth of Nations and Karl Marx's Das Kapital as having greatly influenced economic thinking. Keynes rejected the employment theory of the classicists, yet Keynes, like the classical theorists, remained faithful to deductive logic.

Footnotes

1. McCracken, Harlan L. *Keynesian Economics in the Stream of Economic Thought*, Baton Rouge, La.: Louisiana State University Press, 1961, pp. 30, 97.
2. Ibid.
3. Peterson, Wallace C. *Income, Employment and Economic Growth*, New York: W. W. Norton, 1967, p. 150.
4. Ibid., p. 146.
5. Stewart, Michael. *Keynes and After*, Baltimore: Penguin Publishing Co., 1968, pp. 13, 14, 19.
6. Keynes. *General Theory*, New York: Harcourt, Brace & World, 1936, pp. 20, 378.
7. Taylor, Overton H. *A History of Economic Thought*, New York: McGraw-Hill, 1960, p. 477.

JOSEPH SCHUMPETER

Joseph A. Schumpeter was born in Triesch, Austria in 1883. In his earlier career. Schumpeter administered the estate of a wealthy Egyptian princess. Later he worked as the president of a private bank. In 1918 he served as a consultant to the Socialization Commission in Berlin, and in 1919 he became the Minister of Finance of Austria. From 1909 to 1920, Schumpeter held academic positions at Cernauti and Graz. In 1925 he accepted a professorship at the University of Bonn, and he held that job until 1930. Then he immigrated to the United States and joined the faculty of Harvard University, spending about 20 years as a professor of economics there. During his stay at Harvard, he blossomed into a top economist, respected for his teaching and writing on matters of economics.[1] Some people call Schumpeter the father of the Business Cycle Theory. He died in 1950.

Schumpeter wrote three books at the early age of 31. He was busy with varied economic and political activities even from the years of his university life. Two books he wrote dealt with the history of economic ideas and the third dealt with economic theory. The second book he wrote in 1912, *The Theory of Economic Development*, brought him fame as a first-rate economic scientist. During the political upheavals before and after World War I, the economic condition of Europe was something less than desirable and the ensuing panic attracted the attention of most schools of economics in Europe. Schumpeter analyzed the conditions logically and recommended various steps to avert any major catastrophe. In his book, *The Theory of Economic Development*, he emphasized the "Theory of Capitalistic Dynamics" which is the finest argument in favor of capitalism as a means of economic growth. He explained the dynamics of capitalism with free enterprise, competition based on a price system, and profit as an incentive for upgrading the wages and working conditions of the labor class. Schumpeter used the central theme of this book in most of his later writings.

Schumpeter identified three forms of societies: capitalism, socialism, and communism. Karl Marx influenced his thinking to some extent as one can see in the first part of his work *Capitalism, Socialism and Democracy*. Schumpeter disagreed with Marx and in order to refute Marx's theories he brought out dynamic capitalism as a solution to economic growth and development. Still, Schumpeter did not fail to pay due respect to Marx whenever respect was due him.

In the second part of the work *Capitalism, Socialism, and Democracy*, Schumpeter deals with socialism as a rising form of government. He wrote that, "a socialist form of society will inevitably emerge from an equally inevitable decomposition of capitalist society."[2] Any society can count on its development according to the quality of its citizen. A highly affluent capitalistic society is prone to be discontented with its lot. As a consequence there will arise a spirit of opposition to the existing "establishments," which support the capitalist economy. When these pillars are shaken loose by the discontented elements, society has to come down like a house of cards. Schumpeter wrote, "Capitalism is being killed by its achievements."[3] Looking into the 70s, one can see that these prophesies are not too amiss.

Schumpeter's work, *History of Economic Analysis*, deals with the partial equilibrium theory of the Austrian economists and his own new theory called the *general equilibrium*. The partial equilibrium theory takes into account economic factors alone and works out a system that would give the optimum satisfaction to the people. In the general equilibrium theory, Schumpeter contends that economic factors alone cannot predict meaningfully the best path to choose for economic development. Political and social forces play an important role in defining the economic growth of a nation. Hence the partial equilibrium theory should be replaced by the general equilibrium theory that allows margin for social and political impacts on the economy. The partial equilibrium is based on the essential sterility and static forces of the economy. Schumpeter visualized economics as dynamic and prolific. His writings on the dynamics of capitalism were diametrically opposed to the partial equilibrium theory of the Austrian schools. He said, "I wish to state right now that, if starting my work in economics afresh, I were told that I could study only one of the three (statistics, economic theory, and economic history) and had my choice, it would be history I would choose."[4]

Schumpeter is considered a master of the business cycle theory. He kept a special interest in the causes and remedies of economic fluctuation. He analyzed the history of economics and found the endless wave of economic fluctuations affecting the nations. People accepted the economic cycles fatalistically; the world had a passive view of money as if money controlled man. Schumpeter thought that the attitude of subjection of man to money was not the right order of things. His attempt was to make money subject to man or, in other words, to change from the passive attitude of money's controlling man to the active attitude of man's controlling money. Schumpeter set forth his own version of the causes of business cycles. In his analysis of prosperity he said,

This boom consists in the carrying out of innovations in the industrial and commercial organism. By innovation, I understand such changes of the com-binations of the factors of production as cannot be affected by infinitesimal steps or variations on the margin. They consist primarily in changes in methods of production and transportation, or the changes in industrial organizations, or in the production of a new article, or in the opening of new markets or of the new sources of material. The recurring periods of prosperity of the cyclical movement are the form progress takes in capitalistic society.[5]

Business cycle theorists, as a whole, give many reasons why the cycle comes into being. Overinvestment theory, underconsumption theory, exogenous versus indigenous theory and psychological theories are some of them. But Schumpeter found innovations or their absence to be the major cause of the cycle upward or downward. Schumpeter did not take the term innovation as mere invention. Inventions never go according to a cyclical trend. By innovations he meant application of inventions to commercial pursuits, which do follow a cyclical trend. Innovations can be in a new technology or even in a new method of marketing.

Schumpeter found that an upward trend in the economy is usually caused by a greater volume of investment. When new technology or new products are brought into the scene, the profit-seeking entre-preneurs would invest deeply in these new and unexplored areas of goods and services. As a consequence, investments reduce unemploy-ment, extend more pure purchasing power to consumers, and thus, lend themselves to the upward swing of the economy. Schumpeter thought that one innovation was the cause of more innovations. Competition would force others to seek a faster and better method of producing the same product or even a better product to accelerate the upward swing of the cycle. A wave of innovations would follow until the profit-taking tapers off to the point where the average total cost equals price. When many businessmen run into the same field of products, the heat of selling dampens the price until the production of any more units brings in only negative returns. The same theory of boom deals inversely with the reasons for the downward turning phenomena of the cycle. The expansion in investments would keep up even though there were visible signs of market resistance and loss of profit margin. The idea of competition makes every businessman think that adversity affects others more than himself. It is like talking about highway deaths. The statistics one hears before national holidays always relate to someone else. The politician has many ways of misdirecting the businessman, telling him that the downward trend in the economy is only temporary and the "good old days" will be here again. This is the time when the businessman has overcommitted himself to expensive investments leading him to declare bankruptcy before the upward trend ever looms up on the horizon. Business failures are like an avalanche. One big business going into bankruptcy takes with it a host of small businesses that leaned on it.

In the explanation of business cycles, Schumpeter relied heavily on the money market. He noted: "The pioneering innovator with more efficient processes than his competitors may draw heavily on the banking community for funds to aid in the commercial exploitation of his ideas."[6] Others would also use the money and credit available to keep abreast of the big producer. It is easy to write off the cost of money or interest as the cost of production, just like an increase in wages or the price of raw materials. The result of such a move is a considerable boost in the price level, and, since consumers are very conscious of price, consumer rejection of the overpriced goods results. Such market phenomena lead to recessions and even mild depressions. In order to lift the economy from such a depressed state, the scientist has to work in the laboratory to find a better method of producing a good that can be sold for attractive prices to stimulate the economy.

Schumpeter's formal approach involves the development of a model in two states. The initial impact of the innovation becomes to Schumpeter the "first approximation." The second approximation follows through the original impact of the innovation. The first approximation starts with the economic system in equilibrium state. He describes this equilibrium: "Every firm is in equilibrium with its cost exactly equal to receipts; prices in other words, equated to average costs; interest and profit rates both stand at zero; and there is no involuntary unemployment."[7] One may think that the equilibrium state described by Schumpeter's model is just a utopian stage, but it was necessary for the clarity of the model. In this model, there is no incentive for change anywhere in the system. Since a change can have an adverse effect on the person who changes, nobody dares to make a change. It presupposes that exchange and channels of distribution are also static.

Into this complete quietude of economic doldrums, a new innovation is introduced. Since the innovator is the first in the field, he is able to make a very good profit. This induces the innovator to seek the banks with an offer of higher interest rates and that stimulates banking activities. "Both profit rates and interest rates are positive, with the interest rate closely linked to the anticipated profit rate" according to Schumpeter. With more money on hand, the innovator can lure the scarce resources from other industries. This economic activity is self-perpetuating. The profits become big, prices are high, wages increase, and imitators follow innovators. The stages of increasing return of profits pass into decreasing return of profits and finally to negative returns of profits. As in nature, generation, growth, reproduction, and corruption are innate in every living being, so recycling of the three stages is innate in economy.

The second approximation brings into the picture elements that are reactions to the primary approximations. Schumpeter thought that speculations develop during the primary upswing leading to innovations that are unprofitable and unfeasible in the normal partial equilibrium. This type of launching rather unreasonable innovation gives a sudden upswing to the economy. The whole upswing is predicated on a speculative base and as such is unrealistic and unnatural. The effect of the secondary approximation is that "excesses which have accumulated during the expansion become manifest, the contraction begins, and, because of the excesses which have developed during the expansion, the contraction carries beyond the equilibrium point — beyond the point the wave would have brought it."[8]

The second approximation thus ends with a four-phase cycle. In the first approximation, economy goes through prosperity and recession, but the use of the second approximation brings the economy from prosperity to recession, to depression, to recovery, and finally to prosperity. Thus the complete cycle is warranted by the speculators.

The time to recover from depression depends on the maladjustments the economy went through at the time of sudden prosperity caused by the second wave. "The lower turning point which marks the shift of the economy from depression to revival will occur only after the necessary liquidation has taken place and after the debt structure has been brought into order, with excesses and uneconomic positions eliminated."[9] There is no guarantee under this maladjusted economy that prosperity can be brought in after the recovery shows its signs.

Schumpeter and Capitalism

Schumpeter was a great believer in capitalism, although he worried about the "germs of self-destruction" inherent in the present capitalistic operations. He wrote avidly on "plausible capitalism"—a capitalism that can achieve the many-faced goals ascribed to it by Keynes. He went so far as to predict a deadline for the decay of capitalism, somewhere between 50 to 100 years. He asked the question, "Can capitalism survive?" and he replied laconically, "No, I do not think it can."

Schumpeter thought that capitalism was being attacked by the intellectual critics from within and without. Again, the leaders of business and industry who are the knights of capitalism, either by defect or by excess, destroy the system. The rank and file of ardent proponents only see the immediate gains and selfish interests. Schumpeter believed that depersonalization of men and talents was the most dangerous destructive element of capitalism. He predicted that capitalism would become old-fashioned and uninspiring to the majority after a while. An unbiased critic can see that Schumpeter painted this gloomy picture without any economic foundation to support his statements.

Schumpeter went against his own teacher, Boehm-Bawerk, especially in the theory of capital accumulation. People save due to their personal liquidity preference. These savings, if not hoarded should come back into the circular flow of economy in the form of investment. Additional investments go through the multiplier effect and that is the major cause of economic growth and capital accumulation. The improved production function can also expedite the capital growth. Schumpeter claimed that capital growth can be smooth and orderly without bringing in the undesirable aspects of dehumanization and impersonalization. He persistently held that gradual growth cannot be of any appreciable size. The big changes in the world do not arise from gradual or continuous evolution but are forced intermittently in lumps and clusters.

Conclusion

It is hard to make an objective evaluation of Schumpeter's business cycle theory. Schumpeter differed from the Austrian economists on the premises that the economy is vastly influenced by political and social changes. Thus economy has no independent foothold of its own. Since political and social sciences themselves are mere approximate sciences qualifying another approximate science, economics, there is major leeway for interpretation of any conclusion drawn from the theory of the business cycle. Schumpeter's approach eliminates any room for empirical evaluation and testing. Schumpeter made an unorthodox model of the business cycle marking the total process from equilibrium to equilibrium. His interpretations of the revival phase and the recovery phase are not the same but pertain to separate cycles. The theory needs a "Superman Innovator" to start the cycle all over from the state of depression. Schumpeter might be considered a sociologist using economics as an instrument to prove his points. He used modern sociology and politics and interpreted social organizations according to the construct of political ideologies. He was an avid student of history. His historical perspectives became the dominant guiding light of all his theories.

Footnotes

Harris, Seymour E. *Schumpeter, Social Scientist,* Cambridge: Harvard University Press, 1951, pp. 5-11.

2. Schumpeter, J. A. *Capitalism, Socialism, and Communism,* New York: Harper & Bros., 1942, p. 59.

3. Ibid., p. 63.

4. Schumpeter, J. A. *History of Economic Analysis,* New York: Oxford University Press, 1954, p. 5.

5. Schumpeter, J. A. "The Explanation of Business Cycles," *Economica,* December 1927, p. 295.

6. Schumpeter, J. A. *Business Cycles: A Theoretical, Historical and Statistical Analysis of the Capitalist Process,* New York: McGraw-Hill, 1939, p. 83.

7. Ibid., p. 110.

8. Schumpeter, J. A. "Innovation in the Capitalistic Process," *Quarterly Journal of Economics,* 19 (1951): 423.

9. Ibid., p. 423.

References

Gide, C., Rist, C. & Richards, R. *A History of Economic Doctrines*, Lexington, Mass.: D. C. Heath & Co., 1913.

Heilbroner, Robert L. *The Worldly Philosophers*, New York: Keith Jenneson Book Co., 1961.

Speigel, Henry William. *The Development of Economic Thought*, New York: John Wiley, 1952.

Whittaker, Edmund, *Schools and Streams of Economic Thought*, New York: Rand McNalley, 1960.

ROBERT TRIFFIN

Robert Triffin is one of the architects of modern international monetary planning. He received a Ph.D. from Harvard Unviersity in 1938. After his graduation he spent his time, mostly in government service. He participated in the International Monetary Fund, served as one of the Board of Governors of the Federal Reserve System, member of the Economic Commission to Latin America, member of the Council of Economic Advisors, member of the European Cooperation Administration and member of the United Nations. He was a visiting professor at Yale University and a convocation speaker at many Ivy League institutions. In spite of the many responsible agencies he served, he found time to publish books on the intricate problems of international liquidity.

Economic Thoughts of Robert Triffin

In 1940, Triffin published his doctoral dissertation in book form under the caption, *The Monopolistic Competition and General Equilibrium.* His dissertation proper was a critical analysis of Joan Robinson's work, *The Economics of Imperfect Competition* and his own professor E. H. Chamberlain's *Theory of Monopolistic Competition.* It was not easy to analyze two living authors' works and integrate the findings in a new theory of *general equilibirium.* Triffin successfully combined the two theories into a solid base and built his theories on them. This book is very technical in content. He noted:

Three main problems have been raised that had not been clearly perceived or solved in current expositions of monopolistic competition: the problems of the interdependence of the firms, the problems of the objective or subjective nature of the sales and cost curves, and most important of all, the vital problem of defining exactly the "elementary quanta" of our analysis: commodities and firms.[1]

Triffin gave his own definition of firms. According to him, "firms are not only interdependent with respect to their sales curves; they are similarly interconnected through the mutual influences they may have on each other's costs."[2] Triffin was very cautious in analyzing the merits and demerits of his own professor. Professor Joan Robinson had already achieved prominence as a progressive economist or as many called her, "an institutional economist." So it was not easy to analyze these reputed authors and then uphold his theory of monopolistic competition and general equilibrium. Triffin says:

Product differentiation robs the concept of industry of both its definiteness and its serviceability outside of the limiting cases of pure monopoly and pure competition, the substitutability between any two products, the competitiveness between any two firms varies only in degrees. The grouping of firms into industries cannot be based on any clear cut criterion, nor can it be of any help in a general statement of value theory. The substitutability between any two products, the vulnerability of any firm to incursions from new rivals, are problems outside the reach of theoretical deductions.[3]

Triffin found that there were no simple methods and formulas for solving the problems of competition. It is easy to state in price theory the general distinctions and characteristics of monopolies, monopolistic competitions, firms, and industries. But the basic definition of each term does not meet with the environmental differences that are seen between firm and firm and competition and competition.

In 1957, Triffin published *Europe and the Money Muddle*, in which he described the monetary problems of Europe after World War II. There were loser nations and winner nations. It was expected that the losers' currency would become cheap and the winners' currency dear. Triffin was appointed to the European Payments Union. The contents of his book were really the problems he encountered and the decisions he made in that office. Possibly Triffin relied on the operations of the peacetime settlement of monetary problems after World War I. The members of the Payments Union were not working for a temporary solution to the monetary problems of Europe. They wanted a lasting settlement of the problems that occur periodically after each war. The goal was to create an economic condition that could not be totally affected or destroyed by any war. War debts in themselves are inhuman to the people who survive a war. War destroys the equilibrium of any economy, but especially that of a defeated nation. Then, the imposition of war debt makes it doubly hard to meet the payments of debts and at the same time find a way to reconstruct the economy.

Triffin thought bilateral payments were economically immature ways of paying debts. It is hard to create a balance of trade between two nations only. Possibly a multilateral payment may be more feasible to foster better international trade and the creation of good will between people polarized by the war. Triffin opposed bilateral payments, saying, "this system is destructive of triangular trade and prevents each country from using its surpluses with some of its trade partners to settle its deficits with others."[4]

There were strong opinions about making the payments between states by regional agreements. The regional agreements still create certain monetary blocks and to some extent a spirit of parochialism. When nations get into these economic huddles, it is the first sign of disaster in some part of the world. World history attests to that fact. Understanding this probability, Triffin noted: "Regional monetary arrangements of the EPU type might well be preferable, from the short-run point of view, to nationalistic restrictions and bilateralism, but they would slow down or permanently impede further progress toward world wide competition and currency convertability."[5]

Triffin was not convinced about the ability of the International Monetary Fund to deliver the aid needed to rebuild Europe from the ashes of war or to extend a helping hand to emerging nations in Asia and Africa. "The most glaring defects of the Fund's charter relate to the handling of the widespread but temporary, disequilibria inherited from the Second World War."[6] He found the entire structure of the world economy was deteriorating because of the instability of the major currency during the 20s. There were attempts to covert a weak nation's currency into gold or dollars, thus destroying the rest of the world's faith in that currency. Triffin was very disturbed about the future of European currency. He remarked: "The institutional framework of international convertibility needs to be greatly strengthened if it is to survive the inevitable shocks occasionally to be expected from unfavorable developments and policies in some of the major trading nations."[7]

International Liquidity

International liquidity is, in simple terms, the ability of a nation to pay its bills. Just as a private consumer buys goods and services with the understanding of future payment, so also a nation becomes involved in buying goods and services from other nations with the understanding that it will pay (1) in the seller's currency; (2) in the buyer's currency; (3) in the currency of another country acceptable to the seller; or (4) in gold. Besides the goods and services a nation buys, it stands as a cosigner for its citizens and sometimes for another nation through a "correspondent agreement" with the force of international law. Usually these adjustments are made through the international trade balances. The central banks of each nation carry the currencies of other nations to meet the deficits when they happen. Triffin gives some descriptions of liquidity:

Internationally accepted monetary reserves are the medium used by national monetary authorities to absorb or release the net amounts of each national currency used or needed by all other transactors for payments across rather than within national borders. They contribute the indispensable link between independent national currencies in an internationally trading world.[8]

The reserves of foreign currencies in the control of central banks are very important to liquidity. The reserve requirements are based on the volume of trade between two nations. For instance, the United States does not have to maintain any appreciable amounts of the foreign currencies of Asia, Africa, or Latin America. It is always ahead of these nations due to greater exports and lesser imports from them. But looking into the European Common Market countries, the United States has an unfavorable balance of trade and should have a considerable amount of those currencies ready to meet the payments whenever required. In the 60s, the United States failed to meet some of these obligations and was forced to pay in gold.

If the goal is to have an expanding world economy and increase in world trade, the prerequisite is to establish international liquidity. When an individual nation becomes unable to increase its money supply by its own creative activities, it fails internally and externally. The per capita income cannot be increased unless the domestic production and consumption are capable of growth. A country that can come up with a surplus, over and above the domestic consumption, can launch a foreign trade. By selling the surplus to foreign countries, the seller nation builds up foreign reserve. This reserve makes a nation "liquid."

Some nations fall into the doldrums, economically speaking, and are unable to increase their production due to the lack of technology. They cannot buy sophisticated machinery because they have no reserve of foreign currency. This was the point that worried Triffin. He wrote, "The economic growth is certain to be arrested or slowed down if a way cannot be found to insure a parallel—although by no means proportionate—monetary liquidity."[9] How much of an increase is needed to bring the world as a whole to solvency? Triffin said:

Beggar-my-neighbor reserve policies and pervasive deflationary or restrictive policies on world trade would thus appear well-nigh unavoidable over the long run, if institutional arrangements failed to provide for substantial increases of the pool of world reserves over the long-run.[10]

Triffin did not think that going back to the gold exchange standard would be sufficient to bring back international liquidity. The world's gold supply was held by certain privileged nations at that time. These nations were not actually affected by a shortage of reserves. The world supply of gold was too small to generate the needed supply of reserves. When the world was not in such bad turmoil, the United States dollar and the British pound were used to circumvent this key problem. The world divided itself into dollar belts and sterling belts and the adjustments of accounts were made within each circle first, and then between the two major groups. Small nations were happy with such an arrangement, and by that time Russia and the satellite countries were not participating in world trade.

Right after World War II, many small countries preferred to use the dollar reserve in the forms of stocks and bonds purchased from the United States. This was better than saving the reserves in gold, which remained unproductive. The key currency country like the United States lost its favorable balance of trade situation beginning in 1958. An unfavorable balance of trade was one reason the reserves the United States held until that time started to be pumped out into the hands of foreign nations. The loss of reserves for the United States was a gain of reserves for the rest of the world. The world became better by the diffusion of the frozen reserves caused by the gold flow from the United States. If the United States stops running a deficit balance of payments, the flow of dollars into the world will cease and the international liquidity will cease to expand. Triffin notes:

The key currency countries cannot afford to let their net reserve position deteriorate indefinitely. If they did, their currency would stop, in any case, to be considered the safest, and the time would come when other countries would cease accumulating it, and might even begin converting some of their outstanding holdings into gold or other currencies.[11]

This tendency started showing up in the late 50s to the point where the other nations began converting their dollar holdings into gold. They knew that the gold by itself would not be productive but the intrinsic loss sustained by dollars would offset any gain these nations would receive in the form of interests or dividends from the stocks and bonds they held as reserves for liquidity. Then, to make things worse, the market price of gold began to rise in the London markets, tempting the dollar holders to convert the dollar into gold.

Triffin finds many undesirable features in the system of holding reserves:

1. The state's deficits are underwritten by the local central bank and free credit expansion by commercial banks is permitted by the local central bank, both of which work toward an unbridled gallop toward inflation.

2. The state's credit policies induce a spiraling increase in prices and wages without proportionate increase in goods and services or the real quantity of gold or foreign currencies.

3. The states are not controlled by any external world agency, so that the state may adjust its external expenditures to its internal receipts in lieu of the contracting reserves to exhaustion.

Triffin could approve the artificial mechanisms by which a nation tried to cover up the disequilibrium found in the reserve position. If a country is facing a temporary liquidity problem, the present system uses a redistribution of reserves somthing like borrowing excess reserves of a nation temporarily to cover up the imbalance. This approach is widely used in the banking system to meet the temporary need for money between banks. It can never be counted as a cure for the real problem caused by imbalance between international payments and international receipts. This temporary adjustment precipitates accelerated imports and exports against the real demand of the consuming nation. These measures create an artificial price system, gradually reducing the real price of the products and leading to chronic evils like recession and depression. Triffin said: "During the cyclical depression, however, simultaneous efforts by many nations at maintaining, or increasing, their exports in the face of a shrinking world demand, merely results in an accelerated fall of prices and reduction of exports."[12]

Triffin thought that drastic measures should be taken to resolve some of these troubles that loom in the economic horizon periodically. He believed there should be an effective way to keep a steady growth of international trade and a continuous combat against creeping inflation. He recommended an international effort to find markets for the products of the underdeveloped countries so that they could earn some foreign currency. He wanted to have an international committee watch over the massive shift of international balance from one hemisphere to another serving private gains at the expense of global liquidity.

Triffin believed that most of the goals he pointed out could be met. Some of his recommendations to solve the problem are:

1. The United States and other major countries should bar the use of their currencies as monetary reserves. Instead these nations should use the deposit with IMF in any form as the base of their reserve.

2. The IMF can use the reserve of each nation like the Federal Reserve System of the United States, to establish a lending quota for each nation. In this way, the IMF will truly become a world bank, able to watch over the world liquidity by increasing the world reserve by three to five percent annually to meet the increased need of money in each nation.

All economists of the world did not go along with Triffin. One outspoken critic of Triffin was the then Undersecretary of the Treasury for Monetary Affairs, Robert Roose. He had many objections but the most important were that "the Fund Unit would not accomplish a meaningful net increase in liquidity to be sure, or a corresponding increase in the world commerce," and "methods of creating money, once learned, would be abused through excessive expansion as the 'needs of trade' led to spiraling over issue."[13]

Another critic of Triffin was Professor Robert Aliber, of the Graduate School of Business at the University of Chicago. He was skeptical of Triffin's plan, and wrote:

The dollar became an international currency neither by the Act of Congress nor by the act of god, but rather because it met various needs of foreign official institutions and foreign private parties more effectively than other financial assets could. United States financial facilities provided foreigners with a safe depository for liquid funds.[14]

Looking at world conditions with the intimacy Triffin had under various positions he held, however, it is difficult to discredit any of his statements. He was not a pure theoretical economist but had to arrive at workable solutions to the living problems he faced. Moreover he was under orders to face the problem and in the name of the United States to solve it in favor of all parties concerned. Possibly the dimensions of the problem he encountered far surpassed the abilities of one man. In defense of his recommendations, however, his lament about the fate of gold is worth notice. "Nobody," he said, "could ever have conceived of a more absurd waste of human resources than to dig gold in distant corners of the earth for the sole purpose of transporting it and re-burying it immediately afterwards in other deep holes especially excavated to receive it and heavily guarded to protect it."[15]

Footnotes

1. Triffin, Robert. *Monopolistic Competition and General Equilibrium*, Cambridge, Mass.: Harvard University Press, 1949, pp. 95-96.

2. Ibid., p. 108.

3. Ibid., p. 188.

4. Triffin, Robert. *Europe and the Money Muddle*, New Haven, Conn.: Yale University Press, 1957, p. 94.

5. Ibid., p. 200.

6. Ibid., p. 201.

7. Ibid., p. 303.

8. Triffin, Robert. *Maintaining and Restoring Balance in International Payments*, Princeton, N.J.: Princeton University Press, 1966, p. 89.

9. Ibid., p. 64.

10. Ibid., p. 93.

11. Triffin, Robert. *Gold and the Dollar Crisis*, New Haven, Conn.: Yale University Press, 1961, p. 88.

12. Triffin, Robert. *The World Money Maze*, New Haven, Conn.: Yale University Press, 1966, p. 155.

13. Roosa, Robert V. *Monetary Reform for the World Economy*, New York: Harper and Row, 1965, pp. 87-88.

14. Aliber, Robert A. *The Future of the Dollar as an International Currency*, New York: Praeger, 1966, pp. 8 & 14.

15. Triffin, *Gold and the Dollar Crisis*, p. 89.

GENERAL GEORGE C. MARSHALL

General George C. Marshall was neither an economist nor a politician. Yet his actions made indelible marks on 20th century politics and economy. Marshall is best known for the Marshall Plan and the Colombo Plan that he implemented for the reconstruction of Europe and the economic development of emerging Asiatic nations. The plan was originally suggested by Secretary of State Dean Acheson on May 8, 1947. This idea of reconstruction took better shape and was finally launched under Secretary Marshall. The program needed a lot of speeches and conferences on the part of Marshall, in order to be finally authorized by the Congress.

Marshall was a professional soldier for 45 years. His career began in 1900 when he was commissioned a second lieutenant and culminated with his appointment as chief of staff in 1939. The chief of staff is second only to the president and the secretary of defense. Marshall was in charge of all United States military establishments. Peace conferences were initiated even before the complete termination of World War II, and Marshall accompanied President Roosevelt and President Truman on some of their peace missions. Marshall was supposed to give advice only on military matters, yet many political decisions were made in consultation with him.

In 1945 he was back in the Pentagon for a more peaceful and leisurely life. That peace and leisure never came. Patrick Hurley resigned as ambassador to China, and Truman appointed Marshall to replace him. Before the end of a year as ambassador, Truman called Marshall to accept the onerous job of secretary of state. Marshall accepted the job with a categoric statement about his party relationship: "I'm assuming that the office of the Secretary of State, at least under present conditions, is nonpolitical and I will govern myself accordingly."[1]

Marshall had seen with his own eyes the destruction of the war in Europe, and he had attended peace conferences with Roosevelt and Truman. Besides matters of military administration, Marshall voiced his opinion about the cleanup job left after the ravages of war were over. Since the United States was the only nation capable at that time of doing something constructive to rebuild Europe, Marshall felt that reconstruction works should be initiated by the United States. The experience after Versailles in 1918 was in the minds of all who gathered for the peace mission after World War II. When called to be secretary of state, Marshall had this idea of reconstruction foremost in his mind, and when the red tape unraveled too slowly, he complained, "The patient is sinking, when the doctors deliberate."[2]

The destruction of World War II was far more extensive than that of World War I. Europe lost fertile farms under heavy bombardment. Factories were wiped out during the destruction of cities and towns, and the sources of raw materials and power necessary for industries were reduced to almost nothing. In 1947, to make things worse, the winter in Europe was particularly severe. Food, shelter, and clothing were limited. The United States came forward to save Europe from starvation and disease. Marshall's first job was to recruit world aid to meet the challenge in Europe. Fuel, power, food, and clothing were supplied to save the suffering. But an occasional shot would not effect a permanent cure. The idea of reestablishing Europe's industry became the subject of a world dialogue.

Russia found the time apropos and initiated a policy of extending its domination over the free nations of Europe. The United States Government felt it was obligated to help the free nations defend themselves from the incursions of Russia. It also felt that the vast increase in industrial output required a market to keep up the production under peacetime planning. Europe was a potential market for America, but Europe could not buy from the United States since foreign exchange was depleted to zero in most major nations of Europe. It was necessary to think of reestablishing some sort of political stability and economic independence in Europe. The only practical method was by extending outright financial aid and possibly long-term credit to Europe so that the painful process of rebuilding could be undertaken. George Marshall came up with the European Recovery Program in hopes of achieving "the revival of a working economy in the world, so as to permit the emergence of political and social conditions in which the new institutions might exist."[3]

The new policy set by Marshall demanded that the countries of

Europe should accept voluntary limitations on political, economic, and military growth. It even seemed that some countries, wherever possible, should have military cooperation with erstwhile enemies. It was almost focused on the creation of a United States of Western Europe.

After Marshall made his plan well-known, he called a conference of Western European powers in Paris to "take an inventory of European nations." Each nation was supposed to present a plan for its own growth. They were expected to analyze the maladjustments of people, industry, and commerce caused by war and collectively to find a solution.

The Marshall Plan was intended to achieve the following results:

1. The restoration of the prewar level of bread, grain, and other cereal production;
2. A higher than prewar level of production of sugar and potatoes, some increase in oil products, and a fast expansion of dairy production;
3. An increase of coal output to 584 million tons;
4. The expansion of electric output by 70 million kilowatts;
5. Development of oil refining capacity;
6. An increase in crude iron production;
7. An increase in inland transport; and
8. Restoration of prewar merchant ships.

Most of the capital equipment needed for this expansion would be manufactured right in Europe with technical and material aid from the United States. The cost of the entire plan was computed as 22 billion dollars, and the United States government would contribute 20 billion. The breakdown of the plan set aside, "8.04 billion in 1948; 7.35 billion for '49; 4.65 billion in 1950; and 3.40 billion in 1951."[4]

What did the United States expect from Europe for the help it was rendering? The expected return was not in direct financial payments. It was expected that the strength of Europe would become the strength of the United States. Against the growing power of Russia, Europe would stand as a bulwark in protecting the internal security of the United States. Europe was helpless after the war. It could go to Russia or the United States for help. If Russia gave the help, that would mean a certain type of economic imperialism of Russia over Europe. If the world islands of Asia and Europe fell into the hands of Russia, then the balance of power of the world would be in disorder and world dominance of communism would be possible. This is what Marshall wanted to avert. Russia was invited to share in the Marshall

Plan by contributing something toward the two billion dollars needed to complete the plan, but she, perhaps wisely, declined. Russia was primarily interested in territorial expansion. By the military coup in Czechoslovakia in 1948, Russia was able to annex that independent nation. The increasing menace of Russia in Europe prompted the American people and the Congress to underwrite the plan and allot the necessary funds.

The plan demanded that the countries receiving aid should work wholeheartedly to improve their economic conditions. If possible these countries should work as a group in fostering industry and commerce. To cut down domestic expenses, they were supposed to have a combined military power, instead of a separate one for each. Moreover the restraints to free trade like tariffs and customs were to be abolished to enhance the participating nations' interstate commerce. This idea became the basis of the Coal and Steel Union, which later became the European Common Market.

Italy was one of the hardest hit nations among the war-torn countries of Europe, and she was slow in entering into the Marshall Plan. But the timely aid given to Italy in 1948 avoided the possibility of a communist takeover in Italy. "With 300,000 members, the Italian Communist Party was probably the largest European group outside of Russia. The Party dominated the unions and had gained ground among the impoverished tenant farmers."[5]

The election was a highly contested one. In fact, it was an election in which the Italian nationals of the United States took an active part. They wrote millions of letters to their relatives at home asking them not to vote for the Communist Party. Marshall warned that if Italy voted in a communist government, that government would be denied any help from the Marshall Plan. The Italian Christian Democrats and the Roman Catholic church entered into an alliance to defeat the Communist Party. Faced with such odds, the Party didn't have a chance.

After the election of 1948, the Marshall Plan lavished every form of help that could build Italy into a self-sufficient nation. Southern Italy needed emmigration as a way of keeping the economy in balance. The plan helped Italians to move to Australia, New Zealand, South America, Canada, and the United States. Italy was the first nation to publicly acknowledge President Eisenhower's call for men to defend Western Europe and was also very cooperative in the Schuman Plan. Italy was used to dictatorship. The greatest achievement of the plan was to indoctrinate the people in a democratic form of government. With democracy as the guiding light, the free enterprise system became more active. The industrial output rose, giving jobs and purchasing power to the Italian people, and the Italian currency became healthy.

The crowning glory of the Marshall Plan was the gradual development of the European Common Market. The Luxemburg Coal and Steel Union between Belgium, Luxemburg, and the Netherlands accepted three influential partners in the Rome convention of 1950. Italy, Germany, and France joined the union and the name was changed to the European Common Market. They agreed among themselves about abolishing the customs and tariffs. The greatest benefit was the freedom of movement for labor and capital among the participating nations. The growth of the Common Market was almost miraculous. Europe under the Common Market built some of the most industrial nations of the world. There are seven other nations desiring to join the Common Market, which, if admitted, will realize Marshall's dream, the creation of the United States of Europe. The Marshall Plan showed the best result in Italy. Italy had some basic resources for growth: (1) workers for her large and numerous industrial plants; (2) farmers able to increase the food supply in Italy to feed all Western Europe; and (3) an exportable surplus of manpower to aid other Western European nations faced with a shortage of manpower. The opening of the Common Market gave room for domestic and foreign industrial growth with the wealth of population Italy enjoyed.

With Italy's help, the Marshall Plan enabled the people of Europe to be better fed and to enjoy a higher standard of living. The Marshall Plan was not all money aid. It gave the up-to-date machines and well-trained technicians to initiate the industrial revolution of the postwar era. Economically and politically Europe and the United States became closer because of the Marshall Plan.

Footnotes

1. Graebner, Norman. *An Uncertain Tradition*, New York: McGraw-Hill, 1961, p. 246.

2. Ibid., p. 253.

3. Dean, Vera Michaelis. *Europe and the United States*, New York: Alfred Knopf, 1950, p. 249.

4. Brown, G. Stewart. *Great Issues*, New York: Harper & Bros., 1951, pp. 128-29.

5. Ibid., p. 391.

PAUL SAMUELSON

Paul Anthony Samuelson was born on May 15, 1915, in Gary, Indiana. He attended Hyde Park High School, University of Chicago, (B.A., 1935), and Harvard University, (M.A., 1937, Ph.D. 1941). His classic work, *Foundations of Economic Analysis* was written when he was a graduate student at Harvard. This book was finally published in 1947 to the dismay of the majority of economists who did not have an average grasp of mathematics.

During World War II, Samuelson left the halls of learning to take a job at the MIT Radiation Laboratory where he helped in computer tracking aircraft. He had regrets for those years at the laboratory, only because he missed his field of predilection, economics. In 1941, Harvard awarded Samuelson the coveted David A. Well's prize for the mathematical restructuring of economics he did in his work, *Foundations*.[1]

Samuelson is a born writer. His very erudite articles were read all over the world by 1945. His criticism of New Deal Economics, especially the idea of pump-priming as a cure for economic ills was totally original thinking and a challenge to the well-established teachings of Joseph Schumpeter. In another article, he brought out the incompleteness of Keynesian dynamic economics and brought out his own theory to explain the frustrations of dynamic economics. Samuelson wrote about the accepted principles of saving, consumption, investment, interest, rent, and similar elementary notions of economics in his own version. He found that the interdependence of these functions creates downward or upward business fluctuations causing recession or recovery.

Samuelson taught international economics at Fletcher School of Law and Diplomacy in 1945. In 1947, he was invited to MIT to serve as full professor of economics. During 1948-49, he lectured in

Europe under a Ford Foundation grant. This was a golden opportunity to meet the great economists of Europe, but more than that, the European economists had a first hand look at an American economist. The Guggenheim fellowship that took Samuelson to Europe paved the way for the universal adoption of the textbook he published in 1949. *Economics—An Introductory Analysis* was a book for which the world at large was looking. Marshall's *Principles of Economics* was widely used until Samuelson published his textbook. There were phenomenal changes after Marshall, especially the great depression, World War II, and the prosperity after the war. Keynes and Schumpeter wrote extensively in the line of neo-classical economics, and Pigou and Clark taught the welfare economics of Marshall. The academic world needed another base from which to launch their theories, and Samuelson came up with the answer. No wonder that the *Economics* sold over two million copies in the English version and over another million copies in translations.[2]

Young professors in economics at that time were all Keynesians. Samuelson admired Lord Maynard Keynes from the time he studied with Alvin Hansen, who was one of the greatest exponents of Keynesianism. *Economics* was just what these professors were searching for. Samuelson's analysis of national income, fiscal policy, full employment without inflation, labor legislation, functions of money and credit, and factors of economic growth, to mention a few, were almost memorized by these teachers of economics. The old idea, "thrift is a virtue," was thrown out into the gutter; the idea that prices and wages would reach an equilibrium, if the government, unions, and industry kept their hands off, was not an easy dogma to reject. Protests against the book mounted daily, but more and more universities and colleges adopted it. Today almost 40 percent of colleges in the United States use Samuelson's *Economics*.

Samuelson is not a man for only writing books and articles. He was the man behind President Kennedy during his election campaign and later in his New Frontier economic and political plannings. Samuelson wrote to the president elect in the official report, supporting a tax reduction of two to three percent to revitalize the sluggish economy. He did not believe in the New Deal fiscal policy of creating jobs as a temporary measure. The jobs under the New Deal did not carry the essential feature of continuity. The tax reduction he proposed would primarily benefit business, which in turn would reinvest that amount opening new jobs that would be permanent. Labor called the report, "a well prepared and thoughtful report." Later, however, the AFL-CIO thought Samuelson's program would be inadequate to create the number of jobs essential to lift the economy up and presented their own recommendations to the president. A controversy ensued and surprisingly Samuelson replied with only one statement, "It is just as important to know what not to do, as to know what to do."[3]

When in 1965, President Johnson went on an austerity measure of his own, cutting into half the government deficit spending, Samuelson gave a warning to the nation that "almost one-half million new jobs could not develop." Time has proved the veracity of Samuelson's prophecy. In 1970 unemployment reached almost six percent. President Johnson appointed Samuelson to head the task force to report on the "Great Society." In his report, Samuelson offered an optimistic view of the economic state for years to come. The New York Times in an interview with Samuelson about the economy wrote, "The big change since the thirties is that we will not sit by and do nothing when a chronic slump is developing."[4]

President Nixon came into power inheriting an unwanted war and an economy that was almost reaching a galloping inflationary state. To fulfill the promises of his election campaign, President Nixon dropped the lid on the cookie jar. Samuelson said, "The President is making a tactical mistake, trying to fight inflation." He thinks that the art of economic politics depends on the ordering of priorities:

1. The highest priority is to restore vigorous growth in the economy.

2. It is false to think that long-term unemployment is an inevitable price of winding up a war economy.

3. The end of war should not permit macroeconomic stagnation to permeate the economy.

One can see that Samuelson does not go along with President Nixon's economic policies in spite of 400 economists advising President Nixon. One can call Samuelson a liberal economist, but Samuelson says, "I am a liberal but not a libertarian."

The second Alfred Nobel Prize was awarded to Samuelson on October 16, 1970. The Swedish Academy of Science said in presenting the award to Professor Samuelson, "Professor Sanuelson's extensive production covering nearly all areas of economic theory is characterized by an outstanding ability to derive important new theorems and find new applications for existing ones. By his contribution, he has done more than any other contemporary economist in economic theory."[5] The Nobel Prize is awarded to one man selected from among the greatest men of the world. In the case of Paul Samuelson, the selection was from a hundred men by a five man committee of Swedish economists. The Nobel Prize is a reward for many years of painstaking study and labor. To Samuelson, some of these years were not that painstaking, since his natural talents found room for exposure naturally. Talking about his *Economics*, he says, "Nobody designed it, it just grew; like human nature it is changing, but it has met the first test of any social organ . . . it survived."[6]

Basic Economic Theories

Samuelson defined economics as the study of how men and society try to choose, with or without the use of money, to employ scarce productive resources to produce various commodities and distribute them for consumption. He thought that the labor theory of value can validly predict prices on the basis of labor-hours involved. He resuscitated the idea of the "invisible hand" offered by Smith. As a believer in the free enterprise system, he depends on the invisible hand to determine what to produce, when to produce, and for whom to produce.

Samuelson affirmed the net national product as a dollar flow for the total product of a nation. The net national product (NNP) plus depreciation becomes the gross national product (GNP). Depreciation is an item that is hard to measure and so he recommended that the national income analysis should base the study on GNP, instead of NNP. All these theories should be credited to Keynes. Samuelson is only a reviewer of Keynes' theories. As an ardent follower of Keynes he unconsciously fulfilled or complemented Keynesian economics by paraphrasing the theories.

In the analysis of monetary policies, Samuelson introduced reserve requirements, rediscount rate, and open market operations as effective means of monetary stabilization. Technological innovations are means of keeping a full employment economy. Government spending according to Samuelson, does not have to emphasize military spending as the prime area of concentration. He recommends alternative areas like education, welfare, housing, urban renewal, pollution control, and the space explorations. These additional programs can re-place those who are unemployed due to the reduction of defense spending. When private investment and consumption spending create an inflationary or deflationary gap, it is the task of the fiscal and monetary policy to offset the gap to safeguard price stability, high employment, and growth.

The question of balanced budget was and will be an enigma for many economists. There are reputable economists on both sides condemning, condoning, or recommending the practice. Samuelson spoke about this:

With demand so brisk as to lead much of the time to inflationary gaps then active fiscal policy will probably mean a bias toward surplus financing and a secular downward trend in the public debt. Perhaps the majority of economists feel there is no need to try to predict what the distant future has in store, being prepared to advocate programs that the developing situation calls for.[7]

The public debt should not burden each citizen like his private debt. Imagine the year when the GNP will rise to many trillions; normally one fifth of the GNP would be the revenue of the federal government, to make a very conservative estimate. Today a national debt burden of 435 billion seems to be a millstone around the neck of 212 million people. Given time, the national debt can be a trifle, only in view of the potential growth of this great nation. Looking at the same situation, who knows whether greater demands of expanding population and expanding economy will so spiral deficit spending that the nation becomes unable to liquidate its insolvency.

Dealing with agriculture and its problems, Samuelson gives an alarming picture of the exodus of population from the farms to the cities. The birth rate of the rural population is greater than that of the city. Hence a certain number of people will continue to move into the cities. But the decline in agriculture can grow into a national problem, if it fails to produce enough to support the entire nation. The government has to step in to keep the price of farm products high enough to encourage people to accept agriculture as a mode of life. He discusses the possibility of bringing farm income parallel to industrial income. There are two ways of doing it: (1) by farm support, so that prices of farm goods remain within the reach of the rich and the poor; and (2) by leaving agriculture to the fate of supply and demand, as proposed by Ezra Wilson. The tragedy of the second alternative is that prices may increase beyond the ability of the poor to pay.

During the past quarter century, political, social, and scientific changes have happened beyond the speed of the economist to internalize and suggest adequate remedies. Paul Samuelson is considered one economist who has kept abreast of other disciplines and has come out with salient advice to help his fellow men. That is why he is the foremost economist of the United States and, in fact, the foremost economist of the world. He, himself, defined his position, calling himself "in the age of specialists ... the last generalist in economics."

Footnotes

1. Moritz, Charles. *Current Biography*, New York: Wilson, 1965, p. 357.
2. "Theorist With The Best Seller," *Business Week* 60 (1959).
3. "Economist on Economist," *Newsweek* 63 (1965): 34.
4. *New York Times*, 28 October 1970, pp. 19-20.
5. *New York Times*, 28 October 1970, p. 63.
6. Samuelson, Paul A. *Economics*, New York: McGraw-Hill, 1970, p. 103.
7. Ibid., p. 349.

References

American Men of Science, vol 10, New York, 1960-62.

Coleman, Saunders, Bishop & Samuelson. *Readings in Economics*, N.Y.: McGraw-Hill, 1964.

Facts on File, 1970.

New York Post, 24 February 1961, pp. 87-93.

New York Times, 27, 28, 29, and 30 October 1970.

Samuelson, Paul A. *International Economic Association*, New York: Macmillan, 1963.

Samuelson, Paul A. *Stability and Growth in American Economy*, New York: McGraw-Hill, 1963.

Who's Who In America, Chicago: Marquis, 1964-65.

JOHN KENNETH GALBRAITH

Time magazine describes Galbraith as a "popular economist, a polished diplomat, a veteran lecturer, a fledgling novelist, a former Presidential advisor and a current cynosure of the Eastern intellectual set."[1]

Kenneth Galbraith was born in October 1908 and was raised in a small, rigidly Calvinist immigrant community. He attended Ontario College and later Toronto University where he recieved his undergraduate degree in 1931. The depression was at its ebb, and economics was the universal topic of conversation. Galbraith joined the University of California for his graduate studies, and received a Ph.D. in Agricultural Economics in 1934. He immediately took a job as instructor and tutor at Harvard University. Shortly afterwards he became an American citizen.

While Galbraith was tutoring at Harvard's Winthorp House, he became a close friend of Joseph Kennedy, Jr. and John Kennedy, who joined Winthrop House a few years later. He also met and married Catherine Atwater, a literature student at Radcliff.

Galbraith and Catherine left Harvard the day after their marriage to join Cambridge University in England, where Lord Maynard Keynes was the master of economics. Unfortunately, he suffered his first heart attack the day Galbraith joined Cambridge, so Galbraith missed the opportunity to study with the great master. While at Cambridge, however, he internalized the Keynesian approach to economics.

After his return to Cambridge, Galbraith was appointed assistant director of the Office of Price Administration in 1941. As *Time* puts it, "his zealous, but irritating performance" in this government job came to an end in 1943. The government asked him later in 1945 to study the effectiveness of bombing in Germany and Japan. After

215

World War II, Galbraith was appointed advisor to the occupied countries. In an interview given to the *Playboy* magazine, Galbraith reminisced about the need for air superiority during the war.

It was very important in Europe in World War II that we had control of the air over the battlefields. But the real battles were fought on the ground. On the whole, Air Force claims about the success of strategic air attacks—strategic bombing, in particular—have been vastly exaggerated. I was one of the group set up by Secretary Stimson to appraise the accomplishments of the Air Force after World War II. The strategic air attacks, we learned were far less than expectations. This was especially true in Germany. For example, we attacked all the German Airplane plants in late February 1944. The plants were all hit, but German aircraft production increased that February—the very month of the bombing—by a substantial percentage.[2]

From 1949 on, Galbraith was a professor at Harvard in name only. He was intermittently called on by the government to take over responsible studies. Galbraith, the students say, is only an average teacher and he spends at least four hours a day writing.

Galbraith was one of John Kennedy's earliest supporters and later wrote many speeches for him. Kennedy borrowed Galbraith's lines, "let us never negotiate out of fear, but let us never fear to negotiate," in his inaugural speech. President Kennedy appointed him ambassador to India. While Galbraith was in India, Kennedy asked his opinion of the Vietnam involvement. Galbraith predicted that it would be the biggest mistake of the 60s.

Galbraith's Works

Galbraith's most popular work is *The Affluent Society*. It is not usual to make an economic writing into a best seller, but Galbraith wrote economic principles in everyday style that people in the street enjoyed reading. In the chapter on "Conventional Wisdom," he repeats his criticism of established thought. The economics of the past was intended to fight poverty. Even today many nations struggle under poverty and the main theme of such societies will be "Developmental Economics." But the nations of Western Europe, the United States, and Canada have overcome poverty, and a new type of economics is needed to deal with the conditions of these nations. This should be the work of modern economists. They have to come up with economic principles to administer prosperity and opulence so that the distribution of wealth and continuation of prosperity can be guaranteed to last. Galbraith calls the conservative thinkers, people of conventional wisdom. Galbraith himself is a liberal, yet he says that the ideas of the liberals first have to stand the test of conservatives. Only good ideas would be eventually accepted into practice. According to Galbraith, even a liberal idea put into practice becomes a conservative idea. "He (conservative) can think of himself with justice as socially elect, for society in fact accords him the applause which his ideas are arranged to evoke."[3]

The Great Crash is an analysis of the causes of the great depression of the 30s and an indictment of the economists of the time. He blamed the crash on "established thoughts." He thinks that all economists recognized the fast-approaching depression, but nobody dared to change the traditional economic thinking to avert it. The United States was going through normal prosperity in 1918, and economists and politicians thought that prosperity was self-generating and would not take a downward trend. Galbraith accuses the people of the time of speaking against their own convictions. When everything was fundamentally wrong, the spokesmen of the time said loudly that everything was basically sound. Galbraith thinks that such deceits are worse than communism.

The Liberal Hour is a compilation of the many lectures he gave at Grinnel College in Iowa. He discusses many major menaces that haunt our present day economy. He delves into the causes of the economic disorder. He thinks that the United States has taken a competing attitude toward the Soviet Union and because of that the national goals are limited to economic and military superiority over the world. There are many other finer goals of life that are forgotten in the wholesale attempt to advance financial and military goals. The arts and aesthetics are totally ignored in this rivalry with Russia. The economic and military gains are only transient glories whereas the achievements in arts and aesthetics are eternal contributions to humanity. Galbraith says, "It is possible that our greatest danger, in these days of massive introspection, is from our terrible solemnity. For this is a serious source of inflexibility." He thinks that there should be ways to negotiate with Russia so that our national goals can be revised and pursued.[4]

The New Industrial State was written in 1967. In this work he draws an interesting picture of the modern economic structure. The basis of Galbraith's industrial state is a thoroughly planned economy. He thinks of government as an auxiliary that produces what industry does not care to produce and performs tasks in which industry has no interest. Conflict between business and government would not take place in this planned society and modern classical capitalism with government interventions to protect the interest of all would also disappear in this utopian society. "No Ford executives will ever fight Washington."[5]

Among Galbraith's minor works the leading ones are *American Capitalism: The Concept of Countervailing Power, Economic Development, Resources for the Future, How to Get Out of Viet Nam, A Workable Solution to the Worst Problem of Our Time,* and his own biography, *The Scotch*. His articles written for the leading magazines and papers are too numerous to mention. Once his secretary gave an account of his works, "His works since 1959 consisted of eight books, thirty-two articles, fifty-four book reviews and thirty-five letters to the editor."

The Production Function

Galbraith wrote,

Production remains central to our thoughts . . . it continues to measure the quality and progress of our civilization . . . it has become central to our strivings to reduce insecurity . . . its importance has been buttressed by a highly dubious but equally accepted psychology of want . . . by an equally dubious but equally accepted interpretation of national interest and by powerful vested interest . . . ."[6]

There is tension between rich and poor, teacher and student, employer and employee, and even between doctor and patient. Production in the capitalist system is geared to bridge the inequalities between those who have and those who do not. Insecurity is another reason why the production function receives so much attention. Production is the only way to create full employment economy. Production covers up or maintains the social status. This overemphasis on production has created what Galbraith calls "dependence effect." Is welfare greater at a lower level of production or at a higher level of production? No one knows. If want is the basis of welfare, then at the higher level of production the system enjoys a higher level of welfare.

Economists have glorified the Industrial Revolution for over 200 years. The world has seen great progress in the economic fields due to the industrial revolution. The technology has rendered greater ease in mass production. The reason for cyclical fluctuations is the inability to consume the mass of products rolled out from the mills. This underconsumption leads us to think in another direction now. The industrial revolution has come to the point of diminishing returns. What the world needs today is a distribution revolution or, in other words, a consumption revolution that would operate side by side with industrial revolution. Galbraith pleaded for a deemphasis of the production function. Why not emphasize distribution revolution together with production rather than deemphasizing production?

Technology

Technology is the dominant factor of the new industrial society. Technology has been made extremely costly so that only a few big entrepreneurs can think of using it. This situation cuts off the competition through new products or substitute products. In order to eliminate competition, the technocrats have set the minimum possible price for the goods and services offered in the market. They virtually dictate demand through high-pressure advertising.

Galbraith thinks that the big businesses of the industrial society emancipated themselves from the classical models of supply and demand and also from the chancetaking of the market economy. Big business has excluded the owners from any major decisionmaking through the corporate form of ownership. The millions of owners are strewn all over the world, unable to have any effect on the administration of the industries or firms. The individual stockholder is a passive, functionless figure. By the use of retained earnings, sales of bonds, and accumulation of welfare funds, these corporations are able to keep the bankers at bay. If the corporations are unable to finance themselves, then the state moves in with subsidies and outright grants. The state can find in these businesses elements of public service and permit accelerated depreciation and other technical manipulations of the tax laws to keep the firm in operation. The state also provides a demand for the more risky types of technology such as warheads built at the expense of billions of dollars only to be grounded forever. Galbraith describes a society that is totally artificial and unrealistic. The industrial growth of modern technology carries its own elements of self-destruction. One erratic phase is covered by another that is equally erratic. *The New Industrial State* is a condemnation of the technocracy of today. He thinks, "the present system puts too much emphasis on goods—washing machines, cars, gadgets—and not enough on beauty and man's search for higher values."[7] In 1968 he wrote *The Triumph*, an analysis of administration and the cost of administering. In the book he describes a fictional state department, a foreign service, and a certain Caribbean island in a state of revolution. It is a satire, but he is really laughing at the United States and its approach to the challenge. Galbraith had his grievances against the State Department from the time Franklin

Roosevelt appointed him director of price administration in the 40s. He had to go through congressional investigation time after time, until he gave up that position. During his tenure as ambassador to India, he locked horns with Secretary of State Dean Rusk to the point of undignified epithets. Besides his personal feelings toward the State Department, he saw the tardiness of action and immense waste of time and money in the operation of this machinery. As *Time* evaluated the situation, "the all-purpose critic shows his fangs."

Conclusion

In an age of specialists, John Kenneth Galbraith cannot be enthroned in a special niche. Galbraith states that he is only a writer about economics or politics, not an economist or politician. He does not think he deserves to be called a professor even though he taught for many years. He was in positions of diplomacy but he does not consider himself a diplomat. But his writing makes him economist, politician, professor, and diplomat. The current generation of Americans learned its economic and social thinking from Galbraith. He translated incomprehensible economic ideas into best sellers. As a diplomat he advised presidents from Franklin Roosevelt to Lyndon Johnson. As an ambassador to India, he made India the focal point of the world's attention and interest. As a Harvard professor, he made connections with the leading men of America, in business, in administration, and in education.

It is not easy to make a comprehensive study of all of Galbraith's works. It should be remembered, however, that a study of Galbraith is a study not only of economics, but also of literature, history, politics, and business. As *Time* has said, "There are those, in fact who believe that while John Maynard Keynes was the Darwin of modern economics, Galbraith someday will be considered the Huxley."[8]

Footnotes

1. "The Great Mogul," *Time*, 16 February 1968, p. 24.
2. "John Kenneth Galbraith—Interview," *Playboy*, June 1968, p. 171.
3. Galbraith, John Kenneth. *The Affluent Society*, Boston: Houghton Mifflin, 1958, p. 26.
4. Galbraith, John Kenneth. *The Liberal Hour*, Boston: Houghton Mifflin, 1960, p. 1.
5. "Burying Free Enterprise," *Time*, 6 January 1967, p. 92.
6. Galbraith, John Kenneth. *The Affluent Society*, New York: New American Library, 1957, p. 103.

7. Galbraith, John Kenneth. *The New Industrial State*, Boston: Houghton Mifflin, 1967, p. 92.

8. "The Great Mogul," op. cit., p. 25.

References

Galbraith, John K. *American Capitalism: The Theory of Countervailing Forces*, Boston: Houghton Mifflin, 1956.

Oser, Jacob. *The Evolution of Economic Thought*, New York: Harcourt, Brace & World, 1970.

MILTON FRIEDMAN

Milton Friedman was born in Brooklyn on July 31, 1912. He attended Rutgers, Chicago, and Columbia Universities. He joined the faculty of Chicago University in 1946 and in 1962 became Paul Snowden Russell Professor of Economics. Meanwhile, he has been associated with the United States Natural Resource Committee and the Treasury Department. He was also the advisor to Barry Goldwater during his presidential campaign and later to President Richard Nixon during his successful campaign in 1968.

Friedman openly differed with Keynesian economics. His basic disagreement concerns the government's role in a market economy. He thinks that government intervention is always economically and socially harmful. He thinks that a free democratic state is the outcome of laissez-faire. In his work, *Capitalism and Freedom* he says,

Historical evidence speaks with a single voice on the relation between political freedom and a free market. I know of no example in time or place of a society that has been marked by a large measure of political freedom, and that has not also used something comparable to a free market to organize the bulk of economic activity.[1]

Friedman concurs wtih Adam Smith in his thinking that millions of people cooperate to bring about the national wealth of a free market society.

Friedman has criticized the many reforms the federal government brings into society. He challenged graduated income tax policies as a socialist method of redistributing wealth without explicitly confessing the true intent of tax laws. Housing programs, he says, are initiated by the government not to house people but to reduce juvenile delinquency. Even the social security laws are forcing many

223

people to act against their wills in the name of safeguarding them from hardship after retirement.

Regarding the crucial problems of financing the school system, Friedman made two interesting recommendations: (1) Students should be qualified for the education they are seeking; and (2) students should be willing to pay for their education, " . . . either currently or out of the subsequent higher income that the schooling will make possible."

Friedman recommends negative income tax as a good remedy for the shortcomings of the present welfare system. The present paradox is that if a person is on welfare, he cannot take part-time work because he would lose the welfare payments and possibly not earn as much as he does on welfare; so people on welfare care less about finding a job. What Friedman recommends is supplementing the total income over and above the earned income to bring the level of the standard of living above the subsistence level. He says, " . . . a negative income tax would permit the elimination of the bulk of our present welfare bureaucracy, give those receiving assistance, greater freedom . . ."[2]

Monetary and Fiscal Framework for Economic Stability

Friedman discusses the living problem of economic stability in an essay in the *American Economic Review*.[3] Any fiscal policy has to face the issues on a short-run basis and on a long-run basis. Friedman accepted the long-run objectives of the fiscal policy. Cyclical fluctuations in economy are like sea storms to a sailor, unwanted and hated. Society would be better off if in some way it could ward off cyclical fluctuations. Friedman thought that cyclical fluctuations could be averted, or the bad consequences of fluctuations could be lessened, if a sound fiscal policy were employed. If the fiscal policy is well-ordered, even speculative mismanagement of money by vested groups cannot inflict lasting bad effects on the economy.

Friedman offers a few suggestions for implementing sound fiscal policy:

1. The government must provide a monetary framework for a competitive order, since the competitive order cannot provide one for itself.

2. This monetary framework should operate under the "rule of law" rather than under the discretionary authority of administrators.

3. While a truly free market in the competitive order would yield far less in equality than currently exists, the community should strive to reduce inequality even further.

These proposals have four main parts:

1. A reform of the monetary and banking system to eliminate both private creation and destruction of money and discretionary control of the quantity of money by the central bank authority. The private creation of money can be restricted by 100-percent reserve requirements. Such a proposal would restrict the lending function of the banks and reduce their revenue drastically. Savings and loan organizations serve the society without multiple credit creation clauses and still prosper as sound monetary systems. The legal reserve, excess reserve, and rediscounting now in operation with the commercial banking system gives power of expansion and contraction of money supply at the discretion of banks. Such a credit system can be pernicious to the economy, despite the supervisory power invested with the central banks. The quantity of money is the most vital element of the economy and that should be completely in the power of central banks and no one else.

2. A policy of determining the volume of government expenditures on goods and services (so defined as to exclude transfer expenditures of all kinds) entirely on the basis of the community's desire, need and willingness to pay for public services. Friedman wants the community to pay for many services now offered by the government completely free or with a token payment. The government should extend many services free when the people are unable to pay, but much waste can be eradicated if the payment clause is attached to them.

3. A predetermined program of transfer expenditures, consisting of a statement of the conditions and terms under which relief and assistance and other transfer payments will be granted. Friedman was thinking of the social security plan. The community should know what it wants and what it is capable of doing. Social security and Medicare came from the government to the people rather than from the people to the government. If social welfare plans are to be initiated by the government at all times, it may become burdensome to many who do not care to participate in the various disbursements.

4. A progressive tax system that places primary reliance on the personal income tax. Friedman recommends the need of collecting taxes at the source of income. There can be delay and waste in going through the collection of tax liability.

This fourfold proposal takes into account automatic stabilizers, such as the government's adaptation of its contribution to the balance of aggregate demand and aggregate supply. Under this proposal the entire government contribution would be financed by tax revenue or the creation of new money, in the form of issuance of non-interest-bearing securities. The domestic stability will determine the aggregate quantity of money. If some sort of rigidity in price is maintained, this would help in the attainment of cyclical stability.

Friedman thinks that the proposed fiscal and monetary framework will provide in depth against changes in aggregate demand. The changes in the quantity of money tend to restore prices to an equilibrium level. The following are some positive proposals to balance the economy:

1. Monetary and fiscal measures are the only appropriate means of controlling inflation. Direct control of prices and wages or quantitative or qualitative control over production will have only limited capability to arrest inflation.

2. A surplus budget will offer security rather than easy money; a balanced budget will tend to make money tight; a deficit budget will create even tighter money.

3. Monetary policy should be directed exclusively toward the prevention of inflation. The Open Market Committee can control inflation by the manipulation of the government securities, selling at the time of inflation and buying when the money becomes tighter. Friedman warns that discretionary open market operation cannot be a permanent instrument of the stabilization policy. He thinks that monetary policy suffers a certain amount of discontinuity. A mild measure is insufficient; extreme measures are too much. It is important to arrive at a safe medium measure to stabilize the economy. Some economists object that monetary policy has some undesirable consequences. The primary area of difficulty arises from the conflict between the private sector and the public sector. Friedman seems to think that a rigid price system can bring together the public and private interests.

An acceptable combination of monetary and fiscal policy would consist of a roughly balanced budget in spite of consumer demands, which cannot be limited by the government. Keynes commented on the inflationary disequilibrium felt after World War I and the government attempts to remedy the situation in this way: "A host of popular remedies vainly attempted to cure the evils of the day; which remedies themselves—subsidies, price and rent fixing, profiteer hunting and excess profit duties—eventually become not the least part of the evils."[4]

Friedman analyzed the role of the International Monetary Fund, in an article in the *Journal of Political Economy*.[5] The IMF has created a rigid exchange rate in the international currency. He thinks that the IMF is not capable of converting a nation's domestic currency into a new medium of currency that can be acceptable to all nations. It is impossible to convert the national currency into gold because of its scarcity. Friedman thinks that introducing an artificial medium, "Commodity Reserve Standard," is an attempt to advance the concept of *symmetallism*. This term was coined by Alfred Marshall when he met with the deficiencies of gold and silver. He thought that if all the gold and silver in the world were fused into an alloy and offered at a greater price than silver and a smaller price than gold, it would serve as the basis of currencies in all nations. This idea of blending gold and silver is called *symmetallism*.

The commodity reserve standard is to establish a value on a market basket, consisting of x units of one product, y units of another product and so on. Symmetallism needs a certain amount of silver and gold. Some countries may not have any silver or gold to show. But all countries have some products that are native to their geographical position. Friedman thinks that if currencies are predicated on the reserve of these market baskets, it would be a legitimate and valuable offering of currency for a nation. As in the United States history of banking, the land banks preceded the specie banks. That system worked because the notes were redeemable in land. If the currency is redeemable in market baskets, it becomes a valuable medium of exchange. The currency may carry the symbol of a warehouse receipt, which assures its convertibility.

Friedman does not ask to repeal all the existing currency. He thinks that this commodity reserve currency can be added to the existing currency system. By doing that, the quantity of money can be expanded, regardless of the gold or silver reserve in the treasury. The commodity reserve currency presupposes one important thing, the inflexibility of price of the commodities. Otherwise during the rising prices of a commodity, the reserve currency would be liquidated by the speculators and a new Gresham's Law would be necessary.

Milton Friedman has written about many aspects of economic life. The task of evaluating him now is superfluous as the 57-year-old writer is still passing through the maturation process. He is constantly reevaluating his economic thinking. Given time, the genius of this economist will reveal itself.

Footnotes

1. Friedman, Milton. *Capitalism and Freedom*, Chicago: University of Chicago Press, 1962, p. 9.

    2. "The Market versus The Bureaucrat," *National Review*, 19 May 1970, p. 525.
    3. Friedman, Milton. "Monetary and fiscal framework for economic stability," *American Economic Review* 38 (June 1948): 245-264.
    4. Keynes, J. M. *Monetary Reform*, New York: Kelley, 1942, p. 30.
    5. Friedman, Milton. "Commodity-reserve currency," *Journal of Political Economy* 59 (June 1951): 203-232.

References

    Encyclopedia Britannica Book Of the Year, 1970.
    "Why does more money mean higher interest?", *Business Week*, 14 October 1967, p. 134.
    "The Great Iconoclast has a shocking answer," *Business Week* 19 July 1969, p. 82.

KENNETH E. BOULDING

Kenneth Boulding, Professor of Economics at the University of Michigan, received B.A. and M.A. degrees from Oxford University, London. He has served as vice-president of the American Economic Association, and currently is president of the Society for General Systems Research and a fellow of both the American and the International Academy of Arts and Science.

Kenneth Boulding received the attention of the public for his ability to apply principles of one discipline effectively to other disciplines. Besides many scholarly essays and speeches, Boulding has published two important books, *Impact of the Social Sciences* and *Economics as a Science.*

Boulding is very effective in bringing down the scientific and complex analyses of social sciences to the grass roots so that even lay readers can internalize the contents without expensive tutelage. He writes, "Social systems consist of all human beings on the planet and all their interrelationships, such as kinship, friendship, hostility, status, exchange, money flows, conversation, information, outputs and inputs and so on."[1]

Boulding believes that the knowledge man has gained over his environment is the secret of his success. Man has come to understand more about the world and himself in the last 200 years than in all the time since creation. Boulding groups knowledge in three distinct periods:

1. Folk knowledge is the knowledge we receive without overt learning, like the ideas we pick up from family and friends. It is not gained by conscious effort but given inadvertently by the society in which one is born and reared.

2. Literary knowledge deals with information that is recorded. It helps knowledge to be perpetuated rather than destroyed after the

229

death of a generation. In other words, it is history, the systematic recording of man's actions. There is always a possibility of error in these chronicles, since writing or recording cannot be separated from the presumptions and prejudices of the chronicler.

3. Scientific knowledge is a systematic body of knowledge or conclusions deduced from certain and evident principles. It is the scientific knowledge that flourished during the last 200 years and gave men more understanding of self and the universe. In fact, economic growth is the result of the intellectual growth of man.

Economics came under the category of a science when it was put in the form of theoretical models from which people can infer probable conclusions. The quantity of proven data available tends to help an economist in predicting the future of the economy with less room for error. Ricardo and Malthus did not have the empirical data to prove their points conclusively. Boulding cannot accept physiocrats and mercantilitsts as scientists, since they were operating on the natural wisdom of the times. Yet Boulding has a deep appreciation of Smith, Ricardo, and Malthus who opened a track for their students to investigate. Marx, according to Boulding, has two distinct styles of eminence, the positive and the negative. Marx in some way aroused the stagnant societies to a broad awakening, but, at the same time, the human sufferings visited on humanity by class war are extremely costly.

Boulding sees the post World War II era as the real theater of economic growth. The intermittent depressions that used to ravage nations have been brought under control; the economic failures that used to haunt industrialization have been checked; and the political instabilities that used to rewrite totally the destinies of nations have been mitigated.

Boulding finds simultaneous operation of static and dynamic phenomena in the social systems. Economics is a part of the exchange system visible in the society. Trade of goods, services, wages, labor, interest, rent, and similar human activities are part of the exchange system.

Economics is also an ecological science. Ecology is a term to describe a total system of interrelated populations of different species. Boulding believes that ecosystem is nothing other than ecology. Everything is interdependent; the equilibrium of diverse forces both acting independently and interdependently produce the universal harmony. He describes equilibrium as a state in which the species find themselves neither growing nor decreasing in relation to the size of all other species. Ecological equilibrium can never exist since equilibirum for specific species is not linear. Boulding suggests a few arguments to substantiate his premises:

1. In the first case the species live in mutual competition. The increase of one species has to decrease the other species, as in the case of lions and tigers. If the lion becomes the king of the jungle, then the number of tigers will have to decrease and vice versa.

2. Mutual cooperation is possible when two species complement each other like bees and clover. With more bees, pollination operates better; with more clover, the bees will have plenty to eat. In business, there is a dictum, "business is business's friend." If equilibrium occurs between man and his artifacts, then all parties benefit from the affinity.

3. It can also happen that one species is beneficial to another while the other can be detrimental to the former. Boulding suggests the example of fleas and dogs. The more dogs there are, the more fleas there will be, but in the long run, the more fleas there are, the less dogs there will be. There can be measures by which this conflicting phenomenon can be kept in equilibrium if there is a third agency that has power over the fleas and dogs. The profit maximization of the entrepreneurs, the excessive wage demands of the unions, and the desire for total inertia of the moneyed classes can be brought into equilibrium if the government steps in to enforce certain minimum norms.

Boulding made some analysis of equilibrium level of population. He considers pollution a by-product of population. Man uses the biological profit system by exhausting the natural resources. When natural resources have been cycled through the mill, what remains is the polluted reservoirs. Boulding is admonishing the profit seeker to recycle the polluted reservoirs back into a productive factor. Boulding does not accept the GNP as the measurement of progress since it does not expressly show the amount of pollution in air and water, nor the rate of depletion of natural resources during the process of creating the GNP.

Boulding identifies two rates of progress happening in the world, group A and group B. The countries located in the temperate zone, bearing one third of the world population belong to group A. These are the economically self-sufficient people of the world. Group B consists of underdeveloped nations with a lower growth rate. He thinks that the growth rate of Group A is already on the verge of diminishing return while that of Group B is on consistently increasing return. In the long run these two groups would merge into a single group with identical economic conditions. Boulding does not follow the prediction of Joseph Schumpeter that capitalism carries with it the germs of its own destruction; his ideas more closely resemble the Ricardian prophecy of diminishing returns.

The merger of group A and B is not the creation of an ideal world democracy. It is the period of secular stagnation. There will be no more resources and the world will be filled with the garbage of polluted reservoirs! Boulding believes the human race must come up with newer technology based on recycling raw materials and factors of production. He thinks that the village economy survived for centuries because there was constant recycling, and therefore the time has come for man to revert back to the primitive system with a flair for the new.

Footnotes

1. Boulding, Kenneth. *The Impact of the Social Sciences*, New Jersey: Rutgers University Press, 1966, p. 3.

References

Boulding, Kenneth. *Economics as a Science*, New York: McGraw-Hill, 1970.

MICHAEL HARRINGTON

Michael Harrington was born in St. Louis in 1928, the son of a patent attorney. In 1947 Holy Cross College awarded him his B.A. degree, and the University of Chicago gave him an M.A. in 1949. In between he attended Yale Law School, but he did not complete the works toward a law degree.

Harrington spent his early life as a social worker in St. Louis. His writing ability developed during college made him a reporter for many papers, in particular the *Catholic Worker*. His life as a social worker brought him very close to the real life of many underprivileged people of America. This knowledge became the background of the message contained in his best seller, *The Other America*. Harrington spent some time as the secretary of the Workers' Defense League and editor of *New America*.

As a social worker, he became the champion of the poor and the destitute, and disillusioned by the apathy of the American people, he turned to socialism as an effective way of insuring distributive justice. Twice he was the delegate from the United States to the International Union of Socialist Youth; Chairman of the League of Industrial Democracy; and a recipient of the George Polk award and the Riordan award from the Washington, D.C., Newspaper Guild.

Harrington's works are: *Labor in Free Society, The Other America, The Retail Clerks, The Drive Against Illiteracy, The Accidental Century, The Poor in Our Affluent Society,* and *Conference on Poverty in Plenty*. He is a regular contributor to the national periodicals and magazines, like *The New Republic, Commentary, Harper's, Atlantic Monthly, The Nation, Commonweal, Reporter* and many others.

Michael Harrington believes that the structure of capitalism and its prime goal, profit maximization, are the root causes of the social ills of the world. Harrington blames capitalism for the existence of big nations and small nations, poor people and rich people, and developed nations and underdeveloped nations.

Harrington thinks that the American people are beset with a mental psyche he calls, *traditional optimism*. He thinks that the people implicitly believe that every issue they face will work out. He fears also that the Americans have lost their innovative thrust. There are many problems in the United States to be resolved, like poverty, urban blight, racial hostility, inadequate education, and a rising crime rate. Harrington believes that the people are not doing enough to remedy these maladies, but rest peacefully in the belief that "these too will pass." *Toward a Democratic Left* is a recent book of Harrington, in which he expresses love and hate for this country. He loves his country because he realizes its tremendous potentials for good; he hates it because of the people who are still unwilling to change and remedy its inadequacies.

The New System

A critic who does not offer an alternative solution is not worth his salt. Harrington has an alternative solution, "The New System." He is calling for a system that has more social awareness than the present one. He wants capitalism to rewrite its goals. At present, it is operating on mere pragmatic economics—the most units in the shortest time and at the least cost, yielding the highest profit. The goal of the new system would be to educate the people away form the profit-motive.

Cooperative Ethic

The United States attained its greatness, operating on the competitive nature of capitalism. The competition that built the United States has been emulated by other nations that believed it to be the secret of success. These other nations find that the system that worked for the United States is not working for them, nor is it the most desirable tool to achieve progress. They identify only crude selfishness in the competitive package the United States tried to sell to other nations. Harrington thinks that the mistake of trying to force other nations to accept our system is the fundamental reason foreigners turn against the United States.

Harrington offers the cooperative ethic as a substitute for competition. He thinks that every effort the United States has made to improve the conditions of other nations has had a sinister string attached and has tended to promote war. Nothing has been done to relieve the poverty of the people or improve the sociocultural aspects of human growth.

Harrington challenges the profit motive involved in everything capitalism touches. Can money be spent without ulterior motives of self-benefit? That is what he proposes. He suggests a massive program of social investment out of which would emerge real solutions for the many ills that are encountered. He finds much waste in the present federal poverty program. These programs are tied to the bureaucratic interests rather than the welfare of the people, and little of the money allocated will ever filter down to the grass roots of the poor people. According to Harrington, only a socialist approach can effectively resolve the problems that the United States is trying to resolve in a democratic way. The replacement of this system with socialism is more important than really finding a shortcut in the same democratic dead end plans.

What Is Ahead?

Harrington finds that the future of the United States is well laid out for gradual socialization of the political system. He proposes that a government's primary task is to unify its people. Pride in the unification of all nationalities was a basic tenet in the founding of this country. But it has grown up just enough for the people to have a second look at themselves and find that they are not blended inseparably together. The parochial mentality is very much visible in the way America is crumbling into distinct pieces. There are blocks of young versus old, rich versus poor, white versus black, oriental versus occidental, employers versus employees, students versus teachers, and vested interests against vested interests. Harrington believes the people must be united with an intellectual tie, and he wants the effort toward unity to be first on the nation's agenda.

America is founded on the Judeo-Christian heritage. Harrington believes these grand ideals have lost their flavor and have become irrelevant in the everyday life of the people. The second important function for the United States, therefore, is to revitalize the great ideals effaced from the hearts of American people. If this cannot be done he suggests we give up the epithet of Jew or Christian and be true to ourselves as human beings. It is questionable, of course, whether the Judeo-Christian ideals really have lost their flavor for the majority of people.

As a third point, Harrington seems to be afraid that the present system will not collapse soon enough. There are two ways of looking at this: It may mean that before the natural extinction of this system could happen, possibly the system can be wiped out through armed conflict, like a World War III. The other possibility is that the poor will turn against the rich and destroy capitalism by bloody revolution. Neither result could be called a happy one. The evil of capitalism as seen by Harrington is the inefficiency it shows in eradicating poverty. Harrington wants to achieve that goal by political action.

The New First Party

Harrington hopes to build not a third party but a new first party. The people who will make up the new first party, according to Harrington, will come from the poor, both white and black. In order to give the party sufficient weight, Harrington expects a gradual influx of invigorated labor unions, Galbraithian scientists, technicians, teachers, professors, ministers and priests, and a whole mass of Americans who are disgruntled at the folly of the capitalistic melodrama.

Harrington is not politically naive. He does not want to create his party from scratch. He intends to infiltrate the existing Democratic Party, so that it will evolve in line with his blueprint. The new class has to move into the ranks of the party and change its outlook, policy, and utterances. The new majority will then exclude the racists, the profit hungry, and the warmongers. The electoral code will have to change so that the executive power can be removed by the will of the people, and no president can stay in capital for four years without their continuous approval. Only then will a president become responsible to the people.

The new first party will do everything in its power to rebuild America's slums, provide better schooling for all, decentralize industries according to population, control wages and prices to the advantage of the consumers, retard business fluctuations, and impose taxes so that the recycling of wealth will be guaranteed for the nation. It will be a paradise in which all people able and willing can find jobs and the disabled and elderly will be protected. This kind of utopia is bound to be viewed with a great deal of skepticism, but it is a valid question whether the United States can achieve the goals Harrington pointed out without the means he proposed.

Marx sounded the bugle for the defeat of capitalism; Keynes pointed out the defects of the capitalism he believed in; Schumpeter predicted 50 to 75 years as the life span of capitalism, and that was in 1929. Is Harrington proclaiming the final curtain for capitalism? Only time can tell.

BIBLIOGRAPHY

"A Contribution to the Discussion of the Industrial Revolution in England," *Economic History*. 16 (1956).

Abbott, Thomas Kingsmill (trans.). *Kant's Critique of Practical Reason and Other Works on the Theory of Ethics*. London: Longmans, Green & Co., 1909.

Adams, Lawrence. *Marx in Economics*. New York: Harcourt, Brace & Co., 1961.

Aiken, Henry. *The Age of Ideology*. New York: Mentor, 1963.

Albrecht, William P. *William Hazlitt and the Malthusian Controversy*. Albuquerque: Universtiy of New Mexico Press, 1950.

Alderman, Irma. *Theory of Economic Growth*. Stanford: Stanford University Press, 1961.

Aliber, Robert Z. *The Future of the Dollar as an International Currency*. New York: F. A. Praeger, 1966.

American Economic Review 38 (June 1948): 245-64.

American Federalist, August 1923.

American Federalist, November 1915.

American Federalist, December 1923.

American Federation of Labor, *Convention Proceedings*, 1923.

Aris, R. ed. and trans. *Economic Doctrine and Method*. London: Allen and Unwin, 1954.

Aveling, Elanor, ed. *Marx: Value, Price and Profit Addressed to the Workingmen*. Charles S. Keer Co., 1913.

Bagehot, Walter. *Biographical Studies*. Richard Hutton, ed. London: Longmans, Green & Co., 1914.

Barber, William T. *A History of Economic Thought*. New York: F. A. Praeger, 1968.

Beales, H. L. *The Industrial Revolution, 1750-1850*.

Beer, Max. *Life and Teaching of Karl Marx*. Boston: Small, Maynard and Co., 1924.

238   HISTORY OF ECONOMIC THOUGHT

Bell, John Fred. *A History of Economic Thought*. New York: Ronald Press Co., 1967.

Berlin, Sir Isaiah. *Karl Marx, His Life and Environment*. New York: McGraw-Hill, 1963.

Blake, William. *Elements of Marxian Economic Theory*. New York: Cordon Co., 1939.

Blaug, Mark. *Ricardian Economics*. New Haven: York Union Press, 1958.

Boardman, Fon., Jr. *Economics: Ideas and Men*. New York: Henry Z. Walck, Inc.,1966.

Boehm-Bawerk, Eugen von. *Karl Marx and the Close of His System*. New York: A. M. Kelly, 1949.

Bonar, James. *First Essay on Population*. New York: A. M. Kelley, 1965.

_____*Malthus and His Works,*2d ed London & New York: Macmillan Co., 1924,

_____*Philosophy and Political Economy*. New York: A. M. Kelley, 1966.

Boner, Harold A. *Hungry Generations*. New York: King's Crown Press, 1955.

Bottomore, T. B., ed. *Karl Marx's Early Writings*. London: Watts, 1963.

Boviner, G. A. and Emile Burns, eds. *Theories of Surplus Value by Karl Marx*. New York: International Publishing Co., 1952.

Boyd, Frances & Andrew. *Western Union*. Washington, D.C.: Public Affairs Press, 1949.

Brenton, Crane. *The Temper of Western Europe*. Cambridge, Mass.: Harvard University Press, 1953.

Breuning, Nell Oswald. *Reorganization of Social Economy*. B. W. Dempsey, ed. Milwaukee: Bruce Publishers, 1936.

Broughman, Henry Peter, *Lives of Men of Letters and Science*. Philadelphia: Carey, 1846.

Browder, Earl Russell. *Marx and America*. New York: Duell, Sloan & Pearce, 1958.

Brown, G. Stewart. *Great Issues*. New York: Harper, 1951.

Burns, Emile. *An Introduction to Marxism*. New York: International Publishers Co., 1966.

"Burying Free Enterprise," *Time* 6 January 1967, p. 92.

Business Cycles: A Theoretical, Historical, and Statistical Analysis of the Capitalist Process. New York: McGraw-Hill, 1939.

Cantillon, Richard. *Essai Sur La Nature du Commerce En General*. Henry Higgs, ed. New York: A. M. Kelley, 1964.

Capitalism, Socialism, and Democracy. New York: Harper & Bros., 1942.

Chamberlain, E. H. "Product Heterogeneity and Public Policy," *The American Economic Review*, 40 Proceedings, May 1950.

Chandler, Lester V. *The Economics of Money and Banking.* New York: Harper & Row, 1964.

Clark, J. M. *Adam Smith 1776-1926.* Chicago: University of Chicago Press, 1928.

Clark, John B. *The Distribution of Wealth.* New York: Macmillan Co. 1927.

Cohen, Marshall, ed. *John Stuart Mill.* Chicago: Harcourt, Brace & World, 1961.

Coleman, D. C. "Industrial Growth and Industrial Revolutions," *Economics*, n.s.23 (1956).

Crose, Benedetto. *Essays on Marx and Russia.* New York: F. Unger Publishing Co., 1966.

———— *Historical Materialism and the Economics of Karl Marx.* New York: Macmillan Co., 1914.

Daniels, Robert V. *Marxism and Communism.* New York: Random House, 1965.

Daugert, Stanley M. *The Philosophy of Thorstein Veblen.* New York: King's Crown, 1950.

Dean, Vera Micheles. *Europe and the United States.* New York: Alfred A. Knopf, 1950.

De Cive. Ch. XXIV *Opera Omnia.*

De Conde, Alexander. *The American Secretary of State.* New York: F. A. Praeger, 1962.

Dillard, Dudley. *The Economics of John M. Keynes.* New York: Prentice-Hall, 1948.

Dobriansky, Lev E. *Veblenism: A New Critique.* Washington, D.C.: Public Affairs Press, 1957.

Dorfman, Joseph. *Thorstein Veblen and His America.* New York: The Viking Press, 1934.

Dowd, Douglas F. *Thorstein Veblen.* New York: Washington Square Press, 1966.

Dulles, R. Foster. *America's Rise to World Power.* New York: Harper, 1954, 1955.

Duncan, Arthur L. *The Industrial Revolution in France, 1815-1848. Economica.* December 1927.

Ellery, John B. *John Stuart Mill.* New York: Twayne Publishers, 1964.

Ellery, John. *John Stuart Mill.* Englewood Cliffs, N.J.: Prentice-Hall, 1966.

Encyclopedia Americana. Vols. 8, 9, 22, 17. New York: Grolier, 1963.

Encyclopedia Britannica. Vols. 4, 5, 7, 8, 9, 13, 15, 22. Chicago: 1967.

Ensor, George. *An Inquiry Concerning the Population of Nations.* New York: A. M. Kelley, 1967.

Eshang, Eprime. *From Marshall to Keynes.* Oxford, London: Oxford University Press, 1963.

Farrer, James. *Adam Smith.* New York: Putnam, 1881.

Frandel, S. H. *The Economic Impact on Underdeveloped Societies.* Cambridge, Mass.: Harvard University Press, 1953.

Freedman, Robert, ed. *Marx on Economics.* New York: Harcourt, Brace & World, 1961.

Friedman, Milton. *Essays in Positive Economics.* Chicago: University of Chicago Press, 1953.

Friedman, Milton & Walter W. Heller. *Monetary vs. Fiscal Policy: A Dialogue.* New York: W. W. Norton & Co., 1969.

Fromm, Erich. *Marx's Concept of Man.* New York: F. Unger Publishing Co., 1967.

"The Fundamental Issues," *New York Times* 23 July 1922.

Galbraith, John Kenneth. *The Affluent Society.* Boston: Houghton Mifflin Co., 1958.

_____*American Capitalism: The Concept of Countervailing Power.* Boston: Houghton Mifflin Co., 1952.

_____"Foreign Policy: The Stuck Whistle," *The Atlantic Monthly,* 214 (February 19650: 64-68.

_____ *The Great Crash.* Boston: Houghton Mifflin Co., 1954.

_____ *How to Get Out of Vietnam: A Workable Solution to the Greatest Problem of Our Time.* Boston: Houghton Mifflin Co., 1967.

_____ *The Liberal Hour.* Boston: Houghton Mifflin Co., 1960.

_____ *The New Industrial State.* Boston: Houghton Mifflin Co., 1967.

Garaudy, Roger. *Karl Marx: The Evolution of His Thought.* New York: International Publishers Co., 1967.

Gide, Charles & Charles Rist. *A History of Economics Doctrines.* New York: Heath Publishing Co., 1948.

Gill, Richard T. *Evolution of Modern Economics.* Englewood Cliffs, N.J.: Prentice-Hall, 1967.

Glass, D. V. *Introduction to Malthus.* London: Macmillan Co., 1953.

Godwin, William. *Of Population (1830).* New York: A. M. Kelley, 1965.

_____ *On Population.* New York: A. M. Kelley, 1927.

Goetz, Briefs. "Heinrich Pesch," in *Encyclopedia of the Social Sciences* Vol. 12., 1937.

_____ "I Know Heinrich Pesch," *Social Order,* April 1951.

Golob, Eugene O. *The "ISMS."* New York: Harper & Bro., 1954.

Gompers, S. *The American Labor Movement: Its Make-Up, Achievements, and Aspirations.* A.F.L. Pamphlet, 1914.

Graebner, Norman A. *An Uncertain Tradition.* New York: McGraw-Hill, 1961.

Gray, A. *The Socialist Tradition: Moses to Lenin.* New York and London: Longmans, Green & Co., 1946.

Griffith, Grosvenor Talbot. *Population Problems of the Age of Malthus.* New York: A. M. Kelley, 1964.

Haney, Lewis H. *History of Economic Thought.* Chicago: University of Chicago Press, 1909.

_____ *History of Economic Thought.* New York: Macmillan Co., 1936.

Hansen, Alvin H. *A Guide to Keynes.* New York: MacGraw-Hill, 1953.

Harris, A. L. *Economics and Social Reform.* New York: Harper & Bros., 1958.

Harris, Seymour. *The New Economics.* Oxford University Press, 1947

_____ ed. *Schumpeter, Social Scientist.* Cambridge, Mass.: Harvard University Press, 1951.

Harrod, H. F. *The Life of John Maynard Keynes.* London: Macmillan Co., 1952.

Hart, Albert Gailord. *Money, Debt and Economic Activity.* Englewood Cliffs, N.J.: Prentice-Hall, 1953.

Harvey, Rowland. *Samuel Gompers.* Stanford: Stanford University Press, 1935.

Haxlitt, Henry, ed. *The Critics of Keynesian Economics.* New York: Prentice-Hall, 1960.

Hazlitt, William. *A Reply to the Essay on Population (1807).* New York: A. M. Kelley, 1967.

Heckscher, Eli F. *Mercantilism.* Vols. 1, 2. E. F. Soderlund, ed. New York: Barnes & Noble, 1955.

Hegel, G. W. F. *The Logic of Hegel.* William Wallace, trans. London: Geoffery Cumberlege, 1950.

_____ *The Philosophy of History.* J. Sibree, trans. New York: Dover Publishing, 1956.

Heimann, Edward. *History of Economic Doctrines.* New York: Exford University Press, 1945, 1964.

_____ *The Worldly Philosophers.* New York: Simon & Schuster, 1953.

Heilbroner, Robert L. *The Making of the Economic Society.* Englewood Cliffs, N.J.: Prentice-Hall, 1968.

Hersey, John. "Mr. Secretary Marshall," *Readers Digest,* July 1947, pp. 79-94.

Himmelfarb, Gertrude. *On Population.* New York: Modern Library, 1960.

Hollander, Jacob. *David Ricardo: A Centenary Estimate.* New York: E. P. Dutton, 1911.

Homan, Paul T. *Contemporary Economic Thought.* Free Port, N. Y.: Books for Libraries, 1968.

_____ "Thorstein Veblen," *American Masters of Social Science.* Howard W. Odum, ed. New York: Henry Hold & Co., 1927.

Hook, Sidney. *From Hegel to Marx.* New York: The Humanities Press, 1950.

_____ *Toward an Understanding of Karl Marx.* New York: John Day, 1933.

Horrocks, J. W. *A Short History of Mercantilism.* New York: Brentano's Publishers, 1920.

Horwitz, David. *Marx and Modern Economics.* New York: Modern Reader Paper Backs, 1968.

Hull, C. H. *Economic Writings of Sir Wm. Petty.* Vols. 1, 2. New York: A. M. Kelley, 1963.

Hutt, W. H. *Keynesianism: Retrospect and Prospect.* Chicago: Henry Regnery & Co., 1963.

James, Patricia. *The Travel Diaries of Robert Thomas Malthus.* London: Oxford University Press, 1966.

Jevons, W. Stanley. *The Principles of Economics: A Fragment of a Treatise on the Industrial Mechanism of Society.* New York: A. M. Kelley, 1965.

Johnson, E. A. *The Growth of British Economic Thought.* New York: Prentice-Hall, 1937.

_____ *Predecessors of Adam Smith.* New York: Prentice-Hall, Inc., 1937.

Journal of Political Economy. 59 (June 1951): 203-32.

Journal of Political Economy. 60 (February 1952): 25-33.

Jurihara, Kenneth K. *Introduction to Keynesian Dynamics.* New York: Columbia University Press, 1956.

Kamenka, Eugene. *The Ethical Foundations of Marxism.* New York: Praeger, 1962.

Keynes, John Maynard. *Monetary Reform.* New York: Macmillan Co., 1942.

_____ "Robert Malthus: The First of the Cambridge Economists," in *Essays and Sketches in Biography.* London: 1951.

_____ *General Theory.* London & New York: Harcourt Brace, 1936.

Klein, Lawrence R. *The Keynesian Revolution.* New York: Macmillan Co., 1950.

Knight, Frank H. *On the Method and History of Economics.* Chicago & London: University of Chicago Press, 1963.

Korsch, Karl. *Karl Marx.* New York: John Wiley & Sons, 1938.

Kuhn, W. E. *The Evolution of Economic Thought.* Cincinnati: Southwestern Publishing, 1945.

Laidler, H. W. *A History of Socialist Thought.* New York: Thomas Y. Crowell, 1945.

Lakowitz, Nicholas. *Marx and the Western World.* South Bend, Ind.: University of Notre Dame Press, 1967.

Landsdowne, Marquis of. *The Petty-Southwell Correspondence.* New York: A. M. Kelley, 1967.

Laski, Harold J. ed. *Communist Manifesto—Socialist Landmark.* London: Allen and Unwin, 1961.

Lechtape, Heinrich. "Heinrich Pesch," in *'Staatslexicon* 4 (1931). col. 132.

Leijonhufvud, Axel. *On Keynesian Economics and the Economics of Keynes.* New York: Macmillan Co., 1968.

Lekachman, Robert. *The Age of Keynes.* New York: Random House, 1966.

_____ *A History of Economic Ideas.* New York: Harper & Bros., 1959.

_____ *Keynes's General Theory.* New York: Macmillan Co., 1964.

Lerner, Max. "Thorstein Bunde Veblen," in *Dictionary of American Biography.* New York: Charles Scribner's Sons, 1936.

Leslie, W. C. *Criticism of John Stuart Mill.* Howell, Soskin, 1949.

Levin, S. M. "Malthus and the Idea of Progress," *Journal of the History of Ideas* vol. 27, no. 1 (1966).

Lewis, John. *The Life and Teaching of Karl Marx.* New York: International Publishers Co., 1965.

Lindsay, A. D. *Introduction: John Stuart Mill.* New York: E. P. Dutton & Co., 1965.

Ludwig, H. *Approach to Economics.* Totowa, N.J.: Littlefield, Adams & Co., 1965.

MacKenzie, Norman. *Socialism: A Short History.* London: Hutchinson, 1966.

Malthus, Thomas R. *Definitions in Political Economy.* New York: A. M. Kelley, 1963.

_____ *First Essay on Population.* New York: Sentry Press, 1965.

_____ *On Population.* New York: The Modern Library, 1960.

_____ *Principles of Political Economy.* New York: Sentry Press, 1964.

Mandel, Bernard. *Samuel Gompers.* New York: Antioch Press, 1963.

Marshall, Alfred. *Memorials of Alfred Marshall.* A. C. Pigou, ed. London: Macmillan Co., 1925.

Marshall, Howard D. *The Great Economists.* New York: Pitman Publishing Corp., 1967.

Marx, Karl. *Capital.* New York: Modern Library Press, 1932.

_____ *Capital, A Critique of Political Economy.* Chicago: Charles H. Kerr, 1906.

_____ *Capital, the Process of Capitalist Production as a Whole.* Vol. 3. Chicago: Charles H. Kerr, 1906.

_____ *The Communist Manifesto.* Chicago: Henry Regenery & Co., 1954.

_____ *A Contribution to the Critique of Political Economy.* London: Charles H. Kerr, 1904.

_____ *Critique of the Gotha Programme.* New York: International Publishers Co., 1938.

_____ *Theories of Surplus Value.* G. A. Bonner and Emilie Burns, trans. New York: International Bublishers Co., 1952.

Marx, Karl & Friedrich Engels. *The Basic Writings on Politics and Philosophy.* New York: Doubleday, 1959.

_____ *The German Ideology.* New York: International Publishers Co., 1939.

_____ *Karl Marx: Selected Works.* Moscow: Cooperative Publishing Co., 1904.

McCarthy, Joseph. *America's Retreat From Victory.* New York: Decrim-Adair Co., 1954.

McCracken, Harlan L. *Keynesian Economics in the Streams of Economic Thought.* Baton Rouge, La.: Louisiana State University Press, 1961.

McCulloch, John. *Treatises and Essays on Subjects Connected with Economical Policy.* New York: A. M. Kelley, 1967.

Mehring, Franz. *Karl Marx.* New York: Covici-Friede, 1935.

_____ *Karl Marx—The Story of His Life.* London: Allen and Unwin, 1936.

Mitchell, Wesley C. *Types of Economic Theory.* Vol. 1. New York: A. M. Kelley, 1967.

Moffet, James. "John Bates Clark," in *Colliers Encyclopedia.* Vol. 6. New York: 1962, p. 562.

Morel, George. "The Meaning of Karl Marx," *America* 117 (Oct. 1967).

Murad, Anatol. *What Keynes Means.* New York: Bookman Associates, 1962.

Murray, Robert. *Criticism of John Stuart Mill.* New York: D. Appleton & Co., 1958.

Newman, C. Philip, et al. *Source Reading in Economic Thought.* New York: W. W. Norton, 1954.

Oser, Jacob. *The Evolution of Economic Thought.* New York: Harcourt, Brace & World, 1970.

Parsens, Talcott. *Quarterly Journal of Economics* 39 (1924-25).

Perlman, Richard. *Wage Determination.* Boston: D. C. Heath & Co., 1964.

Pesch, Heinrich. *The Presence of Political Economy.* (Volkswirtschaftslehre der Gegenwart) F. Muner, ed., Leipzig: 1924.

_____ *The Text Book of National Economy.* (Lehrbuch der Nationalökonomie). Friedburg i Cr. Herder, 1905-1925; Vols. 1-3, 2d ed. 1924-26.

_____ "The Theory of Interest," *Magazine for Catholic Thought and Theology* (Zeitschrift fur Katholische Theologie), XII (Heft 1 & II).

Peterson, Wallace C. *Income, Employment and Economic Growth.* New York: W. W. Norton, 1967.

Pigou, A. C. *Economics of Welfare.* London: Macmillan Co., 1952.

_____ *Keynes General Theory.* London: Macmillan Co., 1950.

Place, Francis. *Illustration and Proof of the Principles of Population.* New York: A. M. Kelley, 1967.

Polanyi, Karl. *Primitive, Archaic, and Modern Economies.* George Dalton, ed. Garden City: Doubleday, 1968.

_____ *The Great Transformation.* New York: Reinhardt, 1944.

Postan, M. M. "Recent Trends in the Accumulation of Capital," *Economic History Review* 6 (1935).

Pratt, Julius. *A History of United States Foreign Policy.* New York: Prentice-Hall, Inc., 1955.

Quarterly Journal of Economics, Volumes in the 1950 and 1951 edition.

Reiber, Alfred J. & Robert C. Nelson. *A Study of the USSR and Communism.* Chicago: Scott-Foresman & Co., 1962.

Review of Economics and Statistics 33 (August 1951): 179-200.

Ricardo, David. *Minor Papers on the Currency Question.* Baltimore: The Johns Hopkins Press, 1932.

_____ *The Principles of Political Economy and Taxation.* New York: E. P. Dutton, 1933.

Riesman, David. *Thorstein Veblen: A Critical Interpretation.* New York: Charles Scribner's Sons, 1953.

Rima, I. H. *Development of Economic Analysis.* Homewood, Ill.: Richard D. Irwin, 1967.

Robinson, Joan. *An Essay on Marxian Economics.* New York: Macmillan Co., 1957.

Rogin, Leo. *The Meaning and Validity of Economic Theory.* New York: Harper & Bros., 1956.

Roosa, Robert V. *Monetary Reform for the World Economy.* New York: Harper & Row, 1965.

Ruhle, Otto. *Karl Marx.* Eden and Cedar Paul, trans. London: Allen & Unwin, 1929.

Ryazanoff, D. *The Communist Manifesto of Karl Marx and Friedrich Engels.* New York: Russell & Russell, 1963.

Sabine, George. *A History of Political Theory.* New York: Henry Hold & Co., 1937.

Samuelson, Paul A. *Economics.* Engelwood Cliffs, N.J.: Prentice-Hall, 1955.

―――― *The General Theory—Keynes' General Theory Reports of Three Decades.* Robert Lakachman, ed. New York: St. Martin's Press, 1964.

―――― *Readings in Economics.* New York: McGraw-Hill, 1964.

Schmiedeler, Rev. Edgar., O.S.B. *The Industrial Revolution and the Home.* Atchison, Kan.: St. Benedict Abbey Press, 1927.

Schmoller, Gustav. *The Mercantile System and Its Historical Significance.* New York: A. M. Kelley, 1967.

Schumpeter, Elizabeth B., ed. *The History of Economic Analysis.* New York: Oxford University Press, 1954.

Schumpeter, Joseph A. *The Great Economists from Marx to Keynes.* New York: Oxford University Press, 1951.

Scott, William R. *Alfred Marshall.* London: British Academy Press, 1928.

Semmel, Bernard. *Occasional Papers of T. R. Malthus.* New York: Burt Franklin, 1963.

Senior, Nassau. *An Outline of the Science of Political Economy.* London: W. Clowes & Sons, 1836.

Skow, John. *Is John Kenneth Galbraith Really Good?* Philadelphia: Curtis Publishing Co., 1969.

Slichter, Summer H. "The Passing of Keynesian Economics," *Atlantic Monthly* 152 (November 1957).

Smith, Adam. *The Wealth of Nations.* New York: Modern Library, 1937.

―――― *Wealth of Nations: Representative Selections.* Bruce Mazlish, ed. Indianapolis: Bobbs-Merrill, 1961.

Smith, Howard R. *Economic History of the United States.* New York: Ronald Press Co., 1955.

Somer, Louise. "Cameralism," in *Encyclopedia of Social Science.* New York:

Soule, George. *Ideas of the Great Economists.* New York: The Viking Press, 1934, 1952, & 1953.

Spann, Othmor. *The History of Economics.* New York: W. W. Norton & Co., 1930.

Spengler, Joseph J. *French Predecessors of Malthus.* New York: Octagon Books, 1965.

Spiegel, Henry. *The Development of Economic Thought.* New York: John Wiley & Sons, 1952.

Stangeland, Charles Emil. *Pre-Malthus Doctrine of Population.* New York: A. M. Kelley, 1966.

Stephen, Sir Leslie. *English Thought in the Eighteenth Century.* New York: Putnam, 1902.

Stewart, Michael. *Keynes and After.* Baltimore: Baltimore Press, 1961.

Stigler, George J. *Production and Distribution Theories.* New York: Macmillan Co., 1941.

Stillinger, Jack. *The Early Draft of John Stuart Mill, Autobiography.* Illinois: University of Illinois Press, 1961.

Strachey, John. *Contemporary Capitalism.* New York: Random House, 1956.

Sweezy, Paul. *The Theory of Capitalist Development.* New York: Monthly Review Press, 1956.

Taft, Philip, ed. *Seventy Years of Life and Labor—Sanuel Gompers.* New York: E. P. Dutton & Co., 1957.

Taylor, A. E. *Plato.* London: Constable & Co., 1911.

Taylor, Overton H. *A History of Economic Thought.* New York: McGraw-Hill, 1960.

Ten Great Economists from Marx to Keynes. New York: Oxford University Press, 1951.

"The Great Mogul," *Time* 16 February 1968, pp. 24-28.

"The Other Side of Affluence," *Business Week* 18 April 1964.

Three Years of the Marshall Plan. (News Division of E.A.C.'s., Office of Information) 3 April 1951.

Toynbee, Arnold F. *The Industrial Revolution.* Boston: Beacon Press, 1961.

Triffin, Robert. *Europe and the Money Muddle.* New Haven, Conn.: Yale University Press, 1957.

_____ *Gold and the Dollar Crisis.* New Haven, Conn.: Yale University Press, 1961.

_____ *Monopolistic Competition and General Equilibrium.* Cambridge, Mass.: Harvard University Press, 1940.

_____ *The World Money Maze.* New Haven, Conn.: Yale University Press, 1966.

Triffin, Robert, et al. *Maintaining and Restoring Balance in International Payments.* Princeton: Princeton University Press, 1966.

Tucker, Robert. *The Marxian Revolutionary Idea.* New York: W. W. Norton, 1969.

U. S. Industrial Commission of 1899. *Report on the Relations of Capital and Labor.* Vol. 7.

Usher, Abbot Payson. *A History of Mechanical Inventions.* Rev. ed. Cambridge, Mass.: Harward University Press, 1954.

Veblen, Thorstein B. *Absentee Ownership and Business Enterprise in Recent Time: The Case of America.* New York: Viking Press, 1945.

_____ *The Theory of Business Enterprise.* New York: Charles Scribner's Sons, 1930.

_____ *The Theory of the Leisure Class: An Economic Study of Institutions.* New York: New American Library, 1953.

Viner, Jacob. *Readings in Price Theory.* Chicago: Chicago University Press, 1952.

Wanlass, Lawrence. *A History of Political Thought.* New York: Appleton Century, 1953.

Watson, Donald S. *Price Theory and Its Uses.* New York: Houghton Mifflin Co., 1968.

West, E. G. *Adam Smith.* New Rochelle, N.Y.: Arlington House, 1969.

Whittaker, Edmund. *Schools and Streams of Economic Thought.* Chicago: Rand McNally, 1960 and 1963.

Wright, David M. *The Keynesian System.* New York: Fordham University Press, 1961.